THE WANDERING HERETICS O

CW00363054

How should historians read sources which record inquisitorial trials in the Middle Ages? How can we understand the fears felt by those on trial? By analysing six volumes of depositions in the trials of Cathar and Waldensian heretics in Languedoc between the late twelfth and the fourteenth centuries, Caterina Bruschi challenges old methodologies in the study of dissent. She examines the intrinsic narratological problems related to the sources and, using approaches from the social sciences, analyses the different fears felt by deponents and how those fears affected their actions and decisions. In so doing, she sheds new light on itinerancy within the ecclesial structure of non-conformist movements and contextualises the problem of itinerancy as a benchmark for the definition of heresy. Focusing on the lives and attitudes of trial witnesses, this innovative account is a major contribution to our understanding of the nature of religious non-conformity in the Middle Ages.

CATERINA BRUSCHI is Lecturer in Medieval History at the University of Birmingham.

Cambridge Studies in Medieval Life and Thought
Fourth Series

General Editor:
ROSAMOND McKITTERICK
Professor of Medieval History, University of Cambridge, and Fellow of Sidney Sussex College

Advisory Editors:
CHRISTINE CARPENTER
Professor of Medieval English History, University of Cambridge

JONATHAN SHEPARD

The series Cambridge Studies in Medieval Life and Thought was inaugurated by G. G. Coulton in 1921; Professor Rosamond McKitterick now acts as General Editor of the Fourth Series, with Professor Christine Carpenter and Dr Jonathan Shepard as Advisory Editors. The series brings together outstanding work by medieval scholars over a wide range of human endeavour extending from political economy to the history of ideas.

A list of titles in the series can be found at:
www.cambridge.org/medievallifeandthought

THE WANDERING HERETICS
OF LANGUEDOC

CATERINA BRUSCHI

CAMBRIDGE
UNIVERSITY PRESS

CAMBRIDGE UNIVERSITY PRESS
Cambridge, New York, Melbourne, Madrid, Cape Town,
Singapore, São Paulo, Delhi, Mexico City

Cambridge University Press
The Edinburgh Building, Cambridge CB2 8RU, UK

Published in the United States of America by Cambridge University Press, New York

www.cambridge.org
Information on this title: www.cambridge.org/ 9780521182270

First published 2009
First paperback edition 2012

A catalogue record for this publication is available from the British Library

Library of Congress Cataloguing in Publication data
Bruschi, Caterina, 1968–
The wandering heretics of Languedoc / Caterina Bruschi.
p. cm. – (Cambridge studies in medieval life and thought)
Includes bibliographical references.
isbn 978-0-521-87359-8 (hardback)
1. Albigenses–France–Languedoc–History. 2. Heresies, Christian–France–
Languedoc–History–Middle Ages, 600–1500. 3. Languedoc (France)–
Church history. I. Title. II. Series.
BX4891.3.B78 2009
273'.6–dc22   2009008468

isbn 978-0-521-87359-8 Hardback
isbn 978-0-521-18227-0 Paperback

To the memory of my Mum and Dad, who saw the beginning,
but not the end of this book.
To Martin, Douglas and Amanda, my beloved travel companions.

CONTENTS

ACKNOWLEDGEMENTS

In Parma, my native city, those few 'Parmigiani' who have fled to other cities or countries are called the 'strajè', the 'scattered'. When in 1998 I started this work on 'scattered' Cathars, who had fled France and found refuge in Italy, I certainly did not know that one day I would endure their same fate. Since then, journeying between Italy and Great Britain, from Bologna to York, then to Birmingham, has been a long affair. Both my 'identities' owe much to all those who encouraged my work, believed in my ability to adapt to different cultures and climates, e-mailed me their affection and friendship, and listened to my occasional outbursts of Italian-ness. For this reason, I wish to name here all those whom I would like to thank for helping me keep myself together through such difficult and intensive years.

In Italy, infinite thanks to my Boss and Master, Lorenzo Paolini, for all he has done as a guide and a friend, for his patience and important suggestions; to Luigi Canetti, Alessandra Greco, Riccardo Parmeggiani, Roberta Bertuzzi and Saverio Amadori, first friends, then colleagues; and to all the kind people at the École Française de Rome, in particular to François Bougard, André Vauchez, Cécile Caby, Antonio Sennis, Anne Reltgen-Tallon, Sylvie Barnay and Umberto Longo.

In York, first and foremost, to Peter and Miggy Biller, for everything from my first English bicycle, long chats over a glass of wine, moral and professional guidance and Rabelaisian, succulent meals. To all the people at Centre for Medieval Studies: students, porters and colleagues. Particular, warmest thanks to Shelagh Sneddon, Gwylym Dodd and Chris Liddy, and to Dr Simon White.

In Birmingham, thanks to my students and colleagues. Deserving special mention are Peter Ricketts, and my mentors both official and unofficial, Nicholas Brooks, Robert Swanson, Chris Wickham, Steven Bassett and John Bourne, for their patience and caring attention. Special thanks also to Francesca Carnevali and her mother, Graeme Murdock,

Acknowledgements

Matthew Hilton, Noelle Plack, Leslie Brubaker and Ruth Macrides, for sharing the pains and pleasures of our common burden (and still managing to laugh at it!)

My heartfelt thanks to Robert Swanson and Peter Biller for checking and correcting my English prose throughout the book.

Additional but not less important thanks to Peter Biller and Martin Forster for moral encouragement and discussion of the most controversial points in the book.

INTRODUCTION

A few years ago, in one of the universities where I taught, one of my students was found to have committed what is considered the worst sin in the academic world: plagiarism. I had the job of dealing with this case as a disciplinary matter, according to the university's ordinances and regulations. At the same time I was very curious to know why, despite all my efforts to be available to students to discuss such matters and give them help, this student had chosen the path of crime when writing the essay: copying it from the Internet.

The student was duly summoned with a concise and formal letter, to attend a meeting at which I and one of my senior colleagues would be present. I had asked for this colleague to be there because I wanted reassurance and help. Most important of all, I wanted the backing of the institution, an institution in which I happened to be an authority, even if a minor one, and my student a lesser citizen.

I had prepared a list of questions, which I had put together during the days leading up to the meeting. I brought with me a notebook to take minutes. I also had the evidence: the essay and the website from which it was taken. I asked for the meeting to be held not in my room, but in the more austere and official-looking Head of Department's study.

While sitting there and questioning my ashen-faced student, I suddenly realised that I was in fact acting like an inquisitor. Like a medieval inquisitor, I was a prepared and authorised member of an established institution. I was required by the rules and regulations to take disciplinary action against a fraud perpetrated against the system. At the same time I also noticed that I was – like my student – absolutely terrified and very insecure, even though I possessed the evidence of guilt. I also had mixed feelings: anger, compassion and sorrow. And despite the threat of exclusion from the university, I could not prevent this person lying to my colleague and me, both then and on other occasions.

Our chosen tactic was to scare the student into confessing what we already knew. Our means were legitimate. First of all we presented the student with the worst possible outcome (exclusion), and then the less extreme measures (obtaining an insufficient mark and being required to do the essay again). We delayed providing our decision until the following day. And we asked for a written confession of guilt, which the student duly produced.

Later on, while I was writing up the definitive and official version of what became the 'fair and complete record of the meeting', which the student was required to confirm and sign, I found that almost by instinct I was producing a record much like the hundreds of medieval ones I had been studying for years.

I could not avoid asking myself, 'Am I in some sense creating an offender? Did this person confess what I wanted, write what I needed, and partly act as I expected because driven to do so by the intimidating atmosphere of the meeting and the presence of the Head of Department, by the appearance of incontrovertible evidence, by my notebook, and by my questions?' And at the same time, 'Why did the student *still* lie to us?'

'Am I retrospectively creating an offender now, as I turn our brief meeting once again into a long and bureaucrat-friendly text, one which tries both to establish what they did and also to protect my institution from legal action?'

Apart from my thoughts and concerns, all that would remain of that episode would be a text that I was producing on the basis of my brief and scribbled notes and my own and my colleague's memory. In order to compile this text I was selecting from my notebook what was relevant to my purpose and leaving out what was not...

...something in this meeting, indeed much more than simply something, happened in exactly the same way 750 years ago.

It was not just one of these moments when historians find parallels between events in their own lives and in the past they study. It was a chance to put on the clothes of an inquisitor for a day or two, and to live some of the emotions an inquisitor would have felt while questioning someone about heresy. I started to analyse my own reactions (were they really instinctive?), my actions, the tactics chosen both by my student and by me before the meeting, and the outcome.

On the following day the student produced a written confession, as we had asked, using the words we had suggested and declaring that the record I produced was fair, complete and not distorted. The student had no additions or changes to make. Although that confession was guided by me, even in its wording, I cannot say that it admitted to things that never happened, nor can I say that I falsified or exaggerated my student's wrongdoing. Of course, the text did conceal what lay behind the crime: the reasons for plagiarising the essay, my student's past history, their attitude to the university and writing essays, and the real level of their ability, all of which influenced the student's decision to act wrongly. Nor did the text contain my anger and regret. Nevertheless I can honestly regard it as a faithful record of what happened.

WHY DOAT 21−6?

Since that episode I have rethought my approach. Research has meant acting intellectually, reading sources, taking account of their textual distortions and distilling the information I needed. But I have tried at the same time to think in my skin. What do I mean by this? Well, I have kept this episode in mind, and I have tried to look for the human features of my characters in order to better understand their choices and actions. I do not want to forget that the many inquisitors and deponents I met in the registers of Doat 21–6 were real people. Of course, a historian should always try to be analytically and intellectually rigorous when reading texts, and an attitude of detachment is what the profession expects. But I cannot help feeling that the heuristic process is fundamentally driven by our own identification with the situation itself, by compassion for and curiosity about those lives and those characters.

I am well aware of other possible approaches to these sources and to the interpretation of the records of inquisition trials, and I do believe that the words received from the past have been shaped by the minds and by the roles of those who wrote them and thought them. However, I aim to steer a middle course between radical scepticism and simple positivism. Carlo Ginzburg has taught us that in reading inquisition trials historians can indeed hear some of the original dialogue. Although the voices hidden in the texts, within the many layers superimposed by their writers, are mostly lost, there remain glimpses of them. To some extent they are still audible, at least in part. Although Ginzburg's idea was formulated in the mid-1970s, some scholars still highlight the stubborn silence of the sources rather than the glimpses of voices one can detect. Only a decade ago, for example, Mariano d'Alatri, analysing Inquisition trials from central Italy, wrote: 'In fact, instead of the voice of those under investigation, the judicial records echo the indignant and unconditional silence of those who judge and do not accept a reply'.[1]

---

[1] Mariano d'Alatri, *L'inquisizione francescana nell'Italia centrale del Duecento: con in appendice il testo del 'Liber inquisitionis' di Orvieto trascritto da Egidio Bonanno,* ('Bibliotheca Seraphico-Capuccina' 149) 1996, p. 157.

Not all judicial records are the same. Sentences are much drier and functional documents than interrogation records, and do actually show more silences than voices. However, by underlining this silence of the sources against the voices of the deponents, d'Alatri showed the half-empty glass rather than Ginzburg's half-full one. What a reader will remember is this silence: the unconditional, stubborn silence of a sentence where no reply is allowed. The judges do not leave space to any voice which is not theirs. There are available judicial records which are more talkative than those analysed by d'Alatri, providing us with opportunities to detect fragments of lives behind various screens and superimpositions. Those feeble voices are the reason I am writing this book. Whether voices of power (inquisitors) or voices of fear and anger (deponents), they do not deserve to be treated just as categories, simply as the mouthpieces of a struggle between the powerless and the powerful, or as the cold evidence resulting from an intellectual equation involving the writers, the text and the readers. In other words, they are not only fragments of constructed text. They were and are human, individual and personal voices and as such, what is left of them deserves to be carefully heard.

The volumes of the *Collection Doat* of the Bibliothèque Nationale de France in Paris still offer plenty of temptations and opportunities to the historian wanting to detect snatches of those lives. At the time of writing, most of the volumes are still unpublished, although historians coming from very different areas and backgrounds have recently shown a strong interest in editing such extraordinary material. Jean Duvernoy, during long and passionate years of research, has gathered a huge collection of transcriptions of sources related to Catharism. Among them, excerpts from volumes 21, 22, 24, 25, 26, 27, 28, 32 and 34 of the *Collection Doat* are available for consultation at the Centre d'Études Cathares of Carcassonne, and now also on the Internet, at http://www.jean. duvernoy.free.fr/sources/sinquisit.htm. Duvernoy has recently edited the sentences of the inquisitor Peter Cellan in volume 21,[2] and alongside this there is Jörg Feuchter's forthcoming critical edition of the whole of volume 21. Peter Biller, Shelagh Sneddon and I have prepared a critical edition and English translation of volumes 25 and 26, up to f. 78v, to appear shortly.[3]

Why have I chosen volumes 21–6 among the many? A two-year grant from the University of Bologna allowed the continuation of my research

---

[2] *L'inquisition en Quercy. Le registre de pénitences de Pierre Cellan 1241–1242* (Castelnaud-La-Chapelle, 2001).

[3] P. Biller, C. Bruschi, and S. Sneddon (eds.), *Inquisitors and Heretics in Thirteenth-Century Languedoc: Edition and Translation of Toulouse Inquisition Depositions 1273–1280* (Brill, forthcoming).

outside Italy: I combined the desire to work on the Doat volumes with the opportunity to be supervised by one of the leading specialists in this field, Peter Biller. His knowledge of the *Collection Doat* suggested volumes 21–6 as the ones which had most to offer on the links between Italian and French Cathars.

A dissertation on the contacts between the two areas had already been written in Oxford by Andrew Roach, *The Relationship of the Italian and Southern French Cathars, 1170–1320*.[4] I have deliberately avoided consulting or referring to this work, partly because my intention was to look at the sources afresh (however, I have taken into consideration Roach's more recent views, and discussed them where appropriate in several parts of this book), and partly because my initial interest in the French–Italian connection slowly shifted. I began to look at other, albeit connected things.

These were the methodological issue of text criticism; the topic of heretical itinerancy, in relation to both Cathars and other heretical groups; and the wider topic of fear and risk, to which I adopted an interdisciplinary approach. The link between the three is to be found in this specific collection of texts, Doat 21–6. This has already been used as a repository of information about the geography of heresy in France and Italy. But it can also be seen as the textual result of hundreds of trials, of even more hearings, and of the process of recording them. The judicial events which sparked and justified the production of our records can be looked at as a dramatic performance and psychological struggle at the same time. Here, the codification of the interaction between the two parties into a verbal and written record followed the dynamics of textual genesis, but it also responded to the psychological dynamics of the exchange between inquisitors and deponents, and to the assessments of risk made by the deponents themselves and to the risk-taking strategies they adopted. While looking at the records in these ways, I have tried to stay open to suggestions coming from different disciplines, such as the social sciences, in the hope of new and fresh light being cast on our too familiar material.

The overriding intention of giving back to the deponents – be they heretics or not – their rightful role in this textual and psychological game of hide-and-seek, runs counter to a historiographical orientation which is rather widespread.

---

[4] (D.Phil. dissertation, Wolfson College, Oxford, 1990). In his latest work, Roach has incorporated a great part of the material from his dissertation, but also acknowledged that he has modified his views on some issues: *The Devil's World: Heresy and Society 1100–1300* (Harlow, Essex, 2005), n. 15, p. 219.

Among specialists, in fact, heretics are still mostly portrayed as passive, naive and helpless individuals facing and opposing an all-powerful, well-structured, rich and psychologically overriding institution. Lying beneath this depiction are two major methodological flaws.

The first one is what I shall call 'individuals-versus-institution'. While it is true that *during the trial* heretics were individuals facing a group, our vision and analysis of the relationship between dissenters and the Church must not be restricted to this event. For the sake of completeness, it must take into consideration the fact that individual dissenters were also part of *another* institution, with its organisation, rules and psychological ties. To overlook this is a serious omission.

The second flaw is not a sin of omission. It is a wrong assumption: that awareness and unawareness are states of mind which mirror our own. As obvious as it might sound, it is a rather common assumption, still held by historians who are leading authorities in the field. For instance, Grado Merlo, one of the first to challenge inquisitorial depositions and their recording, offering ground-breaking methodologies for their inter-pretation, still subscribes to this overall view of 'aware-versus-unaware'. Recently, he has talked about an 'ignorant attitude of the heretics', as opposed to the sleekness and professional skills of inquisitors. The papal officials, ever since the 1230s, were effectively the sole leaders of a game between orthodoxy and dissent.[5]

Overall, oversimplification of the much more complex relationship between the Catholic Church and its opponents leads to further sim-plification of the phenomenon of the Inquisition. This attitude is, once again, rather widespread. For example, another Italian historian, Marina Benedetti, in her fine study of the activities of the inquisitor Lanfranc of Bergamo, has insistently underlined a supposed 'functional role of the heretics for wider schemes'. From Benedetti's words it seems that, what-ever their actions, intentions and purposes, heretics embodied an entity who served well the purpose of offering some kind of scapegoat 'for wider schemes' (presumably of the Church/Inquisition).[6]

Although these are certainly short quotations, and do not reflect the whole of these scholars' historical opinion on our issue, they betray a similar view: there is a leading party – the Church, or the Inquisition, or the single inquisitors – who uses the other – the dissenters – to fulfil or

[5] G.G. Merlo, 'Il senso delle opere dei frati Predicatori in quanto "inquisitores hereticae pravitatis"', *Quaderni di Storia Religiosa* 9 (2002), 9–30, at pp. 21–2.
[6] M. Benedetti, 'Le parole e le opere di frate Lanfranco (1292–1305)', *Quaderni di Storia Religiosa* 9 (2002), 111–82, for example at p. 126.

justify their own agenda. The second party appears pliable, ignorant and easy prey to the situation, skilfully dominated by the inquisitors.

I do not believe in what Merlo called the 'unawareness' of the heretics. As for the alleged 'functional role of the heretics', why not then hypothesise, within an all-round analysis of heresy and the Inquisition, a parallel 'functional role of the inquisitors in some heretics' wider schemes'? Because of the mercurial nature of emotions, and because of the dignity due to *all* historical characters, I have tried to suggest – in Chapter 4 – that some form of 'reaction' to the inquisitorial strategies and methods did in fact take place.[7] Besides, the reasons and ways in which it occurred have to be read within their appropriate context and according to case-specific criteria. In order to do so, I have outlined and discussed examples of such 'reaction' derived from our Doat volumes.

The main consequence of the methodological limits discussed above, is the fashionable trend of 'deconstruction' of the Cathar phenomenon and of heresy in general. In other words, by portraying medieval dissenters as individuals and as silent and ignorant actors of what I called the 'game of hide-and-seek' with the established Church, historians inevitably come to several assumptions. First of all, the inconsistency of a dissenting organisation – as in the case of a Cathar church; secondly, the negation of an agency in opposing the existing religious authority; thirdly, they suggest the 'invention' of heresy. This means that the Church itself, and notably thinkers, popes and canonists shaped non-obedience and non-conformity into a new, dangerous category: heresy. By doing so, they were able to justify its repression, which was felt by ordinary people and even by some churchmen to be theoretically contrary to the evangelical precepts of tolerance.

I do believe that a problematic approach that questions pre-existing categories, such as that of heresy, authority, dissent and so on, is necessary for healthy historical research. However, in my opinion this deconstruction has been excessive. On the doctrinal side, it leads scholars to underestimate the dualistic component within Catharism. It is also excessive on the ecclesiological side, because it leads to the denial of the existence of a Cathar church.

There must be a middle way. In studying *a* Cathar church, its ways and methods of religious belief, proselytism and organisation, together with the roles and customs of its affiliates, I wanted to take up the suggestion

---

[7] I am by no means the first one to do so. For example, in the English-speaking world, it should suffice to remember J. Given's analysis of 'resistance' in a whole section of his book *Inquisition and Medieval Society: Power, Discipline and Resistance in Languedoc*, at pp. 91–166; more recently, see Barber, *The Cathars*, pp. 150–64.

made more than two decades ago by Lorenzo Paolini,[8] when he introduced his analysis of *domus* and area ('zona') of the heretics thus: 'This is, in fact, the general historiographical problem: to detect and analyse the "alternative" structures of the heretics, the mechanisms which govern the institutions – or the attempt of the institutions – opposed to the Catholic Church, [i.e.] the practical organisation of the [Cathar] movement. These will be dioceses, deaconries, hospices, itinerant preaching, great mobility, and ultimately even … *domus* and area ['zona'].'

The first response to Paolini's invitation was made many years after his appeal. The topic was tackled from the side of 'de-construction' by a *table ronde* organised in Nice by Monique Zerner,[9] while a first attempt at 're-construction' was made by Roberta Bertuzzi.[10] In Nice, historical evidence for the so-called Council of St-Félix of Caraman was reconsidered. At this council the Cathars supposedly gave a solid basis to their church by organising it into dioceses (or diocese-like structures). This evidence was subjected to close scrutiny, with scholars undermining its authenticity and concluding that there was no coherent Cathar ecclesial structure. On the contrary, Bertuzzi's work stemmed from the assumption of the authenticity of this document, and attempted a detailed reconstruction of the Church of the Good Men and Women, its subdivision and its clergy, within the framework of a proper ecclesial organisation.

My work is a further attempt at developing once again Paolini's suggestion, looking at it from a fresh perspective.

Where possible, I have tried to include dates, but the intrinsic characteristics of the records and the fluid nature of all heretical phenomena mean that this has not always been possible.

The records themselves are inconsistent, if measured by modern notions of chronology and division of time. Our records are not the only ones to show this tendency. Arnold Esch has shown how this inconsistency figures in different ways in many different types of judicial depositions.[11] In general, deponents have difficulty in providing events with a coherent chronology. This tendency appears throughout a deposition, with phrases like 'in the time of the harvest, or thereabouts', 'at the time

---

[8] L. Paolini, 'Domus e zona degli eretici. L'esempio di Bologna nel XIII secolo', *Rivista di Storia della Chiesa in Italia* 35/2 (1981), 371–87, at pp. 372–3.

[9] M. Zerner (ed.), *L'histoire du Catharisme en question: le 'concile' de St Félix, 1167* ('Collection du Centre d'Études Médiévales de Nice' 3), (Nice, 2001).

[10] R. Bertuzzi, *'Ecclesiarum forma'. Tematiche di ecclesiologia Catara e Valdese* (Rome, 1998).

[11] A. Esch, 'Gli interrogatori di testi come fonte storica. Senso del tempo e vita sociale esplorati dall'interno', *Bullettino dell'Istituto Storico Italiano per il Medio Evo* 105 (2003), pp. 249–65.

of her second illness', and 'twenty years after the coming of the crusaders'. In addition, the records suffer from being collections and excerpts of previous registers, from referring to now lost previous depositions, and from the mistakes added by the seventeenth-century copyists. A further point is that detailed chronology is of little importance in one part of this book, my discussion of fear and risk in Chapter 4. I have therefore been sparing with dates, limiting them to those occasions where chronological contextualisation is clearly necessary. It is, in some way, ironic that we as historians face similar difficulties to the inquisitors. Both are trying or tried to overcome the 'fluidity of heretical phenomena' during the interrogations and in the records. This has been demonstrated by Gabriele Zanella and Daniele Solvi on more than one occasion.[12] For the inquisitors and for us, such fluidity made dissent and dissenters a rather ungraspable matter. It has proved hard to understand words and stories through the definitions and schemes which belonged to the medieval readers and writers of those records.

Lastly, a *mea culpa*. There is a lack of German literature in the bibliography of this book. I do not read German sufficiently well: I beg my readers' pardon.

TECHNICAL NOTES

All references to volumes 21–6 in the *Collection Doat* are abbreviated to D21, D22 and so on. It should be noted that D25 stands for D25 *and* D26 up to folio 78v, since they constitute a single enquiry. The Doat scribes kept copying the volume summarising the enquiry led by Raoul of Plassac and Pons of Parnac (D25) into the first 78 pages of the following volume.

I have translated all quotations taken from medieval Latin records and foreign secondary literature. Most translations are mine. The exceptions are D25 and D26 up to folio 78v, where I use Shelagh Sneddon's translation, as it will appear in the forthcoming edition of these volumes, and those existing published translations of medieval sources whose editions are cited in my footnotes. I have made extensive use of the texts translated by Walter Wakefield and Austin Evans.[13]

When referring to deponents and/or inquisitors, the first name is given in English, where translation is possible (e.g. 'Guillaume' becomes 'William'), otherwise in French (e.g. 'Esclarmunda' becomes

---

[12] See Bibliography for references.
[13] *Heresies of the High Middle Ages*, 2nd ed, (New York, 1991) [henceforth Wakefield and Evans].

'Esclarmonde'); when the second name is a surname, this is given in the equivalent French (e.g. 'Bernard Faure' for 'Bernardus Fabri'); when it is an indication of provenance, equally this is modernised to current French (e.g. 'Pons of Gomerville' for 'Poncius de Gomenvilla'). In some cases a precise identification has not been possible: there the Latin version is retained in italics.

Chapter 1

STORIES, AND HOW TO READ THEM[1]

It might seem naive, perhaps superficial, to suggest that a historian's first response to primary sources should be fascination and curiosity. If we are talking about heresy and inquisition, that curiosity drives us to get hold of words, dialogues, in an ultimate effort to salvage fragments of those lives that are so quickly forgotten, so easily moulded into statistics and theories, so often just used as a means to substantiate our statements. Yet names and stories are not enough: inquisition trials remain perhaps one of the few types of sources which allow us to hear people's voices.

This discussion builds upon developments in source criticism of the 1960s and 1970s.[2] Since then, following a period of relative lack of interest in this topic with regard to inquisitorial texts, there has recently been an increase in historians' attention to the application of these methods, in the wake of the development of postmodernist theories of

---

[1] The core of this first chapter has been published, with the title ' "Magna diligentia est habenda per inquisitorem": Precautions before reading Doat 21–26', in C. Bruschi and P. Biller (eds.), *Texts and the Repression of Medieval Heresy* ('York Studies in Medieval Theology' 4) (York, 2002), pp. 81–110. I have introduced more material from the sources, and updated the bibliography. Also, some of my ideas have slightly changed after discussing the matter with colleagues and students at the University of Birmingham. I thank them very much for their suggestions and criticism.

[2] H. Grundmann, 'Ketzerverhöre des Spätmittelalters als quellenkritisches Problem', *Deutsches Archiv für Erforschung des Mittelalters* 21 (1965), 519–75; R. Lerner, *The Heresy of the Free Spirit in the Later Middle Ages* (Berkeley, Los Angeles and London, 1972); G.G. Merlo, *Eretici e inquisitori nella società piemontese del Trecento* (Turin, 1977); G.G. Merlo, 'I registri inquisitoriali come fonti per la storia dei gruhpi ereticali clandestini: il caso del Piemonte' in M. Tilloy, G. Audisio, and J. Chiffoleau (eds.), *Histoire et clandestinité du Moyen Age à la Première Guerre mondiale, Colloque de Privas (Mai 1977)* (Albi, 1979), pp. 59–74; *idem*, 'La coercizione all'ortodossia: comunicazione e imposizione di un messaggio religioso egemonico (Sec. XIII–XIV)', *Società e Storia* 10 (1980), 803–23; C. Ginzburg, *The Cheese and the Worms: the Cosmos of a Sixteenth-Century Miller* (London, 1980) [orig. edn. *Il formaggio e i vermi* (Turin, 1976)]; N.Z. Davis, 'Les conteurs de Montaillou (note critique)', *Annales. Economie, Société, Civilisation* 34 (1979), 61–73.

language and power.[3] Some attention needs to be given to methodo-logical approaches, their relevance and effectiveness, and distinctions need to be drawn between them.

Suggestions coming from historians such as Grundmann, Lerner, Ginzburg and Merlo, now considered as 'classics', were developed because they were confronting very different and peculiar texts, and unusual diffi-culties. While some of their sources equated heretics with other rejected or marginal groups, emphasising their libertine sexual activities and doing this within very rigid and repetitive frameworks and language, others were less shaped by stereotypes and formulas, and offered more of a glimpse of 'untouched' information. Overall, the records of inquisition trials posed to their careful readers the stark and simple problem of trust-worthiness – to believe their contents or not.

The tools produced by such innovative and thorough source criticism in those years, however, because of their sustained application, led then to the replacement of credibility as *the* fundamental theme, and to the shifting of focus onto the reasons for and dynamics of the supply of information in these sources. A weighty inheritance derives from these scholars: they set up the *pars destruens* ('destructive part') of innovative textual criticism, providing a strong basis for the methodology which will be adopted here. Their inheritance has been collected and deepened by modern historians who have become particularly interested in very recent years in taking enquiries a step further, to examining how and to what extent 'reasons for and dynamics of the supply of information' influenced the 'creation' of heresy and dissent. Effectively, through the deconstruction of the text, they sought to deconstruct the phenomenon of heresy.

Such a view, although highly suggestive and to some extent extremely useful for reading heresy trials, risks going too far in the direction of what Del Col calls 'radical scepticism', ultimately an obstacle to reading sources that remain unique and irreplaceable for the understanding of –

---

[3] Perhaps the first publication to tackle this issue afresh since the 1970s has been the collection of studies in J.C. Maire Vigueur and A. Paravicini Bagliani (eds.), *La parola all'accusato* (Palermo, 1991), where the contribution by Jean-Louis Biget has focused on the French records, following a similar path but reaching conclusions which are substantially different from mine (J.-L. Biget, 'I catari di fronte agli inquisitori in Languedoc (1230–1310)', pp. 235–51, esp. pp. 240–2 and 245–51). Among the most recent contributions, M. Zerner (ed.), *Inventer l'hérésie? Discours polémiques et pouvoirs avant l'Inquisition* ('Collection du Centre d'Études Médiévales de Nice' 2) (Nice, 1998), esp. pp. 193–218; *Catharisme: l'édifice imaginaire* ('Collection *Heresis*' 7) (Carcassonne, 1998); J. Arnold, *Inquisition and Power. Catharism and the Confessing Subject in Medieval Languedoc* (Philadelphia, PA, 2001); M.G. Pegg, *The Corruption of the Angels. The Great Inquisition of 1245–6* (Princeton and Oxford, 2001); M.G. Pegg, 'On Cathars, "Albigenses" and Good Men of Languedoc', *Journal of Medieval History* 27/2 (2001), 181–95; J. Théry, 'L'hérésie des bons hommes. Comment nommer la dissidence réligieuse non vau-dois ni béguine en Languedoc (XIIe–début du XIVe siècle)?', *Heresis* 36–7 (2002), 75–117.

at least – religious dissent in the Late Middle Ages and the Early Modern period. A middle position has sometimes been maintained, especially by those historians who, perhaps because of their more traditional cultural formation, have been less inclined to surrender to the charms of the theory of language.[4] This last approach has established a successful *pars construens* ('constructive part') balancing the use of textual and non-textual filters for a fruitful reading of the sources. The next step for historians and social scientists alike is – arguably – a much freer reading of the phenomenon of dissent, drawing from interdisciplinary studies in a conceptual and practical way.[5]

On the whole, the records of inquisitorial trials seem to bring us face-to-face with a process of memory construction, a building-up of an ideal image of a trial, shaped *both* by the deponent and the inquisitor. This does not involve us in striving to discover a 'truth' after stripping away all the 'filters' from the depositions. The starting point is a text in its totality, constructed with a very practical and concrete goal, recorded with techniques and features which are themselves dependent on several practical and subjective features, and created by both sets of actors in the performance. This also makes the process of reconstruction one of creation, reordering and producing another constructed text about the same 'stories'. Moreover, historians should never forget that texts like ours should not be read just as literary products. They still record the lives, deaths, plots, suffering and feelings of people who actually were brought to trial, gave their testimony, and for this were either released or condemned.

At the centre of attention here are volumes 21–6 of the *Collection Doat*, relating to the Toulouse area and containing mainly trial depositions of

---

[4] Together with Ginzburg, who maintained a rather detached view on the problem (for instance in his 'The Inquisitor as anthropologist', in *Clues, Myths and the Historical Method* (Baltimore, OH, 1989) [orig. edn. *Miti, emblemi, spie: morfologia e storia* (Turin, 1986)], pp. 156–64), I shall quote here A. Del Col, *L'Inquisizione nel patriarcato e diocesi di Aquileia 1557–1559* ('Inquisizione e Società'. Fonti 1) (Trieste, 1998); A. Del Col, 'Minute a confronto con i verbali definitivi nel pro cesso del Sant'Ufficio di Belluno contro Petri Rayther (1557)', in *Le scritture e le opere degli inquisitori*, Quaderni di Storia Religiosa IX (2002), pp. 201–37; J. Tedeschi, 'Inquisitorial sources and their uses', in *The Prosecution of Heresy: Collected Studies on the Inquisition in Early Modern Italy* (Binghamton, NY, 1991), pp. 47–88; A. Esch, 'Gli interrogatori di testi come fonte storica. Senso del tempo e vita sociale esplorati dall'interno', *Bullettino dell'Istituto Storico Italiano per il Medio Evo* 105 (2003), 249–65; M.G. Bascapé, ' "In armariis officii inquisitoris Ferrariensis". Ricerche su un frammento inedito del processo Pungilupo', *Quaderni di Storia Religiosa* 9 (2002), 31–110; P. Biller, ' "Through a glass darkly": seeing medieval heresy', in P. Linehan and J. Nelson (eds.), *The Medieval World* (Routledge, 2001), pp. 308–26; see also my comments on the problems of a purely Foucauldian approach in my review of J. Arnold *Inquisition and Power*, in *Journal of Ecclesiastical History*, 55/3 (July 2004), 576–7.

[5] See, for instance, the very interesting suggestions in J. Forné, 'Approche pluridisciplinaire du concept de "dissidence" ', *Heresis* 36–7 (2002), 279–92.

Cathars and Waldensians from 1237 to 1289.[6] Internal features, contents, actors, area and time are variables within each of them. Internal and external characteristics differ quite markedly, with each volume displaying a distinctive and unique pattern that requires in turn its own individual and unique method of reading. Doat material has usually not been regarded this way, because at first sight it does not present the clearly manipulated evidence of other trial records, such as those which preoccupied Grundmann and the others. It sounds so plain and clear in its rhapsodic rhythm and development – it is sometimes even quite boring – that one can easily forget the precautions needed when reading it.[7]

The general approach here is that the original dialogue between inquisitors and witnesses has been modified several times: first of all by the witness, then by a series of selections, dissections and voluntary omissions carried out by the inquisitors and notaries. Our analysis therefore begins by listing and describing the 'filters' through which we should look at the confessions: these can be called 'tools'. Linked to this approach are the two 'truths' that the actors, inquisitor and deponent, bring to life. Fragments of the deponent's 'truth' are visible. These will be referred to as 'objects', specific examples of which can be labelled as 'surplus features'; that is, what, though filtered, appear to be genuine and authentic pieces of the original deposition. All the time we must bear in mind that a first selection took place during the trial itself, while a second is the result of the recording process. Their modes and criteria throw light on the 'building method' employed and chosen by the parties. Going down this path we can hope to arrive at an understanding of the aims of all those who took part in shaping the record and, further, to identify what message – conscious or unconscious – the final stage of the register conveys to modern readers.

TOOLS: 'FILTERS'

What is immediately striking when first browsing through these Doat volumes is the tremendous variation in the nature of the records. Some of the registers are lively, narrative and intriguing, while others appear

---

[6] For a full account of the *Doat Collection*, see C. Molinier, *L'Inquisition dans le Midi de la France* (Paris: Sandoz, 1880), at pp. 34–40.

[7] The reference here is to some classic works on textual criticism: B. Stock, *The Implications of Literacy: Written Languages and Models of Interpretation in the 11th and 12th Centuries* (Princeton, NJ, 1987); B. Stock, *Listening for the Text: On the Uses of Past* (Baltimore, OH, and London, 1990); M.T. Clanchy, *From Memory to Written Record: England 1066–1307*, 2nd edn. (Oxford and Malden, MA, 1993); I. Illich, *In the Vineyard of the Text* (Chicago, 1993); L.A. Finke and M.B. Shichtman (eds.), *Medieval Text and Contemporary Readers* (Ithaca, NY, and London, 1987).

mostly formulaic, mechanical and repetitive documents. How many factors contributed to this differentiation? External conditions relating to the course of the trial and the conscious strategies of each of the two parties could have driven the inquiry and its registration to the stage we now read. At the same time there is the survival among modern historians of a rather old-fashioned notion of these features, and this creates a fixed and static image of the trials: a discourse led by only a single guide – the inquisitor – towards the alteration of the original deposition, shaped *ad hoc* for the purposes of the inquisitor himself.

Filters depending on the enquiry: number, grilles

Most confessions were collected during the so-called 'periods of grace', when mitigation of punishment was granted by the inquisitors to those who voluntarily confessed or gave testimony on matters of heresy.[8] Nearly 6,000 witnesses are recorded by MS Toulouse 609.[9] It is easy to imagine crowds of people waiting for their turn to give their deposition, outside the inquisitor's residence: while waiting for their turn to give deposition, these people could have set up plots, agreements or common

---

[8] The *literature* on procedure is quite wide. An overview of inquisitorial manuals about procedure can be found in C. Molinier, 'Rapport à M. le Ministre de l'Instruction publique sur une mission exécutée en Italie de février à avril 1885', *Archives des missions scientifiques e littéraires*, III ser., 14 (1888), 133–336, at pp. 158–206; and A. Dondaine, 'Le manuel de l'Inquisiteur (1230–1330)', *Archivum Fratrum Praedicatorum* 17 (1947), 85–194; see now R. Parmeggiani, 'Un secolo di manualistica inquisitoriale (1230–1330): intertestualità e circolazione del diritto', *Rivista Internazionale di Diritto Comune* 13 (2002), 229–70. According to Dondaine's list, the earliest manuals are the *Consultatio* of Pierre d'Albalat, known as the *Directorium* of Raymond of Peñafort (1242), the *Ordo processus Narbonensis* (probably 1248/9), and the *Explicatio super officio Inquisitionis* (1262–77). On fluctuation in procedure, see J. Paul, 'La procédure inquisitoriale à Carcassonne au milieu du XIIIe siècle', *Cahiers de Fanjeaux* 29 (1994), 361–96. This shows day-to-day variations in *formule*, following the notaries' notes. On *evolution in procedure* after the 'crisis', Y. Dossat, *Les crises de l'Inquisition toulousaine au XIIIe siècle (1233–1273)* (Bordeaux, 1959), from p. 195. On *defence*, W. Ullmann, 'The defence of the accused in the Medieval inquisition', in G. Garnett (ed.), *Law and Jurisdiction in the Middle Ages* (London, 1988), pp. 481–9; J.C. Maire Vigueur and A. Paravicini Bagliani (eds.), *La parola all'accusato* (Palermo, 1991). Examples of *registers* are J.-M.Vidal, 'Le tribunal de l'Inquisition de Pamiers. Notice sur le régistre de l'évêque Jacques Fournier', *Annales de St Louis-des-Français* 8/1 (Oct. 1903), 377–435; J. Duvernoy (ed.), *Régistre de Bernard de Caux. Pamiers (1246–1247)*, *Bulletin de la Société Ariégeoise des Sciences, Lettres et Arts* 1990, pp. 5–108. On *tempus gratie*, see A.P. Evans, 'Hunting subversion in the Middle Ages', *Speculum* 33 (1958), 1–22. An example of the importance of *numbers in interrogations* is in L. Sala-Molins (ed.), N. Eymerich and F. Peña, *Le manuel de l'Inquisiteur* (Paris and La Haye, 1973), ch. 30, pp. 142–3.

[9] Ms. 609, Toulouse, Bibliothèque Municipal. This contains the depositions of the 1245–6 inquiry held by Bernard of Caux and Jean of St Pierre (see Pegg, *The Corruption*). See also the material collected by the same two inquisitors and partially included in D22 and D24, quoted in Y. Dossat, 'Une figure d'inquisiteur: Bernard de Caux', *Cahiers de Fanjeaux* 6 (1971), pp. 153–72.

lines of defence.[10] They sometimes had to face days far away from home, long waits, expense and probably fear. Bernard Barre of Sorèze has a little argument with some fellow villagers, who try to persuade him not to make accusations against them during his hearing. Finding him reluctant they come up with an old proverb, 'Men catch oxen by their horns, and peasants by their tongues'.[11] Again, in MS Toulouse 609 Pons Stephen gives evidence of agreements on a common line of defence:

He said that when brother W. Arnold was carrying out an inquisition, Raymond of Auriac said to him the witness – in the presence of Raymond Hugh, knight of Aiguesvives, in the diocese of Carcassonne – that when questioned by the inquisitors one should answer 'not yet' to everything; for so all the men of Auriac had agreed among themselves to give such an answer in front of the inquisitors. And then he the witness replied to Raymond Auriac that there was no way he would say 'not yet' to the said inquisitors. Instead, he would tell them the whole truth on everything he knew about heresy.[12]

Undoubtedly, the higher the number of deponents, the shorter and drier the records. Pressure of numbers produced rapid summary proceedings that could have taken weeks in other circumstances. This is the first filter, arising from practical conditions, that could strongly affect the 'factual truth' as it is commonly understood: a powerful and insidious filter, imposing brevity on the record and thereby perhaps limiting and abbreviating to the bare bones the 'ideal' deposition for a historian, one

---

[10] See Ullmann, 'The defence'; J. Given, *Inquisition and Medieval Society: Power, Discipline and Resistance in Languedoc* (Ithaca, NY, and London, 1997), ch. 6 *Manipulation*; on my interpretation of the deponents' 'reaction', see below, Chapter 4.

[11] 'Bovem capit homo per cornu, et rusticum per linguam' D25, f. 296v. See P. Biller, *Heresy and Literacy: Earlier history of the Theme*, in P. Biller and A. Hudson (eds.), *Heresy and Literacy, 1000–1530*, ('Cambridge Studies in Medieval Literature' 23), (Cambridge, 1994), pp. 1–18, esp. p. 9. The author refers to J.W. Hassel, *Middle French proverbs, sentences and proverbial phrases*, ('Subsidia Medievalia' 12), (Toronto, 1982), p. 55, n. B118, 'On prend le boeuf par la corne et l'homme par la langue' (earliest French attestation 1463), and p. 130, n. H50, 'On prende l'homme par la langue'; see also J. Morawski (ed.), *Proverbes Français antérieurs au XVe siècle* (Paris, 1925), n. 225, p. 9 ('Bele parole fet fol lié') and n. 1588, p. 58 ('Par les cornes loye on les buefz'). For a discussion of this proverb, albeit conducted on a different ground, see Arnold, *Inquisition and Power*, p. 110; J. Arnold, ' "A man takes an ox by the horn and a peasant by the tongue": Literacy, Orality and Inquisition in Medieval Languedoc', in C. Cross, S. Rees-Jones and F. Riddy (eds.), *Learning and Literacy in the Middle Ages* (Turnhout, 2001), pp. 31–48.

[12] 'Dixit quod cum frater W. Arnaldi faceret inquisitionem Ramundus de Auriaco dixit ipsi testi, presente Ramundo Hugone milite de Aquis Vivis diocesis Carcassonensi, quod quando inquireretur ab inquisitoribus ad omnia responderet eis 'no[n]dum', quia sic condixerant inter se omnes homines de Auriaco de dicta responsione cum essent coram dictis inquisitoribus; et tunc ipse testis respondit Ramundo de Auriaco quod [n]ullo modo diceret 'no[n]dum' inquisitoribus prefatis, immo diceret eis plenariam veritatem de hiis que noverat de heresi'. This is quoted in W.L. Wakefield, 'Heretics and Inquisitors: the case of Auriac and Cambiac', *Journal of Medieval History* 12 (1986), 225–37, at p. 229.

that is rich in detail and full of information. This first filter can also mislead and distort modern historians' perspectives.

While the written record may be shaped by such practical conditions, it presupposes a pattern of questions. These were not all taken down, and those that were are not necessarily complete. These questions in turn depend on several elements connected to the inquiry: the nature and number of clues, the tracks followed by the investigation, the presence or absence of previous depositions, the inquisitor's and the notary's knowledge of technical and theoretical matters, and the correct stage of development of canon and civil law.[13] Besides these elements, no doubt each inquisitor and notary carried with him his own personal experience, the particular aim of the investigation and the reasons why the witness was brought to trial. In a dialogue there is what we might call the 'psychology of exchange' – anticipating each other's views; for example – and there is deliberate intention – trying to produce a desired result, such as escaping the charge, hiding friends or finding someone guilty. Intrinsic to any dialogue is each party's tendency to manipulate the other party's reactions and hence the path of the discussion itself.

The final result of this various and multiform process of construction is now represented by six volumes of inquiries which differ from one another in their structural features, and also – and more importantly – in their methodology of interrogation. Whereas the focus is sometimes on relationships between the deponents, some other interrogations concentrate on heretical beliefs, on preaching activity, or on ways and modes of the ritual of *hereticatio* (administering the Cathar *consolamentum*). Some are particularly centred on the activities and movements of the Cathar hierarchy, while others' curiosity is directed towards the everyday life of the common 'believers'. Only through a thorough analysis of the volumes *in toto* can one understand how the different filters affect the construction of events. For instance, the structural grid of the interrogation becomes much more visible to the reader when the same episode is seen to recur in different depositions or registers. The case of the massacre of Avignonet offers the most remarkable example. The Doat volumes provide 'multiple versions' of this obscure page of history, differently shaped by different deponents, questions, situations and roles.[14] Even here, the modern historian can do no more than gauge the personalisation of a

---

[13] Quite often, in fact, the questions proposed correspond exactly to the conciliar canons, see Merlo, *Eretici e inquisitori*, and Grundmann, 'Ketzerverhöre'; on 'literary' *topoi*, Lerner, *Free Spirit*, pp. 20–5; more extensively Given, *Inquisition*, pp. 24–51, on the 'technology of documentation'; Esch, 'Gli interrogatori', p. 263 on the difference between the line taken in the inquisition and in other interrogations.

[14] I shall investigate this further down.

story, measure the angle of one human being's perspective on the facts. In the end, objectivity is always hidden in an onlooker's eyes.

Filters depending on the process of recording: procedure, translation, competence

To judge from first appearances, the main feature slowing down and limiting the natural flow of narration is the formulaic mode found in the written record. When taken to the extreme, the text becomes no more than a series of confirmations (or denials) of accusations and questions. One senses a broken rhythm, characterised by short and monotonous sentences, giving a strong impression of a form – a form to be filled in only with 'yes', 'no', or 'I don't know'.

Listing the stages of the interrogation can help in figuring out this element.[15] Even in its simplest form, it contains filters. First of all, there was questioning of the witness, where the questions could be based on the contents of previous depositions (for example, in the case of a heresy suspect, accusations brought against her or him in the depositions of other witnesses). The questions could simply be based on a list prescribed in an inquisitors' manual: 'When did you first see heretics? Where? With whom?', and so on – a grille of questions. This dialogue was held in Provençal. Secondly, the notary wrote a first draft, in Latin, and reread it aloud to the witness, but this time in Provençal. The witness was free to approve or modify the text, and only later on did the notary proceed to the definitive registration, again, in Latin. This last stage is what appears written on the parchment of the manuscript, undeniably differing from the first deposition, if one assumes that in each phase selections, misunderstandings and mistakes will have occurred. Even though the final version had to be ratified, it was always possible that the witness was unable – or did not want – to remember every previous statement, or which version of the facts he gave to the notary, or more simply did not think it necessary to dwell upon details, fearing to bore and annoy the inquisitor.

Viewed from a distance, problems relating to language – many of them common to the genre of records of interrogations under any legal system[16] – lie on the *surface* of our written texts. However, the sheer

---

[15] See for instance *Ordo processus Narbonensis*, in K.-V. Selge, *Texte zur Inquisition* (Gutersloh, 1967), pp. 70–6, p. 71. More specific is J.M. Vidal, 'Le tribunal de l'Inquisition de Pamiers. Notice sur le registre de l'évêque Jacques Fournier', *Annales de St Louis-des-Français* 8/1 (Oct. 1903), 377–435, p. 387.

[16] Many studies tackle the recording process and see it as the main problem responsible for modifying the original speech, and all refer to problems of language. Albeit relative to different contexts

variety of translations within the confessions, the linguistic competence of the officials, and the requirement of complete interchangeability of Provençal and Latin are language problems as well, and ones which also existed at a deeper level of the text, constituting – that is to say structuring and producing – them in a fundamental way.[17] We must not neglect the fact that such a complex structure of translations required a body of quite highly skilled notaries, and that whenever the tribunal lacked such competence a rigid series of formulae and questions could have been very convenient. In addition to this, the more complex the structure and grille of questions, the longer the notary's job, particularly in the case of one who was unskilled or incompetent. Sometimes, therefore, a very formulaic and strict text may be a symptom of inadequate officials in regard to the task they faced.

Composing the written record involved selection. Although impossible to measure, given the total absence of notes taken during the hearing, selection aimed at the deletion of elements, digressions, names, particulars and phrases that were judged superfluous, useless or even inconvenient. Nor could the notes have been taken down word for word. As a consequence, the criteria underlying our records were mostly applied by the notary. Although subordinate to the inquisitor, the notary was trained in law, and able to assess and evaluate the relevant *loca* (important passages) of the confession.[18] His prominent role during the hearing is attested by Peter Ferreol of Trébons, at his third and last retraction. After abjuring and receiving a *penitentia arbitraria* (arbitrary[19] penance), he bluntly claims that in the record of the previous hearing the notary only wrote

---

and periods, some suggest interesting paths of analysis. For the medieval context, a remarkable overview is in Esch, 'Gli interrogatori'; for issues of language and speech, see the Introduction in C. Wickham, *Legge, pratiche e conflitti. Tribunali e risoluzione delle dispute nella Toscana del XII secolo* (Rome, 2000), pp. 21–42, esp. pp. 27–8; also, C. Wickham, 'Gossip and resistance among the Medieval peasantry', *Past and Present* 159 (1998), 3–24 esp. pp. 9, 15, 23; for problems in later sources, see A. Prosperi, *Tribunali della coscienza. Inquisitori, confessori, missionari* (Turin, 1996), esp. pp. 244–57; A. Del Col, '*L'Inquisizione nel patriarcato*', pp. 177–8; see also cases of modern-day interrogations, such as those during the Israeli-Palestinian conflict and Guantanamo Bay (see M. Bowden, 'The Persuaders', *Observer Monthly*, 19 October 2003, pp. 28–40).

[17] In a wider sense, inquisitors used Provençal as an 'exchange language', and Latin as a 'codification language'.

[18] See W.L. Wakefield, 'Les assistants des inquisiteurs témoins des confessions dans le manuscrit 609', *Heresis* 20 (1993), 57–65. As far as I know, Ms Clermont-Ferrand 160 is the only example of a record of notes taken by a notary. The case comes from the Carcassonne inquisition (1249–58). On its features, see Paul, 'La procédure inquisitoriale'. See also the forthcoming S. Sneddon, 'The role of the notary in some heresy depositions from 1270s Toulouse'. For a later period, A. Del Col, 'Minute a confronto con i verbali definitivi nel processo del Sant'Ufficio di Belluno contro Petri Rayther (1557)', in *Le scritture e le opere degli inquisitori*, *Quaderni di Storia Religiosa* IX (2002), pp. 201–37.

[19] = 'Variable, according to the person who imposes it.'

down part of what he said: 'And he omitted to mention these things because of forgetfulness, as he says in his first confession; and because the notary who then received his confession did not trouble to write down anything except the things which he confessed to having committed since the time of peace.'[20] At least a couple more filters are identified by Peter's words. First, the notary uses a chronological criterion to select from the confession: a sort of time-limit separating what is worthwhile from what is superfluous. The notary 'non curavit', 'he did not care' to record what followed the 'tempus pacis', thus erecting a real barrier to our comprehension of the sequence of events. He nevertheless seems to trust the deponent, and to leave him free to carry out his own selection. What has already been filtered by Peter himself in his previous confessions is recorded, while further questions are omitted and the enquiry is not taken further. One can read the notary's attitude as that of a busy official who is in a hurry, and is now hearing somebody who has already appeared before the court. Knowing his previous depositions the notary evaluates as important only the last part of Peter's confession. In essence, what he does is abbreviate – and in doing so, eliminate.

A very similar attitude emerges in the deposition of Baretges, wife of Peter Grimoard, when recalling a confession completely deleted from the records: 'Her confession was not written down because the inquisitors did not want to record it.'[21] Whether this is a note from the inquisitor, interpreting some sort of reluctance in Baretges' words, or Baretges' own statement, whether true or false, this phrase is considered worth recording. Later on, Bernard Gui suggests in his manual:

However, it is not expedient for all questions[22] to be written down, but only those which reach more plausibly the substance or the essence of a fact, and which seem to express truth the most. In fact, if in some deposition one finds such an abundance of questions, another deposition containing fewer questions could seem diminished [in value].[23] Furthermore, it is rather difficult to find any agreement in the inquiry when so many interrogations are recorded – a matter for awareness and precaution.[24]

---

[20] 'Et hec omisit dicere propter oblivionem, sicut dicit in prima confessione sua; et quia notarius qui tunc recepit confessionem suam non curavit scribere nisi ea que confitebatur commisisse citra tempus pacis.' D26, f. 65r.

[21] 'Confessio sua non fuit scripta quia inquisitores noluerunt scribere confessionem suam', D22, f. 43v.

[22] Here the Latin *interrogatio* seems to mean one act of questioning, together with the reply.

[23] *diminuta*: Wakefield and Evans translate as 'too brief', Mollat as 'tronqueé'.

[24] 'Non tamen expedit quod omnes interrogationes scribantur, set tantum ille que magis verisimiliter tangunt substantiam vel naturam facti, et que magis videntur exprimere veritatem. Si enim in aliqua depositione inveniretur tanta interrogationum multitudo, alia depositio pauciores continens posset diminuta videri, et etiam cum tot interrogationibus conscriptis in processu vix

It is worth noting Gui's criteria for a fair record: *substantia facti* ('the substance of a fact'), *natura facti* ('the essence of a fact'), *veritas* ('truth'), some sort of 'balance' of the depositions within the same enquiry or register, and finally *concordia* ('agreement') among them.

Filters depending on narration: linguistic level, will

Further interesting filters depend on the dynamics of narration.[25] Such filters are the only ones arising from the words and will of the deponent. Only when deposing before the judge does he or she have the opportunity to modify the construction of the record. Although important, confessing just what one wants to be known is not the only way to influence the text. Approving or denying the text submitted by the notary is another, powerful one, especially given that the main objective of inquisitorial records is to list, file and preserve. Such intervention by the deponent is one of the determinants of the text *per se* and of its formation.

However many digressions may have come from a deponent, there are few in the record.[26] This is because they will have been seen as redundant and pointless to record, though to the modern reader they are of more significance. Only a comparison between different depositions within one enquiry can highlight what goes beyond the 'set pattern', the main line followed by that specific questionnaire. This highlighted part can be read as an accused person's construction. Here we are going further down the path of Ginzburg's 'untapped level' of narration.[27] In classifying these 'surplus features' or deponent's constructions, the first task is to point out filters that depend strictly on the narrative process itself, moving then to a freer reading of the depositions. Finally, an attempt can be made to sketch the general characteristics of these 'surplus features'.

---

posset concordia in depositionibus testium inveniri, quod considerandum est et precavendum': Bernard Gui, *Le manuel de l'Inquisiteur*, ed. G. Mollat (Paris, 1964), p. 32.

[25] I am greatly indebted here to the interesting suggestions coming from Wickham, 'Gossip and resistance'; P. Zagorin, *Ways of Lying: Dissimulation, Persecution and Conformity in Early Modern Europe* (Cambridge, MA, and London, 1990); A. Gurevich, *Categories of Medieval Culture* (London, 1985); A. Gurevich, *Medieval Popular Culture: Problems of Belief and Perception* (Cambridge, 1988); S. Justice, 'Inquisition, speech and writing: a case from Late Medieval Norwich', in R. Copeland (ed.), *Criticism and Dissent in the Middle Ages* (Cambridge, 1996), pp. 289–322; Ginzburg, 'The Inquisitor as anthropologist'.

[26] Although cautious and manipulative, even Eymerich's manual sets a limit. It states that it is never fruitful to interrupt the suspects while confessing since they could feel like going back to their stubborn silence (*Le manuel de l'Inquisiteur*, ed. L. Sala-Molins, (Paris and La Haye, 1973), p. 10.

[27] Ginzburg, *The Cheese and the Worms*, p. xix.

Awareness of the characteristics of storytelling in popular culture is a prerequisite for this enquiry.[28] Without altering the peculiarity and value of each deposition, the aim has been to identify where and to what extent the discourse was driven by and channelled into a literate-friendly, pre-shaped grille; not merely 'physically' in the context of a trial, but rather through the definitive recording of dialogues.[29]

The cultural 'transposition of language' onto a new cultural level – from popular to literate, and the other way round – generated further filters in the deposition. Whenever a translation, summary or record was required by procedure, the notary had to reshape the deponent's words into a new language. This process did not just translate the words, it substantiated the record with a new terminology, at once more technical yet also revealing a different, more refined perception of the semantic value of the words. For instance, it is interesting to see how the notary – or the inquisitor – interpreted the words of Bernard Laguarrigue for the purpose of the record. When a fellow Cathar came to know that Bernard was living with the inquisitors as their servant, he addressed him angrily: "'It would be much better for you if you lived on your own! ... Have you lost all your good altogether?" – meaning to say "your faith", or "error of the heretics".'[30] The writer here distinguishes three linguistic levels, and puts himself at the end of a treble transposition of meaning, in order to 'decode' Bernard's words to the writer's fellow inquisitors, the only possible future readers of his script. In the first passage, from 'all your good' ('omni bono') to 'faith' ('fide'), we can imagine that the inquisitor asked Bernard to be clearer and explain what he [Bernard] had meant with his general wording; while the second passage – from 'faith' ('fide') to 'error of the heretics' ('errore hereticorum') is certainly a Catholic transposition for the understanding of inquisitors only.

Far from 'fine-tuning' the different 'levels', our aim here is to underline the problem of 'cultural opposition'. Whatever the deponents' sociocultural level, the linguistic technicalities of a functional record suppressed and reshaped the semantics of depositions. Cases like the one above are extremely rare: they show the mechanism that in all the other cases has been deleted from the record. Many a time a highly literate inquisitor had to face a peasant, and even when he did not, a complete uniformity of background can never be assumed. This element of 'cultural opposition' is

---

[28] Again, this is a minefield for historians. I shall limit myself here to the classic works of Natalie Z. Davis: *The Return of Martin Guerre* (Cambridge, MA, and London, 1983), p. 3; *Fiction in the Archives: Pardon Tales and their Tellers in Sixteenth-Century France* (Stanford, CA, 1988), p. 18 and n. 43, p. 19).

[29] See also J. Fentress and C. Wickham, *Social Memory* (Oxford, 1992), chs. 1, 3 and 4.

[30] 'Melius esset vobis si moraremini per vos! ... Evacuavistis vos omnino omni bono? – intelligens dicere de fide, seu errore hereticorum', D26, f. 246v.

something else that either side could take advantage of, or instead perceive as a barrier to understanding the other. Not just a question of variation of content, it is more a matter of forcing language. A sense of cultural non-uniformity provoked in both parties a self-censorship and a shifting of language towards unusual significance. The same mechanism works when speaking foreign languages, or talking to people who belong to different cultural levels: people aim at simplifying syntax and words when wanting to clarify, and tend to complicate them when wanting to hide.

Should we then deduce that richness in detail is proportional to the deponent's desire to distract the interrogator? Not always. Another element has to be considered: popular narrative schemes rely heavily on the use of digression and detail.[31]

Another feature to be taken into account is the intentions and agency of the deponent. Putting aside the pressures of the questioning, we must remember the obvious, namely that the deponent confessed what he or she wished to be known.[32] Scholars and modern media tend to deny any degree of agency, and usually produce a predominantly stereo-typical picture: a witness, petrified and completely passive in front of the sadistic minister of the repressive power. Reconsideration is needed of these sorts of images, which derive only in part from historical evidence and more from our preconceived ideas and emotions about the inqui-sition. The Doat accounts – even at first glance – do not reveal utterly passive or impotent victims deprived of the opportunity to defend and justify their behaviour. This is not to claim that the deponents had equal weight in shaping the dialogue, nor that the inquisitorial tribunals were friendly or harmless. To escape was often the goal; horrible, unforget-table episodes affected life in southern France. Rather, what must be underlined is how wrong it is for the historian always to perpetuate this same stereotype, encouraging the assumption that the same 'emotional reactions' are always found among the deponents. In fact, analysis of the

---

[31] In my perspective 'popular narrative' is a more evident feature than the literate discourse, being farther away from the 'grilles' of *doctores*, and more likely to be spontaneous in one who is under psychological pressure, and therefore suitable for a confession. See also Davis, *Fiction in the Archives*, esp. p. 18, and n. 43. Similar generalisations dictated by excessive intellectual anxiety to file fluid concepts can be seen – as argued by P. Friedmann – in texts *on* peasants, where, 'images of peasants did not form an uncontested or "hegemonic" discourse that serenely justified how peasants were treated. Historians reading literary sources are often tempted to reduce them to ideological state-ments at the expense of their specificity as essentially imaginative works ... doctrinaire though such texts may be, they possess an individuality, seriousness and inner tension that resists ideo-logical simplification' (*Images of the Medieval Peasant* (Stanford, CA, 1999), p. 4).

[32] 'Le plus souvent, ce sont eux qui organisent leur récit à leur manière et sans interruption', Davis, 'Les conteurs', p. 70; 'The would-be supplicant arrived at the royal notary's office, then, with a story in mind and, in the case of a literate person, perhaps with a draft', Davis, *Fiction in the Archives*, p. 20.

depositions shows that any attempt to reconstruct the emotional impact of the 'inquisitorial performance' on any single individual relies on far too many variables for it to be clearly understood.

How resilient are the witnesses? To what extent can their role be defined as 'active' in the construction of the text? The well-known case of the notary William Tron from Tarascon throws some light on the question.[33] As a miserly, disliked and bitter man, William provoked a strong reaction from the people he had harmed in the past. Previous colleagues and enemies conspired to accuse him – falsely – of heresy, in order to have him imprisoned, and thus bring about his downfall. Setting up an elaborate net of cross-testimonies, accusations and clues, they managed to make the powerful criminal law of both the lay and the inquisitorial powers work to their own purposes. Jacques Fournier, in charge of the enquiry, discovered and destroyed the plot.

Should we then suggest that in each case people's perceptions of danger varied, that the levels of fear and risk were always different? Yes.[34] This is proved by the fact that some of the Doat registers are filled with retractions. Apart from any specific reasons for the alteration (perhaps force), this implies in the witness a specific degree of agency in hiding some of the facts at the first interrogation. Although realising the dangers connected to an official hearing, he or she decides to take the risk that the inquisitor, unhappy with the first deposition, might decide to go further, asking more.

Filters depending on copying

Let us move forward to the years between 1663 and 1669, when Monsieur Jean de Doat, supported by a team of copyists and proofreaders, was appointed to preserve and reproduce all the relevant documents and manuscripts kept in the archives of the south of France. The volumes resulting from this large-scale conservation project are copies of the lost registers and still represent the largest and most complete source of information on Catharism.[35] Their selection, transcription, correction, copying, and assemblage mainly followed Doat's personal criteria, but they also depended on the accessibility of the documents, the collaboration of wardens and archivists (who were often suspicious and hostile to the whole operation) and the availability of copyists able to read Latin and to

---

[33] For this case, see J.B. Given, 'Factional politics in a medieval society: a case study from fourteenth-century Foix', *Journal of Medieval History* 14/1 (1988), 233–50; Given, *Inquisition*, pp. 156–63.

[34] The issue is fully investigated in Chapter 4.

[35] See Dossat, *Les crises*, pp. 37–55, for a list of the archival patrimony of Toulouse and Carcassonne.

transcribe it decently. On these matters, in fact, Doat himself had plenty to say, when reporting to the finance inspector in Paris:

One can hardly find people capable of this work: those who read the old documents in Latin, Spanish and vernacular, don't write well at all, and those who write well, cannot read.[36] ... The documents of the archives of Rodez were in very bad state and were rotting away by the day because of the bad condition of the place [of preservation].[37] ... The main vicar did not want to give [to Doat's men] those [documents] belonging to the abbot ... which obliged the said M. Doat to send ... four copyists and the clerk, who remained there until March 4th, and made, corrected and cross-checked the copies; and as the main vicar did not want them to take away the copies, since he had no order from M. de Creussol, the clerk made a third trip to collect them with a letter from M. de Creussol.[38]

What concerns us here are the further filters supplied to the text first of all by the overall chronological sequence of the volumes (itself probably dependent on the steps taken by Doat's mission) and secondly by the selection and sequence of depositions within each volume. Thus, not only the thirteenth-century but also – and possibly more – the seventeenth-century constructed grids. Great care is needed in examining the range of filters produced during this 'second birth' of the registers.

The architecture of the collection, detailed by the inventory of Charles Molinier, mirrors that of the archives, which in fact contained much larger holdings: treatises and trial records were kept together with normative texts, sentences and manuals. The majority of these never survived, often because of the ill-will of the local religious authorities, who strongly opposed the project. For example, the vicar of the archbishop of Narbonne, who had previously declared that the local archive was ordered according to a four-volume index, then offered an 'old inventory of a few pages' to Doat's men, with the feeble excuse 'that the main difficulty was the transporting of the documents'.[39] Omissions aside, the

---

[36] 'On eut peine à trouver des personnes capables de ce travail: ceux qui lisoient les vieux titres en latin, en espagnol et en vulgaire, n'escrivoient pas assèz bien, et ceux qui écrivoient bien, ne scavoient pas lire', H. Omont, 'La Collection Doat à la Bibliothèque Nationale: Documents sur les recherches de Doat', *Bibliothèque de l'École des Chartes* 77 (1916), 286–336, p. 294.

[37] 'Les titres des archives de Rodez estoient en fort mauvais estat et périssoient tous le jours à cause de la mauvaise disposition du lieu', *ibid.*, p. 297.

[38] 'Le grand vicaire ne voulout pas délivrer ceux de l'abbé ... ce qui obligea ledit sr Doat d'y envoyer ... quatre copistes et le greffier, lesquels y demeurèrent jusqu'au 4 mars, firent faire, corriger et collationer les copies, et le grand vicaire n'ayant pas voulu qu'ils emportassent lesdites copies, qu'il n'eust ordre de M. de Creussol, le greffier fit un troisième voyage pour les retirer sur une lettre de M. de Creussol', *ibid.*, p. 298.

[39] 'Un vieux inventaire de peu de feuilles', 'que toute la difficulté consistoit au transport des titres', *ibid.*, p. 332.

material had been catalogued on territorial criteria. Inquisitorial enquiries had likewise functioned in one specific diocese, area or town; thus, both the first and the second 'births' of the registers were based on a geographical principle. According to Doat's reports, his team moved from town to town, following his instructions, chasing after documents, archivists, and therefore reproducing the same pattern of the parochial and municipal collections.

Modern readers inherit two kinds of filters from this double process of assemblage: a selection of material, and quite a high percentage of risk of misunderstanding and mistakes arising from both copyists' incompetence and the numerous steps in the process of reproduction. As Doat complained,

> The work is sometimes delayed by the corruption and laxity of the copyists, who do not want to be subjected to the conditions under which they are employed, so that the documents may end up lost because of their negligence or malice; or they may be removed when we are to return them, because of collusion between those who fear or are jealous of this commission, in order to prevent its outcome and success.[40] ... The ablest readers and the worst writers make the first copies of the most difficult documents ...from which the good writers and the worst readers make other copies of the lesser documents ... There are some who read and write well, who make copies from the originals ... We also employ people able to translate documents into the vernacular, and to correct the copies.[41]

Nevertheless, still transparent and visible through the filter of the Doat copies are the historical memory of the investigation – the records and its geographical pattern – and the inquisitor's library, his knowledge and instruments.

OBJECTS: 'SURPLUS'

What is left, after stripping away all these filters one by one? After conducting our analysis through these lenses, how far do we find a deposition still maintaining the distinctive features of living speech? Paradoxically, it is in the most rigid and repetitive registers that what was not necessarily

---

[40] 'Le travail est aussi quelquefois retardé par la desbauche et le libertinage des copistes, qui ne veulent pas s'assujetir aux conditions auxquelles ils se sont engagés, et les titres peuvent s'esgarer par leur négligence ou leur malice, ou peuvent estre enlevés, lorsqu'on les raporte, par le concert de ceux qui ont crainte ou jalousie de ceste commission pour en empescher les suites et les succès', *ibid.*, p. 334.

[41] 'Le plus habiles lecteurs and méchans écrivains faisoient les premières copies des titres plus difficiles ... sur lesquelles les bons écrivains et méchans lécteurs faisoient d'autres copies de menus titres ... Il y en avoit qui lisoient et écrivoient bien, et faisoient les copies sur les originaux ... On employoit aussy des gens capables à la traduction des titres en vulgaire et à la correction des copies', *ibid.*, p. 294.

required by the interrogation is most immediately recognisable. In the midst of utter desiccation, a particular brightness shines out. This is the part which is most attractive to us.[42]

How can one be so sure of this contrast? A few examples may justify our confidence.

The following quotation, taken from D26, shows how the 'surplus' emerges clearly even when witnesses are 'trapped' in a fairly strict textual framework, that is, when recounting a nocturnal meeting at a dying man's house which is – in the great majority of cases – the prelude to a Cathar baptism. A question about participation in such meetings is one of the commonest questions put to witnesses, as it implies not only contacts but also active involvement with the heretics. The records almost always use the same formula, a real 'form', where only names and places vary. Not in this case, however, where we have a more personalised account. To distinguish the 'surplus' from the formulaic elements, the former are italicised.

When the lord of Cuxac fell ill with the illness he died of, one night, in the early hours, the said sick man ordered him, the witness, to go out of the house with others, and go with them, and then he, the witness, and Bonhom,[43] Raymond Vidal, Bernard Arquer and Roger Ferrolt together went out; *and when they were next to the fishing pond, he the witness and Bonhom and Roger remained there and waited, while B. Arquer and R. Vidal departed, and went towards some place called 'orador', as he thinks. And then after a while they returned, and when they were next to the fishing pond, they whistled as previously agreed on their departure, and so he the witness and the others who were waiting for them near the fishing pond immediately heard them, and left, wanting to be ahead of them,* and went their own way towards the house of the said sick man.[44]

Another striking example of differences in *formule* is given by the following comparison between a standard description of a 'heretication' (on the top), and a non-standard one, a real *unicum* in the records consulted.

---

[42] Arno Borst, although convinced that 'Wir sehen hier nur das den Inquisitoren vertraute Bild des Tatbestandes Ketzerei', admitted that 'nur, wenn die Vernommenen redselig und die Vernehmenden schreibfreudig sind, entrollen sich Sittenbilder, die für die Ketzergeschichte von Wert sind', A. Borst, *Les Cathares* (Paris, 1984), p. 25.

[43] 'Bonhom' seems here a name rather than a reference to a Cathar.

[44] 'Dum dominus de Cucciacho infirmaretur ea infirmitate de qua obiit, quadam nocte circa principium dictus infirmus mandavit ipsi testi, et dixit quod esiret cum aliis extra, et iret cum eis, et tunc ipse testis, et bonus homo Raimundus Vitalis, Bernardus Arquerii et Rogerius Ferrolli simul exiverunt, *et quando fuerunt iuxta piscarium, ipso teste, et Bono Homine, et Rogerio remanentibus ibi et expectantibus; B. Arquerii et R. Vitalis recesserunt ab eis; et iverunt versus quendam locum vocatum 'orador' – ut credit – et post per aliquod spatium temporis redie-/runt et quando fuerunt prope piscarium sibilaverunt prout condixerunt inter se in recessu, et tunc ipse testis et alii qui expectaverunt eos iuxta piscarium, statim intellexerunt eos, et recesserunt inde, volentes alios precedere,* et tenuerunt viam suam versus domum dicti infirmi', D26, ff. 100v–101r.

27

First, the said heretics asked her, the witness, whether she wished to give herself to God and the Gospel, and she the witness replied 'yes'. Then she the witness promised, asked by the heretics, that she would no more eat meat or eggs or cheese or any other grease apart from oil or fish, and that she would not swear an oath or lie or perform any sexual act for the rest of her life; and that she would not leave the sect of the heretics for fear of fire or water or of any other kind of death. Then, the said heretics put their hands and a book over her head and read, and the said heretics genuflected many times and prayed; and then the said heretics made her say the prayer of the Our Father according to the rite of the heretics.[45]

Having laid upon a seat some white towels, they put a book on them, which they called 'the text', and asked him the witness, who stood at some distance from the book, whether he wished to receive God's ordination, to which he the witness said 'yes'. Then he gave himself to God and the Gospel and promised that from now on he would not eat nor be without a companion and without praying, and that – if captured without his companion – he would not eat for three days, nor he would ever again eat meat, eggs, cheese, or any other grease apart from oil or fish, and that he would not lie or swear an oath, or perform sexual acts. Having done this, he came next to them in stages saying 'bless' three times, on bended knee; and then he kissed the book of the said heretics. And having done this they put hands and book on his the witness' head, and read the Gospel.[46]

In the following case, taken from another register (D22), where the different style of the notary produces even more concise records, we have the description of a 'standard' *consolamentum* on the top, where the sick person calls for the heretics through relatives and messengers and then is 'consoled' without any abnormal element being pointed out. Beneath this is recorded what happened during the *consolamentum* of another

---

[45] 'Primo quesiverunt predicti ab ipsa teste heretici utrum vellet se rendere Deo et Evangelio, et ipsa testis respondit quod sic, deinde ipsa testis promisit ad interrogationem dictorum hereticorum quod ulterius non comederet carnes nec ova nec caseum nec aliquam uncturam nisi oleo et piscibus, et quod non iuraret nec mentiretur nec aliquam libidinem exerceret toto tempore vite sue et quod non dimitteret sectam hereticorum timore ignis vel aque vel alterius generis mortis; deinde predicti heretici posuerunt manus et librum super / caput ipsius testis et legerunt et fecerunt predicti heretici plures genuflexiones et oraverunt; et tunc predicti heretici fecerunt eidem testi dicere orationem Pater Noster secundum ritum hereticorum', D23, ff. 283r–v.

[46] 'Impositis in quodam banco manutergiis albis et desuper librum quem vocabant textum quesiverunt ab eodem teste differente a libro aliquantulum utrum volebat ordinationem Domini recipere, et ipse testis dixit quod sic. Postmodum reddidit se Deo et Evangelio et promisit quod ulterius non esset neque comederet sine socio et sine oratione, et quod captus sine socio non comederet per triduum, neque comederet carnes ulterius, neque ova, neque caseum, nec aliquam uncturam nisi de oleo et piscibus, neque mentiretur neque iuraret, neque aliquam libid[in]em exercerat. Quo facto, ipse venit per aliqua intervalla ante ipsos dicens 'benedicite' ter flexis genibus, et postmodum osculatus fuit librum dictorum hereticorum et his comple-/tis imposuerunt librum et manus super caput ipsius testis, et legerunt Evangelium', D23, ff. 272r–v.

dying man, where the witness is allowed to expand the story, and adds unusual details. It is worth bearing in mind that the importance of this rite, considered as the central sacrament for the Cathars, is due to the fact that the *consolamentum*, meant as a last rite, provided a sort of seal of purity to the dying believers. It could also be reiterated in case the ill person managed to get better. The underlying argument was that once a believer went back to leading a normal life, they could succumb to sin and temptation. This would invalidate the condition of purity attained through the rite. If possible, therefore, another *consolamentum* could be required later on, when again at risk of losing one's life.

Item, he said that when Raymond of Flaire, his the witness' grandfather, fell ill in Mirepoix in his own home with the illness he died of, he asked for a heretic to be brought to him. And so he the witness sent [the request] through R. of Turrel to Belestar, and they brought from there Peter of Lisle and his companion, heretics, who 'consoled' the said ill man in the way and modes described above.[47]

[The ill man] lost his speech, and so the said heretics, shouting and shaking the said ill man, were calling him, but were not able to extract a word. Then the aforesaid heretics said that the said ill man had previously agreed with them that in case he did lose his speech, nevertheless they could find in his body a spirit so that they could receive him. And the aforesaid heretics received him.[48]

The 'surplus', therefore, leaps to the fore, particularly when it appears amidst page after page of very similar – if not identical – accounts. Here, when taking on the role of a 'memory builder', we must always bear in mind the risk that these reconstructions may falsify the overall perspective. However, every cognitive process is a reconstruction in itself. What gets through the filters can be further listed in order to categorise these 'surplus features'. A selection of the most indicative examples is given here; it is – once again – arbitrary. As in a philological operation, the ultimate tool is one's own *divinatio*: intuition of what is probable.

As the Cathar faith required complete abstinence from all food deriving from sexual intercourse,[49] the range of foodstuffs allowed in a Cathar

---

[47] 'Item dixit quod cum Raimundus de Flaira avunculus ipsius testis infirma[re]-tur apud Mirapiscem in domo sua illa infirmitate qua obiit, petiit hereticum sibi adduci, et tunc ipse testis misit per R. de Torrelas apud Belestar, et adduxerunt / inde Petrum de Insula et socium eius hereticos qui consolaverunt dictum infirmum modo et forma superius expressa', D22, ff. 193v–194r.

[48] 'Amiserat loquelam et tunc predicti heretici clamando et excuciendo dictum infirmum vocabant ipsum, et non potuerunt excutere verbum, et tunc predicti heretici dixerunt quod dictus infirmus dudum fecerat pactum cum ipsis quod quamvis amisisset loquelam tantummodo invenirent spiritum in corpore quod reciperent eum, et predicti heretici receperunt', D22, f. 192v.

[49] Sacconi's famous statement has been questioned by Bernard Hamilton, who suspects the Cathars of a preoccupation with souls reincarnated into animal bodies. B. Hamilton, 'The Cathars and

community where 'clergy' were present was very limited. Consequently, questions relating to food were favoured by the inquisitors, for their clear evidential bearing on heterodoxy. Very often questions about food were among the first addressed to the witness: 'If you ate together, what kind of food did you prepare?' Together with a series of quite standardised answers, it is sometimes possible to find unusual details about recipes or typical food. The believers' favourite meal seems to have been simple vegetables, fish and bread, but more than once this bread is specified as a *fogacia*, a flat loaf baked without yeast, often served with the main course, or a *panada*, possibly a pudding made with bread leftovers, which (says Raymond Mater) 'will be as good for you as if Saint Peter blessed it'.[50] Bona *de Podio* prepared for a Cathar guest 'a pie of fish or eel'.[51] Bernard of Ravat offered the famous heretic Esclarmonde 'a pipe [= measure] full of wine'.[52] Believers showed their devotion and support for the heretics by sending them presents such as wheat, oil, chestnuts, lentils or spices, especially pepper.

Women's confessions can be more precise on details of clothing; a distinction of fabrics and dressing items can be a means of establishing memories within the registers, showing how precisely the deponent recalls the facts. The same function can be ascribed to the words of a dialogue, the physical description, the confession of feelings. Philippa, the wife of Roger of Mirepoix, remembers how her grandmother, the famous Marquise, several times gave her 'shirts, veils, gloves and other things suitable for wearing'.[53] Peter d'Arvinha received from Vigouroux de la Bacone, Cathar bishop, 'a fleece hat ... some gloves and a linen hat'.[54] Imbert of Salles, particularly fond of objects, remembered the gift of another bishop, Bertrand Martin: 'twenty sous of Melgeuil, gloves, a linen hat, a waistcoat, a tunic, and pepper, salt and oil'.[55] Bona of Puy described her guest's clothes as 'a surcoat and a blue serge hood [lined?] with white fur'.[56] Tools and machines crop up mainly in men's accounts, as for example 'a certain

Christian Perfection', in P. Biller and B. Dobson (eds.), *The Medieval Church: Universities, Heresy and Religious Life: Essays in honour of Gordon Leff* ('Studies in Church History', Subsidia, 11), (Oxford, 1999), pp. 5–23, at pp. 21–2.

[50] 'de quadam panada ad comedendum, dicens eidem testi quod "tamen vobis valebat quod si Sanctus Petrus benedixisset eam" ', D23, f. 91r.

[51] 'Unum pastillum piscium vel anguillarum', D25, f. 84r.

[52] 'Quandam canam plenam vini', D24, f. 259r.

[53] 'Camisias, savenas, cirotecas, et alias res aptas ad portandum', D24, f. 199v.

[54] 'Unum capellum de feutre ... quasdam chirotecas et unum capellum de lino', D24, f. 234v.

[55] 'Viginti solidos melgorienses, et cirotecas, et capellum de lino, et unum gardacors, et unam tunicam, et / piper, et sal, et oleum', D24, f. 179v–180r.

[56] 'Unum supertunicale, et unum caputium cum pellibus blanchis de sarga blava', D25, f. 84v.

wheeled instrument in which fire is normally put',[57] or 'an oven to bake bread', made by the heretics for Faure the *parator* (cloth-finisher?).[58]

Perhaps the longest list of items encountered is that of the stolen goods which the conspirators of the Avignonet massacre were reported to have looted from the inquisitors' residence. As we shall see later on, illicit possession could be enough to incriminate an individual, and their presence in the records may be partially due to this fact; nevertheless, it is worth noting such unusual and precise records of objects:

Also, the witness said that the servants from Gaja had and took away from the house where the friar inquisitors were a Bible and other books and much stuff; and Raymond Bernard Barba of Cueilhe had from there a book which was sold for forty sous of Toulouse; and William of Plaigne a chandelier; and Agut the Catalan a sky-blue tunic with a yellow [piece of ?] silk; and William Laurent of Castelbon two pouches to carry books, and he the witness had white shoes, which he bought for six pence of Toulouse, and Peter Aura a sword of Segovia; and Peter Vidal a pair of clogs, and shoes without the front bit;[59] and William of Plaigne some curtains and linen; and Sicart of Puivert some linen; and *Ferro* some linen stained with blood; and Barrau the squire from St Martin the belt and the knife of brother William Arnold; and William of Plaigne similarly had the horse of Raymond, the [inquisitor's] scribe; and Bernard of Saint Martin a hat; and Peter Vidal a scapular; and William *den Marti* took from there some big clogs.[60]

Physical descriptions impress the modern reader. They aimed originally at concrete visualisation of characters, and the vivid images they produce are typical of oral recording and popular storytelling techniques. Their presence demonstrates how, even under extreme psychological pressure, cultural patterns and narrative schemes tend to be reproduced

---

[57] 'Quoddam instrumentum cum rotis in quo solet poni ignis', D26, f. 197r. Perhaps a brazier on wheels, a forge or a small stove; or even a fire-throwing weapon?

[58] 'Unum furnum ad decoquendum panem', D24, f. 190v.

[59] I have not found the word 'ampes, -dis', which could be the contraction or scribal distortion for 'antepes/antepedes'. Du Cange describes the latter as a kind of sandal or shoe called in French 'galoches'. My conjecture is that this indicates a shoe which does not cover the toes.

[60] 'Dixit etiam ipse testis quod servientes de Gaiano habuerunt de domo ubi erant fratres inquisitores et asportaverunt inde unam bibliam et alios libros et raubam multam, et Raimundus Bernardi Barba de Cuella habuit inde unum librum qui fuit venditus quadraginta solidis Tholosanis, et Willelmus de Plainha unam candeleiram et Agut catalanus unum chiot blau de pers cum cendato croceo, et Guillelmus Laurentii de Castrobono duas peras ubi reponebantur libri et ipse testis habuit caligas albas, quas emit sex denarios Tholosanos, et Petrus Aura unum segovianum, et Petrus Vitalis soculares, et caligas sine ampedibus, et Guillelmus de Plainha quasdam cortinas et linteamina, et Sicardus de Podio Viridi linteamina, et Ferro linteamina sanguinolenta; et Barravus scutifer de Sancto Martino zonam et cutellum fratris Guillelmi Arnaldi, et Guillelmus de Plainha habuit similiter palafredum Raimundi scriptoris, et Bernardus de Sancto Martino unum capellum, et Petrus Vitalis unum scapulare, et Guillelmus den Marti habuit inde magnos soculares', D24, ff. 165r–v.

and faithfully preserved, with no great alteration of the deponent's view of reality and scale of values. The range goes from simple physical description to the depiction of a scene or a role.

William of Tourette portrays the people who came to a Cathar baptism: a young man 'rather fat and rosy-cheeked', 'a dark and tall woman', others 'well-dressed, one of whom was rather podgy, another pale and skinny'.[61] Bernard of Camon, a priest, recalls among the participants in a Cathar ceremony a man 'called Annel *de Bugeria* the fisherman, who could swim and stay under water for a long time';[62] Joan, daughter of Ysarn *de Pas*, remembers a woman, Guillelme Salamone, 'who was scabby'.[63]

A particularly notable witness is Berbegueira, whose deposition stands out for two specific features. In the first place, she likes details, and fills her confession with them; secondly, she is obsessed with illnesses, doctors and health matters. The combination of the two gives life to an extremely unusual and lively record. For a start, she even measures time by reference to illnesses, 'from the time of the last healing', 'when [William Bernard, heretic and doctor[64]] was treating her husband'; but most of all, she marks her actions in relation to her or her husband's sickness, 'and there she talked with the aforesaid heretic about some illness suffered by her husband', 'William Bernard, the doctor of the heretics, was treating the said witness for some illness ... Item, she said that the aforesaid heretic treated her husband Lobenx for three or four illnesses'. She herself probably suffered from arthritis since, before a Cathar priest 'she the witness could not bow bending her knees, except with great difficulty'. Later on, she refused to go and honour the same man in the attic of her friend's house because 'she did not dare to attempt the stairs, and remained downstairs, alone, until the others returned'.[65] But once she met a 'heretic' she depicts him in the most vivid and concise description of all: 'They went into the room to see the said heretic, like a monster who was sitting there on his

---

[61] 'Satis pinguis et coloratus', 'quadam mulier longa et bruna', others 'bene induti quorum unus erat satis pinguis, et alius macillentus', D26, ff. 84v and 93r.
[62] 'Qui vocabatur Annel de Bugeria piscator, qui diu sciebat natare et stare sub aqua', D26, f. 301v.
[63] 'Que erat scabiosa', D23, f. 286r.
[64] Elsewhere William does not enjoy the same degree of popularity, 'William Bernard *de Ayros* who pretended to be a doctor' ('Guillielmum Bernardi de Ayros qui fingebat se medicum'), D24, f. 21v.
[65] 'De tempore ultime cure', 'quando tenebat maritum ipsius testis in cura', 'et ibi locuta fuit dicta testis cum predicto heretico de quadam infirmitate mariti ipsius testis', 'Guillelmus Bernardi, medicus hereticorum tenuit dictam testem in cura sua de quadam infirmitate ... Item dicit quod predictus hereticus tenuit Lobentum maritum ipsius testis in cura sua in tribus vel in quatuor infirmitatibus', 'non poterat ipsa testis inclinari flexis genibus, nisi cum maxima difficultate', 'non fuit ausa committere se scale et remansit sola inferius donec alie redierunt', D24, ff. 136r–143r.

throne, as still as a log.'[66] The importance of Berbegueira's deposition is her complete appropriation of the topical items of inquisitorial questioning: she transforms the hereticातions, the meetings, the rites of adoration, even the illnesses – normally part of a 'classic' deposition for their connection with Cathar baptism – into her own narrative. And her narrative is led not only by her eye for details, but also by her lifelong fixation on disease and physical constraints.

Among the main features of D22 is an interest in beliefs, myths and doctrine. Several depositions, in response to a very succinct series of questions, focus on these matters, sometimes widening the description to direct reporting of phrases and conversations – dare one say 'truthful' reporting?

According to William Feraut, the well-known William Faure gave a colourful depiction of the mission of Jesus Christ. The entire testimony deals with beliefs, and the genuineness of the account is strikingly evident from both content and vocabulary:

He heard W. Faure of Puy *Hermer* saying … that when God saw his kingdom impoverished through the fall of the evil ones, he asked those standing around: 'Does anyone of you wish to be my son, and me to be his father?' And as nobody answered, Christ who was God's bailiff, answered him, 'I want to be your son, and I shall go wherever you send me', and then God sent Christ as his son in the world to preach God's name, and this is how Christ came [to the world].[67]

And further on, 'Item, he said that he heard W. Audebert claiming that the heretics say that oxen and horses ploughed and carried hay and worked in heaven as on earth'.[68] Again W. Audebert is reported to have said the following:

Do you want to know the truth about this world below, and about the one above? I shall tell you. One day, while God was preaching to his people in heaven, a messenger came to him from earth, saying that he would lose this world unless he sent [somebody] there at once; and immediately God sent Lucibel to this world, and received him as a brother. And later Lucibel wanted to have part of the inheritance of the things above and of those below, whereas

---

[66] 'Intraverunt ad videndum dictum hereticum tanquam monstrum qui sedebat ibi in sella sua tanquam truncus immobilis', D24, f. 137v.

[67] 'Audivit W. Fabri de Podio Hermer dicentem … quod cum Deus videret depauperatum regnum suum propter casum malignorum quesivit a circumstantibus, "vult aliquis esse filium meum, et quod ego sim pater eius?" et cum nullus responderet, Christus qui erat baiulus Dei respondit Deo, "ego volo esse filius tuus et ibo quocumque me miseris", et tunc Deus tanquam filium suum misit Christum in mundum predicare nomen Dei, et ita venit Christus', D22, f. 26r.

[68] 'Item dicit quod audivit W. Audebert quod heretici dicunt quod boves et roncini arabant et trahebant finum et laborabant in celo sicut in terra', D22, f. 26v.

God did not want that, and for this reason there was a long war, and still there is now, among them.[69]

Usually we impute to inquisitors any recurrences of the same *topoi*, stylistic elements and accusations. Interestingly, quite a few of these recurrences can be ascribed to the heretics. Rhetorical accusations against clergy and the religious are reported, as well as stereotypical lines of debate, as in the case of Peter *de Noya*:

Item, he said that several times he had heard heretics' sermons, about the errors concerning visible things: that God did not create them; that the consecrated host was not the body of Christ; and that even if it were as big as a large mountain, it would already have been eaten up.[70]

Again, here are the words of R[aymond] of Rodolos, who 'heard Aymeric *de Na Regina* saying that God had not entered the blessed Virgin, but rather had overshadowed her, and that God did not establish the mass, but the cardinals and clergy did so, for the love of offerings'.[71]

The cross-fertilisation of Cathar preaching discourse and peasant images sometimes produces rather vivid images and dialogues. According to another deponent, the wife of Artaud Bos declared:

That the devil had made man with clay, and asked God to put a soul in him. And God said to the devil, 'He will be stronger than me and you if you make him with clay, therefore make him with sea sand!' And the devil created man with sea sand, and God said, 'This one is good: in fact he is not too strong, and not too weak'. And [God] put a soul in him.[72]

However, deponents did not only act passively, 'receiving' and swallowing images and sermons without criticism: 'Bertacius', also known as Matfred of Puylaurens, a knight, had a conversation with Arnaud Bos, heretic and

---

[69] 'Vis tu scire veritatem de hoc mundo inferiori et de illo superiori? / Ego dicam tibi: quadam die, dumque predicaret Dominus in celo gentibus suis, venit ei nuncius de terra dicens ei quod istum mundum amiserat nisi statim mitteret illuc, et statim Dominus misit Lucibel in hunc mundum et recepit eum pro fratre; et postea voluit Lucibel habere partem hereditatis de inferioribus et de superioribus, et Dominus noluit, et propter hoc diu fuit guerra, et hodie est, inter ipsos', D22, ff. 12r–v.

[70] 'Item dixit quod audivit predicationes hereticorum pluries de erroribus de visibilibus quod Deus ea non fecerat, de hostia sacrata quod non erat corpus Christi, et si esset ita magnum sicut mons grandis, iam comestum esset', D22, f. 29r.

[71] 'Audivit Aymericum de Na Regina dicentem quod Deus non venerat in beata Virgine, sed obumbraverat se ibi tamen, et quod Deus non statuit missam, sed cardinales et clerici amore oblationum', D22, f. 31v.

[72] 'Quod diabolus fecit hominem de terra argila, et dixit Deo quod mitteret animam in hominem, et Deus dixit diabolo, "fortior erit me et te, si de argila fiat, sed fac eum de limo maris!", et fecit diabolus hominem de limo maris, et Deus dixit, "iste est bonus: non est enim nimis fortis nec nimis debilis", et misit Deus animam in hominem', D22, f. 32r.

deacon, and acutely 'found that the said heretic disagreed with the other heretics on some things'.[73] There is also the irreverent pair Pons of Alamans and Pons Guilabert of Lantar who, while attending a Cathar sermon 'started laughing and immediately had to go away from there';[74] or the inattentive Matfred of Puylaurens, present at a sermon where 'the said heretic preached there for such a long while that he, the witness, fell asleep'.[75]

Discourses interlace and influence each other. To what extent did preaching develop into a 'lower level' explanation of the Scriptures? Is it a phenomenon to be ascribed just to Cathar or heretical preaching, or to the orthodox as well? Is this simplification – lowering to the level of the everyday – to be seen as a reduction brought about by the deponent's operating within his or her own cultural frame of reference? Or should it rather be considered as an automatic reaction to the *hearing* itself, in a manner and to a degree which are impossible to measure? Is it an instinctive switch from one communicative level to another (i.e. a sort of 'automatised translation' of linguistic level)? Should we assume a higher recurrence of this mechanism arising from the secrecy of most Cathar mythology, which, unlike Catholic preaching, had to be selected and mainly hidden from the common believers?[76]

Among the assortment of 'surplus' features, phrases in the vernacular are probably the most evident.[77] The Doat volumes record quotations from poems in Provençal, excerpts from a translation of the Bible and (most notably) short phrases of direct speech, sometimes linked with the performance of Cathar rituals, which maintain their genuine and authentic character. Arising from a notary's deficient skill in translating into Latin, or from his deliberate decision to leave these fragments in Provençal, or for other reasons,[78] these excerpts can be considered the only authentic remains of the original dialogue.

The Doat mission was concerned about them too. Barbaste, an expert in the field, was employed specifically to 'translate the documents in vernacular into French'.[79] The extent and purpose of these 'translations' is not clear. Possibly they were made for the understanding of the copyists only, or were actually inserted – once re-translated – into the final text.

---

[73] 'Invenerunt quod dictum hereticum discordare in aliquibus cum aliis hereticis', D24, f. 113r.
[74] 'Inceperunt ridere et statim dicesserunt inde', D23, f. 66v.
[75] 'Predicavit ibi dictus hereticus tandiu quod ipse testis obdormuit', D24, f. 115r.
[76] See again Ginzburg, *The Cheese and the Worms*.
[77] I am extremely grateful to Professor Peter Ricketts and Dr Shelagh Sneddon for translating the most intricate passages for me.
[78] On the relevance of vernacular phrases kept untranslated in the record, see Justice, 'Inquisition, speech and writing', pp. 290–6. Justice suggests, among the reasons for this bilinguism, the fact that the scribe may be bored.
[79] See Omont, 'La Collection Doat', pp. 320, 323.

It seems, however, that the amount of material in languages other than Latin (Spanish is also mentioned) required at least the expertise of somebody who was able to collaborate with the copyists in structuring the final registers.

Although differing in nuance, volumes 22, 24, 25 and 26 contain most of this evidence. Where we find a slight degree of 'construction' in some of these depositions and unusual attention to speech being shown by the officials, there is usually a higher concentration of data. The range of phrases in Provençal runs from interjections – normally 'broad dialect' – to lively and animated dialogues, fragments of prayers, old sayings and quotes from texts that we might not have, but which we can see were codified in that language.[80] The significance of this bilingual structure, where we find it, is that it provides an open window into the trial scene and its original development. With the sole exception of D24, f. 231v, all the following passages are taken from D25 and D26. This is because volume 25 displays keen interest in particulars, with the redactor choosing to leave them as they were actually stated, while D26, although quite similar in character, adds rather a lot in direct speech.

Notable is the dialogue, which is said to have occurred during a Cathar *hereticatio*, when the *filius minor* says, 'Pregatz ne aquest pro home quen pregue Dieu', and the sick man replies, 'Senher, pregatz en Dieu'; the *filius maior* then carries on, 'Dieu nesia pregatz'.[81] Far from using standardised and ritualistic formulas, a believer is reported to have expressed his thoughts about the afterlife, 'Si ego morior in die veneris, perduz so, si passa lo divendres, eu so sals'.[82] More obviously, there is literal citation of the *incipits* of vernacular texts, whose possession, quotation or use provoked suspicion, such as the satire written by the (Catholic) Guiot de Provins, who ended his days as a Cluniac monk, 'About the stinking and terrible world',[83] or a book of auguries, 'If you wish to know what is *cofres*'.[84] Again, translations of the Bible assume great significance here, both in incriminating the suspect, and in providing specific and 'internal' information to the inquisitor:

[80] See G.G. Merlo, 'Sulla cultura religiosa dei primi Valdesi', in *Identità valdesi nella storia e nella storiografia* ('Valdesi e Valdismi medievali' II), (Turin, 1991), pp. 71–92; see P. Biller and A. Hudson (eds.), *Heresy and Literacy*,, esp. P. Biller, 'The Cathars of Languedoc and written materials', pp. 61–82, and L. Paolini, 'Italian Catharism and written culture', pp. 83–103.

[81] 'Pray that this good man prays to God', 'My lord, pray to God', 'Let God be prayed to', D26, f. 248v.

[82] 'If I die on a Friday, I am lost [damned], if Friday passes, I am saved', D25, f. 171r.

[83] 'Del segle puent et terible', D25, f. 201r/v. Compare J. Orr, *Les oeuvres de Guio de Provins, poète lyrique et satirique*, (Manchester, 1915), p. 10: 'Du siecle puant et orible'. Merlo quotes some of these passages in *Identità valdesi*, pp. 90–1.

[84] 'Si vols saber que ez cofres'. I have left untranslated this last word, which may be a technical term.

'That no one should ascend to heaven except the Son of the Virgin who descended from heaven',[85] 'Today you will be with me in Paradise'.[86]

The requirements of an enquiry and consequent possible incrimination of the suspects make the recording of vernacular statements rather an obvious and functional option in some cases. Waldensians made great use of the vernacular in translating the Bible, and in general felt the urge to communicate with ordinary people in their own native language. More generally, through the pressure of non-conformist and reforming religious groups, there tended to be a widening linguistic discrimination between Latin, the language of the Church, and vernacular as the language of those who wanted to criticise, contrast or even replace this distant institution. To hold assemblies, celebrate sacred rituals and perform sermons in the vernacular became a distinctive feature of these groups, thus any occurrence of this was highly suspicious in the eyes of the Church ministers. When vernacular phrases are connected to ritualistic expressions or excerpts from the Scriptures, they identify obvious areas of enquiry. While there would seem to be less point in looking for the vernacular in other cases, however, abstracts of poems and invectives were indeed also important. The literal recording of pieces of satire which were intended to be invectives against the Roman Church and its ministers could be enough to incriminate a suspect.

Dossat has already identified an excerpt from a *sirventes*[87] ascribed to Guilhelm Figueira, which in Doat runs thus: 'To make a *sirventes* in this key which pleases me … [one line from the original is missing here] and I know without doubt that I shall attract ill-will from [amending the original reading 'dels' = 'about'] the false deceitful people of Rome, the head of decadence where all good decays.'[88] Equally important for indicating the personal involvement of two suspects is a dialogue which occurred after the massacre of Avignonet in 1242. Walking together, William Faure, who was among the conspirators, asked his friend Stephen, 'Would you like to hear some good verses (coblas), or a good *sirventes*?' He carried on, 'Brother William Arnold "the cuckold" is cuckolded and broken!' Stephen replied, 'These coblas are so good that the …[?] text *or* parchment is cut.'[89] Finally,

---

[85] 'Que degus no poja [*MS has* 'poia'] el cel mas lo fil de la Verge qui del cel dechendet', D25, f. 199v.

[86] 'Hoi seras ab mi en Paradis', D25, f. 199v.

[87] A satyrical or heroic composition, performed by the medieval troubadours.

[88] 'Du sirventes far en est so que magensa et sai ses doptar que naurai malvolensa dels fals de manples de Roma que ez caps de la chaensa que dechai tots bes.' It is mentioned by Y. Dossat, 'Les Vaudois méridionaux d'après les documents de l'Inquisition', *Cahiers de Fanjeaux* 2 (1967), pp. 207–26, at p. 222 and n. 61. On Figueira, see also *Cahiers de Fanjeaux* 4 (1969), pp. 136–7.

[89] 'Vultis audire bonas coblas vel unum bonum sirventes?' 'Frater W. Arnaldi Cogot es escogotatz, et pesxiatz!' 'Sic bone sunt iste coble cocula [*or* cocu la] carta es trencada', D22, f. 11v. The translation

37

one can feel the original flavour of living speech in the instinctive response of a man to his potential accuser and neighbour, while waiting for his hearing: 'Pros hom vos a votz dias, no fassatz mal a vostres besins!'[90]

Although these quotations are no more than a tiny fraction of the totality of the depositions, what is important here is the opportunity they provide for investigating why and how the original speech has passed through the filters. Vernacular evidence, although driven by the inquisitor's questions, is the only authentic survival of the first act of the 'deposition performance'.

The 'surplus', that which is beyond the functional schemes of the depositions, is often what we might call the 'affective feature'. Remarks about feelings or personal involvement are a symptom of the 'openness' of the text for its modern readers. We can imagine an individual – either acting freely or under psychological compulsion – eventually providing *us* with something beyond the ordinary and common standardised answers. Whatever the hidden intention of the person questioned, the scarcity of such evidence speaks for itself: nearly all of even the most 'free' interrogations lack personal comments on feelings or intimate matters. The unusual tone of personal involvement that is displayed in some depositions could simply be eloquent characterisation of someone's connections with heretical communities and individuals, but it could also be an attempt to justify someone's absence or presence on the scene, diverting the inquisitor's attention to other things.

Precisely because it is uncommon, and not required by the series of questions, the presence of such material in the records is a clear sign of the official quite deliberately putting it into writing. With most of this sort of evidence, we should assume that the words were actually spoken, and that the emotions they expressed were true or plausible.

Within a long deposition and the usual lists of names and reports of meetings, the rare occurrences of emotions are gifts to us: gifts of human presence and healthy reminders. In the deconstruction of texts we are liable to treat them as abstractions, objects to be sectioned with mathematical precision. But the trials and depositions can pass on to us the lives and deaths of real individuals.

Bertrand of Alamans, probably a 'messenger', was allegedly asked by Bernard Faure to act as a go-between with his daughter. He was to go and

---

and meaning of this last sentence are uncertain. Duvernoy (*Histoire*, p. 281) translates it as 'la f... charte est déchirée', and identifies the 'paper' ('carta') as any parchment, document or record kept by the inquisitors. My reading is different: the modern colloquial English catch-phrase 'so sharp he cuts himself' might possibly approach the flavour of the original – suggesting 'These coblas are so sharp they cut the parchment'.

[90] 'Good man, for the days of your life, do not do any harm to your neighbours!', D25, f. 296v.

talk to her, now a heretic, to convince her to return to her father. Bertrand agreed, and arranged a meeting during which she was urged 'at all costs to give up the sect'. The daughter refused to betray her new beliefs, and Bernard had to back down and accept the unwelcome new situation.[91]

A few folios below the inquisitor allows Raymond Aiffre space to display sentiments of brotherhood and love. He and a sibling were called to the deathbed of a third brother, who asked for Cathar baptism. After the ceremony was completed, they did not feel like going and honouring the heretics, as commonly required by the ritual, 'because of the grief for their brother'.[92] Later, Raymond confesses his feelings for a Cathar woman, the widow of one of his friends. 'Veziada, the wife of the later Peter Carracier, was heretic at the time, and he the witness loved her passionately.'[93]

Way beyond the impact of the interrogation on an individual, there is another kind of psychological pressure which is visible in these accounts of feelings. In a Cathar's life the ideal conclusion of the soul's earthly pilgrimage was the moment of the *consolamentum* in which, through the purging of all the imperfections of human nature, the soul regained its lost purity and was prepared for the succeeding higher stage of its life. Whether as a collective and personal experience, such a moment would be of the highest emotional significance. As Cathars, and as human beings, Raymond of Mireval and his brothers avoided their father's 'heretication' 'as, because of [their] lament and grief at the death of the father of this witness, they were driven from the house'.[94] Another witness recalls the moving image of a woman at a heretication: 'Algaia, then wife of the late Pons of Villeneuve, who was crying extraordinarily.'[95] Again, in relation to a Cathar baptism, there is the remarkable account of a grieving woman. Peter Pictavin and Raymond Petri 'got to the house of the aforesaid ill man, where, as he had just died, his sister Ermesende was hitting her cheeks with her palms, not daring to cry out until the aforesaid heretics had gone a long way away'.[96]

In their textual structure as a whole, the narratives abruptly change the rhythm of the writing, interlacing it with dialogues, as in the popular

---

[91] 'Quod modis omnibus desereret dictam sectam et rediret ad domum patris sui', D23, ff. 67r–v.

[92] 'Propter dolorem dicti fratris', D23, f. 83r.

[93] 'Veziada, uxor quondam Petri Carracier, tunc temporis erat heretica, et ipse testis adamavit eam', D23, f. 84v.

[94] 'Quia propter planctum et dolorem de morte patris ipsius testis erant a domo excussi', D23, f. 234v.

[95] 'Domina Algaia, uxor tunc Poncii de Villanova, que flebat mirabiliter', D24, f. 105v.

[96] 'Raymundus Petri et ipse testis [Peter Pictavin] accesserunt ad domum predicti infirmi, ubi, cum iam obisset, Ermesendis, soror eius, percussiebat genas suas cum palmis, non / audens clamare donec heretici supradicti longe se absentassent', D25, ff. 253v–254r. Peter Biller drew my attention to this passage.

manner of recounting. Larger fragments of stories are mostly included in D22 and D24, the registers relating – not by chance – to the cases of Avignonet and Montségur, in which the purpose of leaving long depositions was to provide the most extensive survey of the facts. The political importance of these two examples both allowed and recommended a freer enquiry and partly explains the higher proportion of passages in direct speech. As already pointed out, if a high number of deponents caused a restriction of narrative freedom, the contrary applied here. Given the significance of the circumstances, a relative latitude was accorded to the deponents, as the inquisitors limited the questionnaire to four or five major points. The deeper the probing, the larger the gaps in the grille or sieve.

The incidence of anecdotal features in a deposition is the best litmus test of how far the text retains the 'narrative level' of the deponents. Anecdotes and details in storytelling belong to and are recognised by the textual community:[97] they can also provide chronological references external to the official techniques of reckoning time, and they are a mental code of everyday popular stories.

The massacre of inquisitors at Avignonet in 1242 is a well-known and dark episode in the opposition to the Catholic Church and its ministers in Languedoc. Six long depositions provide us with a detailed report of the murder of William Arnold, Stephen of St Thibéry, the Minor (= Franciscan), and their servants, providing an account that is memorable not just because they offer six different points of view, but because each storyteller maintains his own character and style within his deposition. The inquisitor's interrogation, based on four or five questions, 'formats' very genuine and convincing reports, entangled with direct speeches, dialogues and descriptions. The same grille of questions put to all the deponents guarantees an unvarying recording style. The *chronological boundaries* go from the initial plot to the last stages of the massacre. The *questions* relate to identity and links between the conspirators, and to the practical details of the attack itself, which were highly relevant to its reconstruction. Despite the obvious reduction and summarising of the depositions, the individuality springing out of them is striking. It can be used to strengthen the theory of 'filters'.

Emphasis on pictorial details characterises Peter Vignol's deposition. He met the vociferous group of conspirators on their way back home and now recalls their clothes stained with blood, their rude and coarse language. One can 'see' this grotesque-looking parade, riding their stolen horses and

---

[97] The concept of 'textual community' comes from the works of Brian Stock, among them *Listening for the Text*, esp. pp. 140–58.

carrying precious items taken from the inquisitors' trunks. Some of them, walking along the path, dressed as Dominican friars, were shouting,

He the witness ... heard it said by the above-mentioned [men] that they had killed brother William Arnold and his companions at Avignonet, and then William of Plaigne, who had brought letters, led along some black horse which he had taken from the brothers, or from their companions. Among the servants there were some wearing the scapulars of the said friars preachers who had been killed. They were shouting as they approached, saying, 'Tell Peter Roger and Raymond of Péreille to come and hear the sermon of brother William Arnold!'[98]

Alzeu of Massabrac gives a completely different perspective. Left outside Avignonet (so he claims) he had the task of controlling the entrance to the village. He therefore met the group of conspirators leaving the scene of the murder, and now recited a list of people and of the spoils stolen from the inquisitors' residence.[99] Alzeu was able to describe by whom and with what weapon each person was killed: a chilling list of swords, clubs, hatchets and even a crossbow. His personal selection of the elements in the story highlights weapons and macabre details. He refers to an astonishing dialogue between two of the conspirators:

Item, Peter Roger questioned John Acermat, saying, 'Where is the cup?', and John Acermat said to him, 'It's broken'. And Peter Roger said, 'Why did you not bring it [with you]? If I had it, I'd put a golden band on it, and always drink from it!' Asked which cup he was speaking about, he replied [that it was] the cup of brother William Arnold's skull.[100]

The most complete and vigorous account is recorded in the deposition of Imbert of Salles, the only deponent to report striking details about the massacre itself. He was there when some people smashed the heavy door of the building, and killed two servants with hatchets, on the stairs to the main hall. He remembers details about the slaughter, and saw the bodies of the two murdered friars, their servants and wardens.

---

[98] 'Ipse testis audivit dici a predictis quod interfecerant fratrem Guillelmum Arnaldi et socios eius apud Avinionetum, et tunc Guillelmus de Plainha, qui aportaverat litteras, adduxit quendam palafredum nigrum quem habuerat de fratribus vel de sociis suis, inter quos servientes erant aliqui qui portabant induta scapularia dictorum fratrum predicatorum qui fuerant interfecti, clamantes in adventu et dicentes, "dicatis Petro Rogerii et Raimundo de Perella quod veniant ad audiendum sermonem fratris Guillelmi Arnaldi!" ', D22, ff. 257v–258r.

[99] Such abundance of detail has to be seen in the light of (but not explained away by) the fact that possession of stolen objects makes the individual liable for prosecution (see W. Ullmann, 'Reflections on medieval torture', in ed. G. Garnett, *Law and Jurisdiction in the Middle Ages* (London, 1988), pp. 123–37).

[100] 'Item Petrus Rogerius quesivit a Iohanne Acermat dicens, "Ubi est copa?", et Iohannes Acermat dixit ei, "Fracta est", et Petrus Rogerius dixit, "Quare non aportasti eam? Nam si haberem eam, facerem in ea cuiculum [*mistake for* circulum?] aureum, et semper biberem in ea!" Interrogatus de qua copa dixit, respondit quod de cupa capitis fratris Guillelmi Arnaldi', D22, ff. 286v–287r.

He remembers some of the murderers taking pride in their handiwork, shouting and laughing. An attitude of horror emerges through his words, as he confesses to what he saw and did.

They came to the hall of the Count of Toulouse, where the friars inquisitors were lying, and smashing the door they went in, and killed brother William Arnold and Stephen, the inquisitors, and their fellows, and the servants. Yet, he the witness remained outside, and Arnold Roger said to him, 'Imbert, why did you not go to where the others are? Maybe, in fact, they will be seizing stuff from there, stuff [Perhaps earlier taken from *or* for the] heretics, or something else.' And then he the witness replied to him, 'Sir, where shall I go? I don't know where to go.' And then two men from Avignonet said to him, 'We'll take you there.' Having heard this, he the witness, and all the foot-soldiers who had come to the castle of Avignonet, together with those two men from Avignonet, went up to the highest point in the castle, and when they were there, they found the friars inquisitors and their fellows and servants dead ... [and those who were there] were stealing the things and clothes and books belonging to the inquisitors, and were smashing the chests. And then he the witness had from there a pyx of 'gingerite',[101] and more than ten pence for the transportation of the objects which he and some others had from there. He the witness also added that he heard that Raymond Dalfaro, who then was wearing a long, white doublet, was boasting that he had hit the friars inquisitors with a wooden club while saying, 'Be well, Be well!'[102]

Another very famous case is the learned dispute held in 1247 between two Garcias relatives: Peter Garcias, the Cathar sympathiser, and William Garcias, the Franciscan, in the *schola* (chamber for teaching and study) at the convent in Toulouse, a discussion overheard by a small group of other Franciscans, well hidden from sight, and able to act as witnesses against Peter by quoting some of his declarations and heretical tenets to

---

[101] I use a neologism, 'gingerite' for *Zinziberacum* – seemingly a derivative from *zingiber/i*, 'ginger' – which I have been unable to find in any dictionary of medieval Latin. My conjecture is that it was a word for some metal alloy, and is here used to signify metal of little value. (Another possible explanation would be a pyx containing ginger powder.)

[102] 'Venerunt ad salam Comitis Tholosani ubi fratres inquisitores iacebant, et frangentes hostium intraverunt et interfecerunt fratrem Guillelmum Arnaldum et Stephanum inquisitores, et socios eorum, et familiam. Tamen ipse testis remansit extra, et Arnaudus Rogerii dixit eidem testi, "Imberte, quare non accedistis vos ad locum ubi sunt alii? Nam forte hereticis inde raubam vel aliquid aliud occupabunt." Et tunc ipse testis dixit eidem, "Domine, quo ibo? Nescio quo eam." Et tunc duo homines de Avinioneto dixerunt eidem testi, "Nos ducemus vos illuc", et hoc audito ipse testis et omnes servientes pedites qui venerant in Castrum de Avinioneto simul cum illis duobus hominibus de Avinioneto ascenderunt in caput castri, et quando fuerunt ibi, invenerunt fratres inquisitores et socios eorum et familiam interfectos ... [and those who were there] non [*sic*] occupabant res et raubas et libros inquisitorum et frangebant arca [*sic*]. Et tunc ipse testis habuit inde unam pixidem de zinziberaco, et ultra decem denarios pro portatione rerum, quas cum aliis quibusdam inde habuit. Adiecit etiam ipse testis se audivisse tunc quod Raimundus Dalfaro, qui portabat tunc perpunctum album longum, iactabat se quod ipse cum quadam clava lignea percusserat in fratres inquisitores, et dicebat, "Va be! Esta be!" ', D24, ff. 163v–164v.

the inquisitors.[103] Naturally, the multiple interrogation of these witnesses followed some predetermined guidelines established (probably *ad hoc* for this case) by the inquisitors; and equally naturally the answers were 'personalised' versions of what everybody had heard from their hiding place. But here lies the interesting element for us. As in the several accounts of the Avignonet massacre, the witnesses are allowed to display individual features in their depositions, which at the same time overlap in some other parts, demonstrating either a preliminary agreement over 'what to tell the inquisitors', or the ability to remember and report Peter Garcias's statements accurately. In both cases they had the opportunity to give a personal reconstruction of this extraordinary episode.

Surprisingly enough, the most loquacious of the six main deponents is not William Garcias (see below, A5), the direct antagonist of Peter, but one of the other friars, Déodat of Rodez (A3), who remembers – possibly understands – more of the discussion, including a long invective against the Roman Church which none of the others recalls. For instance, where brother Arnaud Daitz synthesises the question-and-answer on the belief of a double deity as 'asked whether or not there are two gods, [he replied] that ... he could not be certain up to now',[104] Déodat of Rodez expands this point, saying that when asked 'whether he believed in his faith that there is one Good God who created everything, as it is told in the Scriptures, Peter replied that he did not and would not believe those things; but that there is a Good God who created all that is incorruptible and everlasting, and another God, an Evil one, who [created] all corruptible and transitory things'.[105] William Garcias remembered more concisely: asked 'whether there are two Gods, Peter replied "yes, one Good and one Evil" '.[106]

---

[103] This case has been well known to heresiologists for a long time, being fully edited in C. Douais, *Documents pour servir l'histoire de l'Inquisition dans la Languedoc* (Paris, 1900),vol. II, pp. 90–114. Most recently, both Mark Pegg (*The Corruption*, pp. 52–6) and Carol Lansing (*Power and Purity: Cathar Heresy in Medieval Italy* (NewYork and Oxford, 1998, pp. 87–8) have devoted some space to this episode, reaching very different conclusions. While Lansing uses the depositions as repositories of information on Cathar belief, Pegg's opinion is that, albeit striking – for the different interrogation technique applied by the inquisitors to the deponents, which leaves them free to 'follow surprisingly individual tangents' (p. 54) – the case is important (a) to show the weight of such a technique on the end result, the record; and (b) to show how the declarations of the different witnesses is a sort of 'literate translation' of Garcia's beliefs into a Franciscan-friendly scheme of thought.

[104] 'Cum interrogaretur ... utrum essent duo dii, quod ... de hoc non potuit habere certitudinem usque modo', D22, f. 92v.

[105] 'Si ipse crederet in sua fide quod esset unus Deus Benignus qui creasset omnia cum hec inveniretur in scripturis, respondit ipse Petrus quod hec non credebat nec crederet, sed erat unus Deus Benignus qui creavit incorruptibilia et permansura et alius Deus erat Malignus qui corruptibilia et transitoria', D22, f. 96r.

[106] 'Utrum essent duo dii, et ipse Petrus respondit quod sic, unus benignus et alius malignus', D22, ff. 100r–v.

It would be interesting to show how not only the interrogation follows different paths, but also how much the six depositions differ among themselves. Unfortunately, that would take up too much space, so only a couple more concise examples can be given.

Question:[107] 'Where were you? [this question is not always present in the record]'.

A1: Above some wall, above the *schola* from which place he the witness saw and heard.[108]	A2: Upstairs, between the roof and them, in a place from which he could listen and see.[109]	A3: He was staying above the *schola* of the friars Minors of Toulouse, between the roof and the said William Garcia and Peter Garcia.[110]	A4: In the place mentioned above, between the roof and the *schola*.[111]	A6: On some wooden floor, from which he could see and hear them.[112]

[Question: What did Peter say?]

A1: and about he who howled while singing.[113]	A2: [not mentioned]	A3: that he who held the cross on Good Friday howled while uncovering it ... Item, the same Peter also said that all those who howled in the church singing with unintelligible voice deceived the simple people.[114]	A4: of those who sing in church with unintelligible voice.[115]	A5: [not mentioned]	A6: [not mentioned]

[107] The names of the deponents are as follows: (1) Arnaud Daitz; (2) William Cogot; (3) Deodat of Rodez; (4) William Garcia; (5) Imbert; (6) Peter Raymond; (7) Raymond Ferreiras, rector of the church of St Mary in Aurat; (8) William of Montot; (9) Bernard Prima.

[108] 'Super quadam parietes super scolas, de quo loco ipse testis videbat et audiebat', D22, f. 91r.

[109] 'Superius inter tectum et ipsos in loco de quo poterat audire et videre', D22, f. 92v.

[110] 'Et erat existens super scolas fratrum Minorum Tholose inter tectum et prenominatos fratrum Guillelmum Garcia et Petrum Garcia', D22, f. 97v.

[111] 'In loco superius memorato inter tectum et scolas', D22, f. 99v.

[112] 'Super quodam tabulatu de quo poterat ipsos videre et audire', D22, f. 104r.

[113] 'Et de illo qui ululabat cantando', D22, f. 91r.

[114] 'Quod ille qui tenebat crucem in die Parasceve discooperiendo eam ululabat ... Item dixit idem Petrus quod omnes illi qui ululabant in ecclesia cantando voce non intelligibili decipiebant populum simplicem', D22, f. 97v.

[115] 'De illis qui cantant in ecclesia voce non intelligibili', D22, f. 101v.

CONSTRUCTION METHOD, AIMS:
SOME CONCLUSIONS

An earlier version of this chapter[116] offered some preliminary reflections about the construction method of each register, starting from the assumption that there must have been a direct consequential link between 'what a trial is' and the method of registration chosen by each official or inquisitor. This still appears to be the case, although a more thorough reading of the registers has revealed that this kind of schematisation (that is, by register) is neither possible nor helpful if taken to such an extreme. There are several reasons for this. First of all, the assembling of the registers was mainly due to the work, aims and necessities of the seventeenth-century mission. Secondly, the material given to Doat's agents was already selected and at times 'cleaned up' by those responsible for its conservation. Thirdly, the registers were not always genuine records of a whole enquiry, but something similar to a collection of previous documentation – such as, for example, what remains of the Toulousan enquiry led by Pons of Parnac and Raoul of Plassac, collected in D25 and the first part of D26.[117] Fourthly, sometimes even within one enquiry the method of interrogation and recording cannot be considered wholly consistent, either because of immediate problems imposed by the necessities of the interrogation, or because the officials considered it more crucial to adapt their method (if a structured method was there at all) to the unexpected turn of events.

Behind some very evident and general features – for instance, the focus on Italian and French relationships in D25–6, the beliefs of D22 and the Provençal of D25 – there therefore remains a virtually endless range of precautions and filters, with their fluidity and mutability over time. Nevertheless, the various examples of 'surplus', especially when set against the extremely formulaic nature of the standardised and dominant chunks of text, now appear even more indicative and interesting.

Interrogations and their records attest the presence of two Truths, inseparably entwined in the text. The 'textual building' which the inquisitors ended up shaping (knowingly or not) does not need to be established here. One could imagine, as past scholars did, a 'top-down' thrust which modified the original dialogue: the inquisitors, driving the discourse along a set path of questions, are therefore the agents solely responsible

---

[116] "'Magna diligentia'", pp. 105–6.

[117] For a deeper analysis of this, see my 'Gli inquisitori Raoul de Plassac e Pons de Parnac e l'inchiesta tolosana degli anni 1273–80', in *Praedicatores Inquisitores I, The Dominicans and the Medieval Inquisition: Acts of the 1st International Seminar on the Dominicans and the Inquisition (Rome, 23–25 February 2002)* (Rome, 2004), pp. 471–93.

for the registration of material that is 'factually incorrect'. The need to justify their urge to repress required proof of how strongly dissidence was threatening the unity of the true Church. It seems increasingly likely that such an attitude would have required a full and objective knowledge of the social, political and cultural context in its entirety, awareness of the inquisition's own role within it, and a sharp evaluation of the risks and responsibilities related to it: an external overview so broad that we could hardly ascribe it to anyone. Furthermore, such an interpretation would imply that the inquisitors had a profound perception of their own capacity to influence the registration, and complete and lucid awareness of possessing a 'portion' (or a 'whole') of the Truth. Here not only common sense but also a serious reading of the depositions should make us wary. A will to drive the dialogue, to select the facts, is detectible in the heretics as well as in the inquisitors. The assumptions of ignorance, unconsciousness, stupidity and powerlessness do not do them justice.[118] They were actors – in every respect – in this sharp dialectic fight between the parties.

To moderate the biases attributed to the churchmen, historians should keep in mind that the registers themselves were meant for internal use only. Their promotional and publicising value was virtually non- existent outside the trial context, even when they had some wider circulation beyond the inquisitors.[119] A more balanced approach is required. We

---

[118] Compare with e.g. Given, referring to 'inert and pliant mass, waiting passively to be shaped by their [the inquisitors'] techniques' ('The inquisitors of Languedoc and the medieval technology of power', *American Historical Review* 94 (1989), 336–59, p. 357); Merlo, on 'victims, individuals labelled as heretics: victims- heretics who very often could not even understand what was going on around them and – most of all – upon them', 'heretics who are not in the game anymore' ('Il senso delle opere dei frati Predicatori in quanto "inquisitores hereticae pravitatis" ', *Quaderni di Storia Religiosa* 9 (2002), pp. 9–30, esp. pp. 21–2).

[119] The old scholarly debate about the 'nature' of inquisitorial registers is still alive: historians argue whether they were an instrument of public manipulation by and promotion of the inquisition as an institution, or rather public records of inquisitorial activity, often acting as a 'protection' against over-subjective application of the norms. What Merlo described as the 'public role' of the inquisitorial texts (*Eretici e inquisitori*, pp. 11–12), cannot be ascribed to our sources: rather, it is a strong feature of the *sentences* and *sermons* pronounced during the open declaration of allegations and penances. The judicial connotation of trial records was clearly and deeply investigated by Lorenzo Paolini in his Introduction to the edition of L. Paolini and R. Orioli (eds.) *Acta S. Officii Bononie ab anno 1291 usque ad annum 1310*, ('Fonti per la storia d'Italia' 106) (Rome, 1982), pp. xiii–xxxiii, which has been too quickly forgotten. It is my impression that although conciliar prescriptions and a precise set of papal norms tried to discipline the praxis of interrogations, it is the confused and indecisive *application* of the law that puzzles historians. If it is true that canonists could not prevent the subjective interpretation of the norm, the historiographical analysis of juridical science and analysis of its practical effects should consequently be considered as different enterprises. There is evidence that some inquisitors themselves, in fact, after or during their assignment, were submitted to trial for having read too subjectively the prescribed norms, or for having been too slack in their application. It is the historian's duty, however, to determine some 'average-feature' in these sources, and it seems quite clear to me that normally the registers were intended to be

need to discard the monolithic image of a repressive structure of power opposed to an unarmed group of believers who – we should never forget – were able to hold that structure in check for decades. The depositions actually tell against this image, especially the series of long retractions in them.

The aim of reading with 'precautions' is to find tools for comprehension. Most of the textual differences identified in each register must be contextualised considering the purposes of each single inquiry. As has already been emphasised, each situation, inquisitor, officer, or witness, imposed a personal approach and a different method on the conduct of any particular interrogation. This is why, in the end, the elements of similarity in the volumes are very few.

Stepping back to a 'general' reading of the sources, we should note that the functional nature of trial accounts is underlined by a further element. As noted earlier, these records follow a geographical criterion.[120] As is well known, the medieval Inquisition in southern France was a fragmented but well-structured institution, whose officers, responsible for different enquiries, were mostly unconnected to each other. There is no evidence of any concerted action, or of a common strategy of action. The pope or his legates initially sent one or two inquisitors to the main centre of a problematic area, in an attempt to restore control and re-establish the Church's power. The more institutionalised 'tribunals' are only a later consequence of this initial and patchy strategy. The inquisitors' main task consisted in a detailed enquiry, backed up by special and exceptional powers, in strict collaboration – where possible – with the lay government. This is one reason why these special papal officials mainly concentrated on facts and names, rather than reasons and behaviours, and recorded them as accurately as they could.[121]

One last example helps underline contemporary perceptions of written material, together with the 'surprising' reaction of the deponents. Its implication for us is that we should handle the concepts of 'fear' and 'risk' with care. Saving one's life – or, even more importantly, one's patrimony – induced witnesses to display extraordinary opposition to the churchmen. This example will be used again later, in Chapter 4. Here,

---

a tool for the investigation and record, despite the fact that some sort of access to them was also provided to the accused, in order to provide an opportunity to defend their position.

[120] As shown – although with a different purpose – by Given, *Inquisition*, pp. 35–6.

[121] See Dossat, *Les crises*, p. 195. The situation is not uniform: we cannot talk about one model of 'inquisition', but rather of 'inquisitions', as has been shown by L. Paolini in 'Inquisizioni medievali: il modello italiano nella manualistica inquisitoriale (XIII–XIV secolo)', in P. Maranesi (ed.), *Negotium fidei. Miscellanea di studi offerti a Mariano d'Alatri in occasione del suo 80° compleanno*, ('Bibliotheca Seraphico-Capuccina' 67) (Rome, 2002), pp. 177–98, esp. pp. 177–80.

our point is that these 'records of stories' were treated as crucial by the contemporaries, too.

Our story is about the theft of the Carcassonne registers. According to the depositions, in 1282 Cathar 'priests',[122] lay government members, and officials of Carcassonne, joined together to defend the city from the overpowering influence of the inquisitors, whom they perceived as a threat to their freedom and autonomy. After going over various possible diplomatic and political solutions – all discarded – they arrived at a more radical and illegal one: to steal 'all the inquisition's books relating to this land, that is the Carcassonne region, in which the confessions are written'.[123] Although the precise wording may have been superimposed, it underlines the importance of the episode and shows how the process was perceived by contemporaries.

First, the feeling that *this* written material is hostile and dangerous does not depend on the false nature of the accusations, or on the falsified confessions. The registers are dangerous *as registers*, a threat to the citizens' freedom of worship. They are a written proof of guilt, and therefore indisputable evidence of illicit connections and ties. People, then, did not fear the registers as something twisted and counterfeit: their very existence was a danger for freedom. Evidence of this can be found in the choice of books meant to be stolen. The dangerous ones are the records of trial interrogations ('the books of the depositions of witnesses who gave testimony about the fact of the inquisition into heresy'),[124] and not (as we would perhaps expect) the sentences as being the last acts of the trials and firmly linked to punishment and repression.

The high level of danger ascribed to these particular books and records suggests further thoughts. The citizens did reckon that to steal them would stop inquisitorial activities, at last putting an end to the inquiries which threatened the tranquillity of the city. We need to go beyond a simplifying correlation between theft and liberty, with its consequent identification of a quasi-totemic destruction of the evidence in order to regain freedom. It is much more interesting to look into the perception that contemporaries had of a deep bond between liberty and the writing down and conservation of records. In this way we move further, beyond the recently proposed connection between punishment and freedom.[125]

---

[122] I have chosen to refer to Cathar 'priests', or Good Men/Good Women, rather than to 'perfects' (*perfecti/perfectae*) as this terminology is closer to the original text.

[123] 'Omnes libros inquisitionis qui pertinent ad terram istam, scilicet de Carcassesio, in quibus sunt scripte confessiones', D26, f. 211v.

[124] 'Libros depositionum testium qui deposuerunt super facto inquisitionis heresis', D26, f. 262r. We would expect here 'super facto heresis', not 'super facto inquisitionis heresis'.

[125] See Given, *Inquisition*, pp. 25–51.

This bond arguably also represents a symptom of a different sense of 'community'. From the citizens' point of view, in fact, inquisitorial activity violates the boundaries and territory of a community of residents, villagers or relatives, structured both on a territorial and a familial basis. However, 'community' as understood by the ecclesiastical power is a synonym for Christianity, diocese or parish district. This is a totally different concept, whose ideological assumptions rely on a substantially doctrine-based frame of reference, a religious set of principles and laws. In the light of these different approaches, every action by either party clashes with the opposite party's frame of thought and collective perception.[126]

Eventually the citizens of Carcassonne, together with their noble leaders, a number of Cathars and knights, drew up an effective plan to steal the registers, a plan based on the crucial involvement of a literate man, able to distinguish the key books from the others kept on the inquisitorial shelves.

What can be concluded, after this 'deconstruction' of the records? I suggest that the dialectic between the two parties was much more equal, a more 'balanced' affair than has often been supposed. The two parties' worlds, languages, aims, beliefs and realities inevitably clashed, and shaped both the dialogue itself and its recording. Unfortunately, their fundamental opposition, far from providing historians with a simple path leading in only one interpretative direction, has left traces of much more involved and astonishingly complex interplay. Its true understanding requires meticulous and refreshed textual analysis. In the end, all of this leaves more questions than answers, one of which is particularly nagging. Was it the behaviour that shaped the accusations, or the accusation that 'framed' behaviour?

---

[126] See the fundamental S. Waugh and P. Diehl (eds.), *Christendom and Its Discontents: Exclusion, Persecution and Rebellion, 1000–1500*, (Cambridge, 1996).

Chapter 2

CATHARISM AND ITS MOBILITY

A STARTING POINT[1]

Most of the depositions of Doat 21–6 deal with actions, the majority of them – as one would expect – patently incriminating acts which bring individuals into contact with the 'pollution' of heresy. Being present at public or private preaching, helping well-known heretics or sympathisers, but especially sharing ritual celebrations or meals with them, all constituted possible grounds for suspicion, and led to further investigation. This is why answers dealing with such things pepper our texts, whether they are recorded together with the questions or not. At the same time, however, the interest of the inquisitor identified another very important area, which is frequently investigated in the records: the mobility of the heretics.

Nearly all the evidence deals with deponents talking about moving from one place to another. They themselves or their neighbours and relatives are depicted strolling down the roads of a village, but also planning long trips, moving simply from one village to the next, going with a companion on a pilgrimage that could be as far as Rome or the Holy

---

[1] Heresiologists have marginally tackled the issue of the extreme mobility of heretics, and categorised it either as a reaction to persecution (the topos of the 'fugitive heretic' as in the great majority of studies), or – more rarely – a 'mental attitude' (see, for example, C.Violante in 'Eresie nelle città e nel contado in Italia dall'XI al XIII secolo', in P. Zerbi (ed.), *Studi sulla cristianità medievale. Società, istituzioni, spiritualità*, (Milan, 1975), pp. 349–79, esp. pp. 369–70; and G. Zanella 'Malessere ereticale inValle Padana (1260–1308)', *Rivista di Storia e Letteratura Religiosa* 14/3 (1978), 341–90 [now in *Hereticalia. Temi e discussioni*, ('Collectanea' 7) (Spoleto, 1995), pp. 15–66], esp. pp. 50–51, where the author recalls the words of Dupré-Theseider, who talked about 'a sort of affective circulation among exiled' – [translation is mine]). Some innovative ideas appeared in Merlo, *Eretici e inquisitori*, pp. 87–97. Peter Biller has pointed out the importance of this topic, and of the restrictions imposed by historians when selecting the evidence regarding heretical travels in 'Heretics and long journeys', in *Freedom of Movement in the Middle Ages: Proceedings of the 2003 Harlaxton Conference*, ed. Peregrine Horden, Harlaxton Medieval Studies 15 (Donnington, 2007). I am grateful to him for showing me the typescript of this article.

Land, riding on an ass to visit some ill acquaintances, and so on. Distances vary, as do the destinations and purposes of their trips.

What is surprising is not the frequency of movements in the records – as we have said, this was a selection of each deponent's everyday activities for the purpose of the interrogation. Rather it is the very existence of such a mobile community, which was engaged in a whole variety of 'movements', and accepted its inevitable impact upon the normal rhythms of life. Such a degree of mobility is remarkable, especially taking into account the fact that most of our deponents come from rural areas: many were from peasant families, where the boundaries of a lifetime were often limited to one region, if not to a single village. A medieval community tied to the seasonal rhythms of the land could envisage a certain amount of travelling, mainly involving family affairs and business, where each traveller presumably considered in advance and with extreme care the impact of absence on both work-place and family. But what appears in the sources is much more than this. Even if what is recorded in a deposition is a selection of – say – 'what Bernard did in the winter of 1274', excluding all he had done in the fields, or his sedentary, non-suspicious activities, Bernard and his fellows will have certainly done a lot of travelling to and fro, and they can account for it.

Evidently, the men and women whose depositions are recorded in the Doat registers, rich and poor, were prepared to face risk, uncertainty and the consequences of travelling on both a large and a small scale. They calculated the disruption to their family (for example, parents leaving their offspring), the incurring of expenses, and all the restrictions consequent on their status of travellers. In other words, they were prepared to create, for themselves and their loved ones, a new spatial horizon where they might be obliged to find a new role for themselves, at times even a new identity, in the places they visited.

Unfortunately, the sources severely limit our research. Their inconsistency is such that they do not allow us to follow properly all of the characters in their travels. The Doat volumes record exclusively the voices of those who either never left France, or who came back to France, if previously abroad; and they are the voices of only *some* of those who eventually fell into the inquisitors' net. Many more have escaped either the inquisitors' or our 'hunt' for evidence. Among them are the individuals who left and did not come back, those who were never caught by the inquisitors or their spies and those who appear in our registers only briefly and nowhere else. Last in this list are those who provided depositions and whose words were recorded, but whose testimony was not deemed sufficiently interesting by the Doatists, and is now lost to us. In a great number of cases it is impossible, therefore, to cross-check what happened during such people's 'other lives', whether in another village or town, or in another country. In the case of long-distance travellers, did they recreate some sort of micro-community within these remote milieux? To what extent was their integration acceptable or normal, and when did they begin to fall under suspicion? Indeed, did they ever become suspect to the local population? In what ways and through what channels did they find employment in the new communities? How successful were they?

Regrettably, the answers we can give to these questions provide no more than keyhole glimpses of the past actions, events and words of these travellers. The aim here is to look at them fairly generally, to put these lives into the wider context of the struggle between two conflicting systems, and to outline possible paths for further research.

Our deponents did indeed travel: on differing scales, with different purposes and in different ways. Caveats aside, the records of their hearings create a picture in which members of the Cathar community moved a lot. Movement was a constant feature of their lives. Looking closer, we can distinguish different typologies of itinerancy; use of the plural 'movements' allows the pieces of the puzzle to be arranged according to two main criteria. The first permits analysis of 'movements' according to their purpose. Here we must distinguish the 'positive' from the 'negative' ones – the former voluntary movement, the latter movement brought about by external factors. The second criterion of analysis is quantity. This opens the way to discussion of movements as 'macro' – movements such as migrations or a series of individual journeys on long-haul routes – and as 'micro'. 'Micro-movements' include all the short-distance trips from village to village, from one 'hospice'[2] to the next – the category reported most commonly (and at times in an extremely lively manner) in our depositions.

The stories told by travelling Cathars lend a sort of visibility to the mobility of our characters. As our knowledge of the events develops, it is like looking at Harry Potter's *Marauder's Map*, where flashing dots move on the parchment, as the different characters walk by.[3] However, another, 'invisible' series of movements is implied by the very existence of our texts: the movements of the inquisitors.

The active nature of the inquisitorial office can be confirmed not only by looking at what glimmers through the depositions. Direct sources are also available. The Vatican Archivio Segreto series of *Collectorie*, an uneven collection of inquisitorial registers which includes disciplinary

---

[2] The meaning of this term will be investigated later in this chapter.
[3] J.K. Rowling, *Harry Potter and the Prisoner of Azkaban* (Bloomsbury, 1999).

actions against inquisitors and registers of expenses, preserves copies of documents provided by individual inquisitors to the papal curia, as evidence of their financial conduct.[4] Only a couple of them refer to France, and only one is a register of expenditure,[5] but they are unpublished. Still largely unknown to historians, these records have not been studied in enough depth to provide an all-round picture of the inquisitorial movements. Case-studies, such as Marina Benedetti's recent work on the activity of the inquisitor Lanfranco of Bergamo[6] (fourteenth century), are the exception. The *Collectorie* registers provide an enormous quantity of very 'clean' evidence on the inquisitors' movements, which are recorded not as main items, but in relationship to the expenses inquisitors and their *familia* had to meet.

Although the Italian inquisitors of the fourteenth century appear to have been constantly moving around, to pursue the search and prosecution of heretics, one must draw a distinction between their activities and the earlier periods, especially in France, where the newly recognised papal Inquisition was still embryonic. In the late twelfth and early thirteenth century, in fact, the papacy usually reacted tentatively and patchily to the mobile and lively expansion and proselytism of heretics. It has been demonstrated that the replacement of lay and episcopal tribunals with special purpose-directed ones, directly answerable to the pope and structuring their own techniques of inquiry, was a long and gradual process, uneven in its results, and greatly complicated by local politics. Such an image is very different from that of a 'Holy Office' task-force, which owes much to an outdated historiographical perspective.[7]

---

[4] *Collectoriae, Camera Apostolica,* Rome, Archivio Segreto Vaticano (ASV), on this collection see G. Biscaro, 'Inquisitori ed eretici lombardi (1292–1318)', in *Miscellanea di Storia Italiana,* III ser., 19 (1922), 447–557; G. Biscaro, 'Inquisitori ed eretici a Firenze (1319–1334)', *Studi Medievali,* n.s., II (1929), 347–75, and III (1930), 266–87. Much evidence from the *Collectoriae* features in my recent article 'Inquisizione francescana in Toscana fino al pontificato di Giovanni XXII', in *Frati minori e inquisizione. Atti del XXXIII Convegno internazionale (Assisi, 6–8 October 2005)* (Spoleto, 2006), pp. 287–324. The role of spies and their relationship with the inquisitors will be one focus of my further work.

[5] They are nn. 50 (a criminal trial from 1351–2) and 145 (a register of *subsidii* against the Italian heretics in the provinces of Narbonne, Toulouse and Aix, 1327). See M. Benedetti, 'Le finanze dell'Inquisitore', in *L'economia dei conventi dei frati minori e predicatori fino alla metà del Trecento. Atti del XXXI Convegno Internazionale (Assisi, 9–11 October 2003)* (Spoleto, 2004), pp. 363–401.

[6] M. Benedetti, 'Le parole e le opere di frate Lanfranco, to read as follows: Lanfranco, pp. 111–82. M. Benedetti, 'Frate Lanfranco da Bergamo, gli inquisitori, l'Ordine e la curia Romana', in *Praedicatores Inquisitores,* pp. 157–204.

[7] On interpretations and misinterpretations of the Inquisition, see G.G. Merlo (ed.), *Eretici ed eresie medievali nella storiografia contemporanea,* Bollettino della Società di Studi Valdesi 174, (Torre Pellice, 1994), esp. the contributions by P. Biller for Britain and the USA. (pp. 39–63, esp. pp. 39–41, 55–8) [Engl. edn. '*The historiography of Medieval Heresy in the USA and Great Britain, 1945–92*', in *The Waldenses, 1170–1530* (Aldershot, 2001), pp. 25–48], and W. Maleczek for the German-speaking

The tribunals established in the south of France originated as locally based structures,[8] relying on the *ad hoc* presence of just one or two inquisitors, assigned to coordinate enquiries in that area. At least initially,inquisitors were deliberately sent to a specific place to handle the spread of heretical ideas or preaching in that location. In some cases they were local friars, whose task was to establish the tribunal within an existing political, social and ecclesiastical framework, to sink their roots in the local soil, to mix and mingle with various and changing patterns of power, and with social dynamics mostly alien to them, such as the relationships between families, or the existence of a long-lived *fama* enjoyed by individuals in villages and towns. There is very little evidence of cooperation between different tribunals, of correspondence between them, or of collaboration in solving a case.[9] As always happens, the hunters are a step behind their prey. They have to tune in to the rhythms and habits of that prey, whom they will meet only when the inquisitors and the deponents physically get together. The Catholic officials succeeded eventually by employing spies, men and women within the alien system they were fighting; in other words, only when they adapted to the movements of their adversaries. Meanwhile, the Inquisition had to pay the price of being an evolving structure whose beginnings (if we can really pinpoint them) seem ill-coordinated and lacking larger-scale planning.

This, then, is the grid on which to plot the analysis of the various 'movements', each of which will be studied here through the Doat depositions.

'POSITIVE' MOVEMENTS

Thanks to Bernard Hamilton's numerous and fundamental contributions it is now feasible to think that the longest and most important 'movement' in the history of Catharism was that very first 'migration' of ideas and people from the East.[10] Through a slow and gradual diffusion,

---

world (pp. 64–93, esp. pp. 75, 85, 93). See also D. Solvi, 'La parola all'accusa. L'Inquisizione nei risultati della recente storiografia', *Studi Medievali*, III ser., 39 (June 1998), 367–95; O. Capitani, 'DaVolpe a Morghen: riflessioni eresiologiche a proposito del centenario della nascita di Eugenio Dupré-Theseider', *Studi Medievali*, III ser., (1999), 305–21. Most recently, however, the idea of an extremely organised body of officials is enjoying somewhat of a revival among historians. See for instance the opinions of J. Given, J. Arnold and M.G. Pegg; a different perspective in Roach, *The Devil's World*, who highlights the initial 'confused and inadequate response by the Church' (p. 83) and shows a more moderate position on the development of the Inquisition at pp. 132–58 .

[8] J. Guiraud, *Histoire de l'Inquisition au Moyen Age*, vol. II (Paris, 1938), p. 246.

[9] See below.

[10] The debate on the supposed Eastern filiation of Catharism is old and connected to the derivation of Cathar doctrine from dualistic religions coming from the East (Manichaeism, Bogomilism, Paulicians). Although opinions still differ (see, for instance, the completely different angle recently

following the routes of commerce and pilgrimage, Cathar doctrine reached Europe, up to Germany and Britain, and to Spain, in the West. Although limited and uneven evidence led past historians to concentrate mainly on French, Italian and German Catharism, apart from some scarcely documented examples in other European areas, it is now established that the doctrine of the two principles did indeed have widespread success throughout most of Europe. Sources of a different nature attest its presence from the early twelfth century. Its message, in both the double version of a 'popular' one (shared in public and private preaching) and an 'elitist' one (revealed only to the Cathar clergy), appealed to all strata of society. Women and men, rich and poor, literate and peasants joined the *Gleisa de Dio* ('the Church of God'), entranced by powerful preaching, introduced to it by friends and relatives, or pushed by the lax and mundane attitude displayed by the clergy, to look for a more genuine and honest way of living a true faith. Never again were substantial numbers of Cathars to be mobile over such a vast geographical span. It was a real migration of men and their ideas, a process whose diverse and numerous means and ways is as impossible to reconstruct satisfactorily as it is to reconstruct the beginnings of the Christian faith itself. We can label it as the 'positive' movement *par excellence*. As a missionary enterprise, it had the energy of a fresh start and a positive, new ideology, both of which feature typically at the origins of all religious movements.

Strangely enough, however, the memory of the dawn of Catharism, of its Eastern foundations, does not feature in the Doat depositions, with the sole exception of the confession of Peter Perrin of Puylaurens, who 'had heard Anglesia, the wife of the late Peter Ratier, who [Anglesia] was burnt for heresy, saying that the "heretics" had a certain book which

suggested by R.I. Moore in his 'Postface' to *Inventer l'hérésie?*, pp. 263–9, esp. p. 266), the prevalent argument seems to support the idea of a continuity with Eastern doctrine, most famously introduced, among others, by A. Dondaine ('L'origine de l'hérésie médiévale. A propos d'un livre récent', *Rivista di Storia della Chiesa in Italia* 20 (1950), 47–78); S. Runciman [*The Medieval Manichee* (Cambridge, 1947)]; A. Borst (*Les Cathares* (Paris, 1984)), [orig. edn. *Die Katharer* (Stuttgart, 1974)]; and borne out in recent years by the contributions of B. Hamilton ('The origins of the Dualist Church of Drugunthia', in *Monastic Reform, Catharism and the Crusades (900–1300)* (London, 1979), VII, pp. 115–24); 'The Cathars and the seven churches of Asia', in J.D. Howard-Johnston (ed.), *Byzantium and the West c. 850–c. 1200* (Amsterdam, 1988), pp. 269–95; 'Wisdom from the East', in *Heresy and Literacy*, pp. 38–60; (with C. Hamilton) *Christian Dualist Heresies in the Byzantine World c. 650–1405* (Manchester, 1998); *Crusaders, Cathars and the Holy Places* (Aldershot, 1999). See also F. Zambon (ed.), *La cena segreta. Trattati e rituali catari* (Milan, 1997), at pp. 25–51; Roach, *The Devil's World*, pp. 65–7. On the debate, see Biller's thoughts in Merlo (ed.), *Eretici ed eresie medievali nella storiografia contemporanea*, at pp. 50–1 and relative notes, and B. Hamilton, 'The legacy of Charles Schmidt to the study of Christian dualism', *Journal of Medieval History* 24/2 (1998), 191–214, esp. pp. 196–201.

they looked at when they saw such weather – and this in Bulgaria'.[11] It seems as if the later thirteenth- and fourteenth-century believers lost interest in the past of their own Church; as if the far Eastern lands had been erased from the consciousness of being a Cathar, and had ended up embodying, as all 'far', 'lost' and 'past' things do, something detached from everyday life.

Why this absence? Can one really attribute loss of memory to the Cathar communities of Languedoc? Or is it rather the result of lack of interest by the inquisitors in any doctrine and belief, apart from that element that marked (or 'made', according to some) one out as a heretic? Yet, it is hard to conceive that what constitutes the soul of a community, its common past, the memory of its origins, the collective remembrance of what shaped that community in its beginnings, could not interest the inquisitors. Catharism was indeed a religious group naming and considering itself as *the* Church;[12] and the inquisitors certainly did not ignore the importance and repercussions of the transmission of this specific collective identity.

However, the absence of memory is not limited to our depositions. Those Cathar texts which survive focus strongly on ritual and prayer. Again, this could be the result of the vagaries of historical selection. However, we must consider the *Gleisa de Dio*. This text can be considered the manifesto of the Cathar community, and yet it makes no mention of the original migration from the East; rather, it frames its teachings in a completely scriptural and a-historical context. The depositions of Waldensian brothers too, do not mention a historical past as their origin. Is this common absence solely due to lack of interest on the part of the inquisitors? The case of the Waldensians has in fact been studied. It seems that in the process of memorisation, the image of the founder progressively blurred and then became identified with that of the apostles, so that the identity of the lay founder within the fraternity was forgotten. The purpose of the writers, who 'constructed' this absence, was to make the order 'different', not because it was founded by a layman, but because, as equal to the apostles, it was thus unjustly persecuted by the authorities. The presence of Valdès in depositions and texts was functional to the construction of the identity of the group: a persecuted community.

---

[11] 'Audivit Anglesiam uxor[em] quondam Petri Raterii, que fuit combusta propter heresim, dicentem quod heretici habebant quendam librum quem respiciebant quando videbant tale tempus; et hoc in Bulgaria', D25, f. 216v. This snippet is also quoted by Hamilton ('Wisdom', pp. 55–7). Although he does not make the connection explicit, the deposition was probably referring here to the famous *Secret Book* quoted in Anselm of Alessandria, which was a highly contentious issue among churches in Italy, and which was related to the mysteries of the universe.

[12] See below, paragraph 2.4.

In this way, and this only, the believers were referring to a shared ideological patrimony.[13] These elements can shed some light on the different reasons for the 'absence of a past', which we cannot ascribe simply to the inquisitors' lack of interest. What about this absence in Cathar sources, then? If we bring together and reflect upon the Cathar texts and our depositions, however selective and biased, we gain the impression that we are studying a religious community which did not rely greatly on the construction of a shared past, but which was instead living a strong *present*. In this present, the group's identity was created by communication, contact and mutual support between the living members. Preaching and rituals were the two foci of the communities, as evidenced by both texts and depositions.[14] According to Cathar doctrine, in fact, humanity is the incarnation of evil, an inevitable concomitant of the captivity of the souls; all that is material and human holds an intrinsic negativity. The only value in being human lies in its 'instrumental' function: human bodies, in the shape of the 'priests', provide a means of transmitting the

---

[13] P. Biller, 'Medieval Waldensians' construction of the Past', *Proceedings of the Huguenot Society of Great Britain and Ireland* 25 (1989), 39–54. A more extreme position is G. Merlo's in *Identità valdesi*, p. 39, and nn. 34–6, where he talks of a 'questioning' and later on of the 'cancellation' of the identity of a founder in Italian Waldensian sources. On the Waldensians and journeys, see P. Biller, 'Heretics and Long Journeys', in *Freedom of Movement in the Middle Ages: Proceedings of the 2003* Harlaxton Conference, ed. P. Horden, Harlaxton Medieval Studies 15 (Donnington, 2007), pp. 86–103.

[14] In the case of the Cathars, there is only one element which can be labelled as a typical 'indicator' of memory, and this is the cult of the martyrs, of which the theoretical ground lay in Cathar texts, 'This Church suffers persecutions and tribulations and martyrdom in the name of Christ' (*Gleisa de Dio*, in T. Venckeleer, 'Un recueil Cathare: le manuscrit A.6.10 de la "Collection Vaudoise" de Dublin', *Revue Belge de Philologie et d'Histoire* 38 (1960), 815–34, ch. X, p. 828; Wakefield and Evans, p. 603). This cult appears when believers confess to collecting human remains from the ashes of a stake. It has an eloquent parallel in the later obsession of the Church with wiping out all possible memory of the deceased through the exhumation of bodies and further burning of the remains. However, both behaviours can be an 'unconscious heritage' of the received Catholic education, and a superposition of its cultural framework on Cathar and other groups' practices. See, for instance, *Acta SS. Officii Bononie*, 'Index', at the entry 'reliquie hereticorum' p. 84; the notes by Pseudo-David of Aubsburg (W. Preger (ed.), Pseudo-David of Augsburg, *Tractatus de inquisitione hereticorum*, 'Der Traktat David von Augsburg über die Waldesier', *Abhandlungen der histor. Cl. der Kgl. Bayerischen Akademie der Wissenschaften* 14/2 (1876), 183–235, p. 222); and the comments in Gui (G. Mollat (ed.), Bernard Gui, *Le manuel de l'Inquisiteur*, 2nd edn. (Paris 1964), [V], IV, 7); Wakefield and Evans, p. 430, where the authors indicate this behaviour among the ways of spotting suspicious individuals. Other interesting examples are Guillaume Pelhisson's depiction of the Dominican Roland of Cremona, who in the late 1220s and early 1230s was already performing semi-ritual exhumations for the benefit of believers in Toulouse (J. Duvernoy (ed.), Guillaume de Pelhisson, *Chronicon (1229–1244)* (Paris, 1994), pp. 40, 42); and the inquisitor Lanfranc of Bergamo, who makes 35 *solidi* from the bones of Mia, exhumed and burnt, possibly by selling them to her family or to other Cathars (quoted in Biscaro, *Inquisitori ed eretici lombardi*, pp. 456–531). See also D. Solvi, 'Santi degli eretici e santi degli inquisitori intorno all'anno 1300', in P. Golinelli (ed.), *Il pubblico dei santi. Forme e livelli di ricezione dei messaggi agiografici, Atti del III Convegno di studio dell'Associazione Italiana per lo studio della santità, dei culti e dell'agiografia (AISSCA) (Verona 22–24 Ottobre 1998),* (Rome, 2000), pp. 141–56.

doctrine and administering the sacraments. Cathars perceive themselves as a lively, moving and completely historicised group of believers.

The weight of the first, foundation 'mass-movement' from the East in deponents' minds was, therefore, surprisingly slight. A mythical first missionary migration had little place in Cathar memory.[15] Yet there is knowledge of a shared patrimony of a different type of myth. The *secreta* feature – more or less explicitly – both in some of the depositions and in several anti-heretical treatises.[16] This elitist character of the doctrine, its secret knowledge, refers back to the origins of the world, to the Creation, to the origins of a lost purity and to the beginning of captivity for all souls. By keeping it secret the Cathar hierarchy made it an element of identity for the higher community only; it was not a cultural patrimony available to all. Again, common believers, the great majority of our deponents, can only refer to the present to identify their common heritage.

In contrast to this genesis, other large-scale movements have left a greater mark. As mentioned above, there is evidence not only about places but also of proper 'routes', or privileged itineraries linking distant areas and putting dispersed communities in contact with each other. The two destinations most frequently quoted in the Doat depositions are Italy and Catalonia, in the north-east of Spain. Given the geographical proximity of Catalonia and Languedoc, one could suppose natural, virtually continuous exchanges through the Pyrenees, for reasons connected to commerce, personal relationships, pilgrimages and so on. However, proximity was not the only reason which drove southern French residents to Italian destinations, mainly located in the north of the peninsula. When the southern French deponents, notaries, or both, refer to 'Lombardy', they seem to envisage an area much larger than Lombardy as it was understood by Lombards, and they often include cities in Piedmont, Liguria and the Venetian region. There are also a few mentions of Sicily and Apulia, in the south, and Rome.

---

[15] With two minor exceptions. Anselm of Alessandria's introductory paragraph to his *Tractatus de Hereticis*, which refers to connections between northern French conquistadores and Constantinople. Here, according to Anselm, they met some adepts of a Manichaean sect, were converted to its creed and took the doctrine of the two principles into France. The history of this filiation is likely to have come to Anselm from the hearing of Cathar priests (*Tractatus de hereticis*, in *La hiérarchie Cathare en Italie*, vol. II, *Archivum Fratrum Praedicatorum* 20 (1950), 308–24, [reprinted in A. Dondaine, *Les hérésies et l'Inquisition, XIIe-XIIe siècles*, ed. Y. Dossat (London, 1990), IV, pp. 234–324], p. 308). The second exception is a passing reference in Eberwin of Steinfeld's *Letter* to St Bernard of Clairvaux, where he refers to a cluster of memory still persisting in Greece, 'those who were burned told us ... that this heresy ... has persisted thus in Greece and certain other lands' (*PL* 182, 676–80, p. 680).

[16] The most recent general account of Cathar myths is A. Greco, *Mitologia Catara. Il favoloso mondo delle origini* (Spoleto, 2000), esp. pp. 133–221.

Needless to say, these contacts were extremely interesting for the inquisitors, not only because they demonstrated links between suspects, relationships which became suspicious especially when associated with at least one dangerous activity or person. They confirmed the existence of a recurrent pattern connecting two areas known to inquisitors as hotbeds of heresy. The interest and aims of the inquisitors were undoubtedly crucial for the preservation of this information and for the wording of these portions of the depositions. Details of the trips to Italian cities were preserved because they mattered in the precise establishing of contacts with heresy; equally, the choice of vocabulary in the records reflects the inquisitor's knowledge of the matter. For these reasons, we must allow for a relatively high level of 'contamination' in the sources. However, it would be hard to argue that these movements did not occur, at least in the majority of cases. Deponents might have lied about the number and names of people participating in a trip. Inquisitors may have exercised pressure in order to gain a more accurate description of factual details, or the naming and shaming of more individuals; they may have even forced speech into mental categories better known to them. Notaries could have translated the Occitan speech inaccurately, polishing it into more literate and Latinised expressions; or they may have omitted chunks of an excessively long narration. However, one's impression is that the core of these confessions is real and that the events reported in them did, for the most part, actually occur.

Our evidence confirms that an acknowledged route linked the south of France and the north of Italy not only during the renowned 'mass migrations' following the hardening of inquisitorial policy after Montségur and up to the 1270s, but also in earlier decades. People embarking on such a long trip appear to have known of the existence and location of a series of houses where they could find shelter, and equally they seem to have known of specific individuals able to organise those trips. These people could lead them to a chosen destination.

As long ago as 1938 Jean Guiraud suggested that such routes were not established simply as a direct consequence of the recrudescence of papal measures against heresy. He claimed that although they may have been less organised and frequent, communications between Languedoc and 'Lombardy' were already pretty active.[17] Through commerce, especially

---

[17] Jean Guiraud (*Histoire de l'Inquisition*, pp. 245–65) devoted a whole chapter to the emigration from France to Italy which is still the standard reference work on the topic. Historiography mostly agrees on his chronology – that the highest incidence of contacts between the two destinations occurred between Montségur (1244) and the 1270s – and on his interpretation, which is mainly a 'negative' one (mobility induced by the persecution). See, for example, Douais, *Documents*, I, p. xxxii; M. da Alatri, *L'inquisizione francescana nell'Italia centrale del Duecento: con in appendice il testo*

the cloth trade, a complex pattern of relationships was already in place.[18] It is not hard to imagine numerous people travelling along these commercial routes several times a year, carrying money and goods, but also messages, and possibly acting as guides for those who required expert companions during their trips.

In fact, there had long been an association between cloth-makers and heretics, which is recorded as early as the mid-twelfth century. Writing about Saint Bernard's miracles in Toulouse, Geoffrey of Auxerre quotes a linguistic connection between weavers and heresy ('weavers, whom they call Arians').[19] Evidently, in Toulouse the identification between 'Arians' (an old synecdoche for 'heretics') and weavers was so deeply embedded in local knowledge that it needed interpreting by the writer. Eckbert of Schönau, in his sermons against the heretics of Cologne, refers in fact to the same linguistic association (heretics-weavers) which is common throughout France. 'France calls them *texerant*, from the habit of weaving'; these people state that only where their meetings are held, 'that is, in cellars and weavers' workshops', can one find true belief and practice of Christian values.[20] Further, this association owes much to the brief heretical life of the Italian religious cloth-makers, the Humiliati

---

del '*Liber inquisitionis*' *di Orvieto trascritto da Egidio Bonanno*, 2nd edn. ('Bibliotheca Seraphico-Capuccina' 149) (Rome, 1996), pp. 28, 111; Y. Dossat, 'Les Cathares au jour le jour. Confessions inédites de Cathares Quercynois', *Cahiers de Fanjeaux* 3 (1968), pp. 259–98, esp. pp. 290–7; Y. Dossat, 'Les Cathares d'après les documents de l'Inquisition', *Cahiers de Fanjeaux* 3 (1968), pp. 71–104, esp. p. 75; Merlo, *Eretici e inquisitori*, pp. 89–93; E. Dupré-Theseider, 'Le Catharisme Languedocien et l'Italie', *Cahiers de Fanjeaux* 3 (1968), pp. 299–316 [also in 'Il Catarismo della Linguadoca e l'Italia', in *Mondo cittadino e movimenti ereticali nel Medioevo* (Bologna, 1978), pp. 233–59, 345–60]; A. Pales-Gobillard, 'Passages du Languedoc en Italie a l'occasion du jubilé du 1300', *Cahiers de Fanjeaux* 15 (1980), pp. 245–55, esp. p. 247; E. Griffe, *La Languedoc Cathare et l'Inquisition (1229–1329)* (Paris, 1980), pp. 111–2, 127, 133, 188–9; J. Duvernoy, *L'histoire des Cathares*, (Toulouse, 1979), pp. 304–314; J. Duvernoy, *Inquisition à Pamiers. Interrogatoires de Jacques Fournier, 1318–1325, choisis, traduits du texte latin et presentés par Jean Duvernoy* (Paris, 1966), pp. 9–10; J. Duvernoy (ed.), *Le régistre de Jacques Fournier, évêque à Pamiers (1318–1325)*, 2nd edn. (Toulouse, 1978), pp. 13, 14–6; Zanella, 'Malessere ereticale', p. 49, M. Lambert, *The Cathars* (Oxford, 1998), p. 222. Roach, *The Devil's World*, pp. 38–9, has the merit of pointing out in detail the strength of pre-existing links based on economic patterns and routes.

[18] Guiraud, *Histoire*, p. 248.

[19] 'De textoribus, quos Arianos ipsi nominant', Geoffrey of Auxerre, *Vita Prima Bernardi*, PL 185, col. 411D. However, Grundmann's paraphrase of this excerpt is slightly different, as he makes a different use of punctuation and capital letters. 'Paucos quidem habebat civitas illa, qui heretico faverent: de Textoribus, quos Arrianos ipsi nominant, nonnullos; ex his vero, qui favebant heresi illi, plurimi errant et maximi civitatis illius', which Grundmann paraphrases thus, 'The heretic Henry had few followers in Toulouse; but there were some heretics, who are called 'Textores' by us, but 'Arriani' in Provence, in Toulouse; and these heretics had very many adherents, even among the most important residents' (Grundmann, *Religious movements*, pp. 260–1, n. 35).

[20] 'Gallia, texerant, ab usu texendi appellat', Eckbert of Schönau, *Sermones tredecim contra hereticos*, PL 195, col. 13; 'in conventiculis suis, quae habent in cellariis et in textrinis, et in hujusmodi subterraneis domibus', *ibid.*, col. 14. However, the issue of the association between heretics and weavers is still debated by current scholarship, as accounted for by L. Kaelber ('Weavers into heretics?

(1184–1201). Even after their reintegration into the Church by Innocent III, the Humiliati were always looked upon with suspicion by local clergy and population for their unconventional behaviour: their mixed-sex houses and their unorthodox contacts with the lay world of national and foreign markets. This connection added to the penumbra of heresy/ cloth- making; it seems that cloth-makers had enjoyed a negative reputation with religious authorities for at least a couple of centuries.[21] Indeed, the Doat depositions confirm both the interest of the inquisitors in this aspect of religious and working life, and the existence of a grey area around the Humiliati as well as all cloth-making communities that were in repeated contact with people and ideas travelling from abroad.

Several deponents highlight connections between those suspected of Catharism and the craft of cloth-making. Among them is William of Elves, known also as William Donadieu of Maserac, who knows of some *perfecti* who 'run a textile workshop'.[22] Another deponent mentions 'two heretic weavers in the house of the Barra, near Puylaurens, who wove for him a piece of fabrics'.[23] One very keen traveller is Raymond 'the weaver', who would like to return to Lombardy 'if he finds good company'.[24] Another weaver, Peter Guiraman, hosts people at his place (perhaps a hospice?) in Figeac.[25]

The connection in the case of the Humiliati is evident in the deposition of the famous Raymond Baussan, hospice landlord and traveller, who meets in Genoa 'Arnaud Copa, a smith of Toulouse, who became a Humiliatus'.[26] Again, Arnaud Copa 'from Toulouse, and lives in Genoa

---

The social organisation of early thirteenth-century Catharism in comparative perspective', *Social Science History* 21 (1997), esp. pp. 111–17).

[21] See Roach, *The Devil's World*, p. 69, Lansing, *Power and Purity*, p. 69, and notes 63–4. Lansing also lists the occupational environment of heretics in Orvieto: furriers, shoemakers, smiths, tailors and woodworkers (p. 67). For the Humiliati, the traditional starting point is L. Zanoni, *Gli Umiliati nei loro rapporti con l'eresia, l'industria della lana ed i comuni nei secoli XII e XIII sulla scorta di documenti inediti*, 2nd edn. (Rome, 1970); followed by R. Manselli, 'Gli Umiliati lavoratori della lana', in *Produzione, commercio e consumo dei panni di lana (nei secoli XII–XVIII), Atti della II settimana di studio dell'Istituto di Storia Economica F. Datini* (Florence, 1976), pp. 231–6; L. Paolini, 'Gli eretici e il lavoro: fra ideologia ed esistenzialità', in *Lavorare nel Medioevo: Rappresentazioni ed esempi dall'Italia dei secoli X–XVI, XXI Convegno storico internazionale (12–15 October 1980)* (Todi, 1983), pp. 111–67; L. Paolini, 'Le Umiliate al lavoro. Appunti fra storiografia e storia', *Bullettino dell'Istituto Storico Italiano per il Medio Evo e Archivio Muratoriano* 97 (1991), pp. 229–65; a recent review of relevant literature is in F. Andrews, *The Early Humiliati* (Cambridge, 1999), pp. 29–32.

[22] 'Tenuerunt operatorium artis textorie', D23, f. 209v.

[23] 'Duo textores hereticos in domo den Barra apud Podium Laurentium, qui texerunt eidem testi unam telam', D24, f. 137r.

[24] 'Si haberet bonam societatem', D25, f. 79r.

[25] 'Item he said that near Figeac they had been in the house of Peter Guiraman, weaver' ('Item dixit quod apud Figeacum fuerunt in domo Petri Guiraman, textoris'), D25, f. 189r.

[26] 'Arnaldum Copam fabrum de Tholosa qui fecerat se de Humiliatis', D25, f. 146v.

and was of the Humiliati'[27] is quoted by another renowned hospice land-lord and traveller, Peter of Beauville. Both depositions refer back to events that had occurred in 1273–4. The 1270s can be seen as the highest point of the Humiliati's economic and political power in Italian cities; they were not under suspicion any more. Given this, it is intriguing that there was a Humiliatus among the dozens of believers and fugitives whom Raymond Baussan and Peter of Beauville met.

Guiraud's suggestion of an earlier link between Languedoc and 'Lombardy' has not enjoyed much popularity. With the exception of Andrew Roach's, the most recent works tend to explain such a connection as an Inquisition-driven movement towards safer areas: it was because of persecution that Cathar believers started to travel to and from Italy. I am suggesting, however, that the larger picture needs to be taken into account. Lively commercial routes provided the starting point: Catharism quite naturally used the existing network of relationships and people as a vehicle and a means of spreading its message. Roach states that 'the growth of heresy in Languedoc and north Italy took place against a background of increasing economic links between the two regions'.[28] Ideas travel with people; one does not need always to assume a planned and/or a subtle intention of deliberate proselytism.

I now turn from large- to small-scale movements. On the 'positive' side, the Doat depositions have preserved very rich and very circumstantial accounts. Under this heading I shall group all freely undertaken short-distance movements. There is plenty of evidence here. The constant itinerancy from village to village, from town to town, is at the core of being a Cathar, and is therefore well recorded in the depositions. Movement from place to place was highly necessary for a Church with no official places of worship: for preaching, maintaining contact with brethren and administering the sacraments. Frequent movements involved not only preachers and 'priests' but also all common believers who wanted to hear them preach; in general, anyone who needed to visit someone who was dying, or who simply wished to get in touch with their companions and bring them help, food and money in times of need.

It is hard to single out examples to illustrate this section, since virtually every deposition contains some. The evidence is varied and abundant – this is the most immediate and striking feature of our depositions. It must be considered *en masse* with the aim of discerning any recurrent patterns, and suggesting general hypotheses about Cathar itinerancy – but,

---

[27] 'Arnaldus Copa, qui fuit de Tholosa, et solet morari apud Ianuam, et erat de Humiliatis', D25, f. 306r.

[28] Roach, *The Devil's world*, p. 38.

beforehand, a few general points about its interpretation are worth making.

First, and most immediately, travel from one place to another met a practical pastoral need. Preaching, rituals, charity, care of souls and missionary support are the most recurrent motives for travel, and these involved both the hierarchy – as ministers of the cult – and the believers and sympathisers, who attended celebrations and collaborated with the ministers. Such activities in turn necessitated specific roles and functions, as the communities increased in number, and the need to respond to their requests increased. However, we must try not to confine people and their roles within too rigid categories, since a linguistic categorisation of functions (as we shall see later) can be semantically slippery.[29] Nevertheless, it is legitimate to think that within these groups of believers some members did enjoy more defined roles, due to their positions within the local community or their professional competence. Moreover, it is not unjustified to suppose that, as in all religious groupings (especially newly constituted ones) people tended to share jobs and tasks, to distribute the burden of needs, genuinely wanting to help their brethren.

Second, an organised community posed and poses ecclesiological problems. Medieval polemicists (Ranier Sacconi, Anselm of Alessandria, the anonymous author of the *De heresi Catharorum*) and modern historians[30] have long argued not only over the hierarchy of the Cathar church, but also over the very existence and (assuming that it did exist) the organisation of *a* Cathar church as an ecclesiastical structure. As has already been said, the problem of its existence – I am firmly convinced it did exist – will not be discussed.[31] Nevertheless, it is legitimate to raise the issue, given the heavy contamination of records, especially depositions, by inquisitorial and notarial discourse.

Records of the interrogations were kept for their technical and instrumental value, in order to be used as legal evidence by lay and ecclesiastical authority. Notaries and inquisitors undoubtedly imposed a series of 'cultural translations' on the Occitan confessions, intending to make them more bureaucrat-friendly, and pertinent to their own legalistic requirements. At the same time, a reverse process was also possible – that is, Cathar communities, in need of a linguistic and practical framework

---

[29] See Arnold, *Inquisition and power*, pp. 37–47.

[30] A. Dondaine, 'La hiérarchie Cathare en Italie', *Archivum Fratrum Praedicatorum* I 19 (1949), 280–312; II-III 20 (1950), pp. 234–324, esp. part I; F. Šanjek, 'Le rassemblement hérétique de Saint-Félix de Caraman (1167) et les églises Cathares au XIIe siècle', *Revue d'Histoire Ecclésiastique* 67 (1972), pp. 772–9; Bertuzzi, *Ecclesiarum forma*, pp. 51–113; P. Jimenez, 'Relire la charte de Niquinta', *Heresis* 23 (1994), pp. 1–28; Zanella, *Hereticalia*, throughout.

[31] See the conclusions of this chapter.

to define and organise their life, were in a position to 'borrow' what was already available to them. Not all believers and hierarchy, in fact, were born into a Cathar-only *mentalité*. After all, they were in contact, although to differing degrees, with the culture, language and rituals of a predominantly Catholic environment. When necessary, they could easily adopt categories and their definitions from this rich patrimony of meanings, and adapt them to their own, alternative, community. When looking at depositions, therefore, we must consider 'Catharisation' of discourse alongside its equally feasible 'Catholicisation' and 'notarialisation'.

Can our confessions be reliable sources for the study of an ecclesial structure, through the analysis of the mobility of the Cathars and the internal relationships of their communities? Can they add to or modify the information we gather from anti-Cathar writers? Sources like Ranier Sacconi[32] and Anselm of Alessandria[33] have been extensively dissected and analysed in order to understand the ecclesiological problem.[34] It seems that we should posit an autonomous and well-organised ecclesiastical structure from as early as the second half of the twelfth century (or even from the mention of the Cathars of Cologne in 1144).[35] We cannot assume the existence of a single Church, but rather 'several co-existing ecclesiastical cells'.[36] Among these, the Italian ones (except perhaps the Orvietan and Florentine ones)[37] originated from doctrinal differences, while the French ones were structured on a territorial basis, replicating more or less the boundaries and divisions of local Catholic dioceses.[38] Through cross-referencing polemical treatises, inquisitorial records and papal documents, it has been possible to construct a list of all the senior members of the clergy – bishops, deacons, *filii maiores, filii minores* – and to fit them chronologically and geographically into an ecclesiastical frame.[39]

---

[32] A. Dondaine (ed.), Raniero Sacconi, *Summa de Catharis et Leonistis seu Pauperibus de Lugduno*, in *Un Traité néo-manichéen du XIIIe siècle, le Liber de duobus principiis, suivi d'un fragment de Rituel cathare* (Rome, 1939), pp. 64–78 [also edited by F. Šanjek, 'Raynerius Sacconi O.P. Summa de Catharis', *Archivum Fratrum Praedicatorum* 44 (1974), 42–60]; transl. in Wakefield and Evans, pp. 329–46.

[33] A. Dondaine (ed.), Anselm of Alessandria, *Tractatus de hereticis*.

[34] On this issue, I shall limit my reference to Dondaine, *La hiérarchie Cathare*; Roach, *The Devil's World*, pp. 78 and 82 (about the difference between Italian and French communities, and some degree of 'loose-knit organisation'); and the most recent monograph, R. Bertuzzi, *'Ecclesiarum forma'*.

[35] Bertuzzi, *'Ecclesiarum forma'*, pp. 51–2.

[36] Bertuzzi, *'Ecclesiarum forma'*, pp. 51–62 (on the origins and progressive structuring of organisation); p. 104, the translation is mine.

[37] Lansing, *Power and Purity*, pp. 7, 9, 71 ('every Italian community has its own history' and the stress on source-related problems).

[38] As first theorised by R. Manselli, *L'eresia del Male* (Naples, 1963), pp. 190–243, esp. p. 219; Bertuzzi, *'Ecclesiarum forma'*, pp. 65, 104–5.

[39] Bertuzzi, *'Ecclesiarum forma'*, pp. 37–113; pp. 66–100 for the list of Italian 'clergy'.

This effort will not be replicated here.[40] The information given in the Doat evidence taken on its own (as in this study) is too narrow and uneven. It is sufficient here to point out that there are no fundamental contradictions to Bertuzzi's analysis. The Doat evidence for the existence of dioceses, the presence and activity of bishops, deacons and other members of the clergy, confirms her reading. (The Conclusions section of this chapter supplies further information.)

Instead, the aspect which will be put under the spotlight in our reading of the 'positive movements' is the internal organisation and day-to-day management of the communities, which relied strongly on movements and contacts between individuals.

A 'LIVING CHURCH'

Macro- and micro-movements, taken together, build up the image of a 'living church'. How did it work? This living community shaped itself as an organised church through the gradual creation of a network of private houses where Cathars lived, were hosted for brief periods and found shelter; and through the connections and communications between them. As a result of the very existence of this network, Cathars felt they belonged to a group based on a territorial structure, which also evolved very effective methods to keep itself active and alive.

Postmodernist and Foucauldian historians have dismissed our depositions as a scarcely reliable (if not completely unreliable) guide as to how the structure of Catharism worked. They argue that inquisitors and their notaries, in writing up these records, created an artificial and one-sided categorisation of people and their roles in Catharism. The powerful operated a cultural transposition of categories onto the words of the powerless, and in so doing, gradually created 'confessing subjects'. Inquisitors' perceptions drove the interrogation and wording of the dialogue. As a result, historians can now see a progressive distinction developing between heretics as a 'lump' – an indistinct mass of corrupted 'others' – in the early years of the Inquisition, and the later 'leaven' – individual corruptors of the uniform body of Christianity.[41]

Although this theory has the merit of highlighting a crucial connection between power and language, and has shown the limitations inherent in our sources, it should be adopted only with care, and never applied

---

[40] See the table of Cathar 'clergy' in A. Borst, *Die Katharer* (Stuttgart, 1974), pp. 231–35; Duvernoy, *Histoire*, pp. 347–51.
[41] The terminology is taken from Arnold, *Inquisition and Power*, pp. 19–47. Similar approach in Pegg, *The Corruption*; Pegg, 'On Cathars'; Théry, 'L'hérésie des bons hommes'; see above, Introduction.

too literally. It is, however, something to bear in mind when talking about categories or classification of groups/individuals.

To return to our Cathar organisation of the 'living church', the key personnel to make it work effectively were those called *nuncii* or *receptatores* by inquisitorial records, or simply *receptatores* in manuals. Such a discrepancy in nomenclature shows how inquisitorial discourse did indeed influence the formalisation of our categories, while at the same time it highlights the significant distance between the depositions and other more prescriptive or didactic texts.

The earliest inquisitorial 'manual', the so-called *Directorium* attributed to St Raymond of Peñafort (1242), throws significant light on the connection between messengers and 'houses' (here called *receptatores* and *receptacula*) in the mind of a polemicist.[42] Its author defines the *receptator* as one who deliberately hosted heretics at his (or her) own place or in some other house. A *receptaculum* is described as a 'house or hospice where heretics, or *insabbatati*, have come together twice or more for preaching, meeting or prayer, or also where heretics or *insabbatati* were hosted more than once'.[43] Here *receptaculum*, as a derivative from *receptator*, corresponds to the functions of a *hospicium* or *domus hereticorum*, as we find in Doat. The author of the *Directorium* is surely aware of the existence of the other two names for it, but is simplifying and connecting the subject to his function by creating a third synonym.

In 1242 the author of the *Directorium* had already heard many depositions in which witnesses referred to messenger-figures and to the practice of mutual support and hospitality in 'houses'. They probably recalled memories of different stages of the evolution of the practice and of Cathar organisation, or – who knows? – perhaps they were not aware of an evolution in itself. Possibly for this reason their language was not always precise, or they used a rigid labelling of people and their functions inappropriately. The information the inquisitors received, therefore, was already translated into an a-chronic dimension by the deponents, careless (or unaware) of different chronological sequences and their respective language. Everything was a bit confused. Possibly for this reason the inquisitor felt the need to give definition and, consequently, legal boundaries to his information, to label it again.

---

[42] Selge (ed.), *Texte*, pp. 50–9. The text is discussed in Dondaine, 'Le manuel', pp. 96–7, and in Parmeggiani, 'Un secolo', p. 233. However, the most quoted authority in the definition of *receptatores* is the slightly later *consultatio* of Gui Folques (1255), more popular and absorbed into the manuals, especially fourteenth- century ones.

[43] 'Domum vel hospicium in qui heretici, vel insabbatati, bis vel pluries convenerunt ad predicationem, collationem vel orationem, vel etiam ubi heretici vel insabbatati pluries hospitantur', in Selge, *Texte*, p. 51. Here the *Directorium* refers mainly to Waldensians.

In doing so, the *Directorium* provides guidelines for future inquiries and a framework for understanding Cathar organisation and roles, but it also 'freezes' in a text and 'photographs' a practice that had been evolving over time.

While Catholic texts are precise in defining this function, which they limit to just the 'reception' of heretics, the Doat records are not so clear-cut, using more names to indicate similar functions. Whether they were actually identified in this way or not within the Cathar language is a question which seems – once again – marginal. What counts here is the idea of individuals within these communities who, because of their familiarity with the territory or professional needs (or for some other reason), were accustomed to moving around rather frequently, and handled messages, money and other transfers of goods. Naturally, they were the first people to whom one would refer when needing to communicate with someone else, or to carry messages and items around. One could say that their function was quasi-'telephonic': in fact, the function of a 'messenger'.[44] From Doat depositions we gather that an individual labelled as *nuncius* (sometimes *receptator*) would also be in charge of checking in advance over security. They would know about the availability and reliability of houses to stop in overnight, the best routes to follow, and the way to escape in case of danger, when needing to transfer a Cathar priest to a new location to administer sacraments or perform rituals. Sometimes it seems that single communities or individuals relied on one trusted messenger, presumably a local man or woman, as a sort of private employee. The examples, again, are numerous and varied. There are 'personal' messengers, such as Raymond Ysarn's William Cathala,[45] Helis of Mazerolles' Peter John,[46] Guilabert of Castres's Domingo/Dominic,[47] Arnold, 'messenger' for Willam of Narbonne,[48] William Faure's 'messenger',[49] and the one recorded when a group of Cathar clergy 'sent their own messenger to Cuneo for Peter Regis, weaver, [saying] that he should come with his wife to Genoa to run a house there, so that they could stay with him'.[50] Peter Maurel is named as 'the faithful messenger of the believers of the

---

[44] J. Duvernoy, *La réligion des Cathares* (Toulouse, 1976), pp. 249–50, calls them 'agents', but restricts their role to the financial management of offers, deposits or bequests.

[45] 'Guillelmus Cathala, nuncius dicti Raymundi', D23, f. 141r.

[46] D23, f. 173r.

[47] D22, f. 183v.

[48] D24, f. 187r.

[49] D22, f. 7r.

[50] 'Miserant nuntium suum ad Cuneum pro Petro Regis, textore, quod veniret ad Ianuam cum uxore sua, conducturus ibi domum, ut possent morari cum eo', D25, f. 307v.

heretics, and of the worthy men of Lombardy'.[51] Among the others, more or less famous, are Peter of Beauville,[52] Raymond and Bernard Hugues of Roquevidal,[53] Peter Guillaume of Roquevidal,[54] Peter *de Flaira* of Mirepoix,[55] Raymond and Jordan Pereille of Toulouse,[56] Peter *de Roseto* in the area of Cahors, near Montalzat,[57] the two anonymous characters who live in the Bastide of the (not yet identified) 'Seven Springs',[58] Bernard of Laval of the Lantarès,[59] the Lombard woman Placentia,[60] Bernard Garrigue's son, from Maurenx,[61] and the fugitive Amblard Vassal.[62] Although the name *nuncius* or *receptator* is not attributed clearly to all of these characters, they are listed here as their functions and tasks were the same. In addition to activities already cited, they also handled the blessed bread, which was brought to believers on behalf of the 'priests'. Because of the large number of people they got to know during their various missions, entire communities were in danger if one of them was captured. In one dramatic example where a famous 'messenger' was suddenly arrested, a group of believers eventually turned to a fortune-teller to find out how to avoid falling into the inquisitors' hands.[63]

Peter of Beauville's case, perhaps one of the best known, warns us of the dangers of attaching too much importance to categorisations of individual heretics' functions. Peter seems to act as *nuncius* on many occasions, yet it is over-restrictive to call him simply a 'messenger'. In his own deposition he confessed to a series of activities which are far more wide ranging than a messenger's simple tasks. He was tirelessly on the move for business, either his own or somebody else's, and he was himself in charge of a series of residences, where he variously lived for up to several years at

---

[51] 'Petrus Maurelli est nuncius fidelis credentium hereticorum, et proborum hominum de Lombardia' D25, f. 46r. He is quoted several times in D25 acting as a messenger of the Lombard heretics, for example saying that he 'often came to the friends and believers of the Toulouse region on behalf of the same believers and worthy men of Lombardy, because they placed enormous trust in him' ('veniebat frequenter ad amicos et credentes de partibus Tholosanis/ex parte dictorum credentium et proborum hominum de Lombardia, quia de ipso quam plurimum confidebant', D25, ff. 46r–v), and in D26, f. 33r as 'nuncius ecclesie [Lombardie]'. Peter was also known with the pseudonym of Peter Raymond (D26, f. 22r).
[52] D25, f. 297 and ff.
[53] D25, f. 67v–125r.
[54] D25, f. 130v and ff.
[55] D22, f. 171v and ff.
[56] D22, f. 201r and ff.
[57] D25, f. 186v and ff.
[58] D25, f. 188r–v.
[59] D25, f. 322v.
[60] D25, f. 37v.
[61] D25, f. 79v.
[62] D25, f. 7r
[63] D25, f. 123v.

a time. From these residences he planned trips and managed hospices for the benefit of other travelling Cathars. 'He, the witness, running his own hospice in Pavia, was travelling up and down the region of Lombardy on business.'[64] Peter's other three hospices were in Avignon, Cuneo and Piacenza.[65] One was in France, three in Italy: Peter had established them at both ends of a very busy route. Another example of multi-tasking within Cathar communities is Gaucelm, 'bishop of the heretics running a hospice' in St Paul around 1204, recorded in D24.[66] The point is that, owing to the uncertainty arising from discourse pressures on the inquisitorial records, and also (and perhaps more importantly) owing to the flexibility of roles within the Cathar church, one could be not only a messenger, but also a host, or even a bishop; and the role of messenger itself was not yet restricted in any highly sophisticated manner.

It has been demonstrated that, where hospitality was so crucial a need, these houses constituted the axle of the system; and that Cathar communities were not an isolated example.[67] Their practice of offering safe refuge to sympathisers is recorded as a common habit from the beginning of the thirteenth century. This is shown in the oldest of our Doat volumes – D23; though collected in 1244, its records referred back to episodes occurring thirty or forty years before. Once again, we should assume a natural evolution from the practice of hosting people in one's own house to a more organised form of hospitality. It was a common pattern in medieval cities, where principles of hospitality and communality generated several kinds of similar structures, like hospices for pilgrims of one nation, whose existence is often recorded.[68]

---

[64] 'Ipse testis tenens hospitium suum Papie, discurrebat negotiando per terram Lombardie', D25, f.304r; see also D26, f. 15v.

[65] D25, f. 323r (Piacenza), D25, f. 310v (Avignon), D25, f. 319v (Cuneo).

[66] 'Episcopum hereticorum tenentem hospicium', D24, f.112v.

[67] See Paolini 'Domus e zona', p. 375 and n. 16; D. Corsi ' "La Chiesa nella casa di lei" '. Eretiche ed eretici a Firenze nel Duecento', *Genesis. Rivista Italiana delle Storiche* I/1 (2002), 187–218, p. 198; Bertuzzi, '*Ecclesiarum forma*', pp. 110–1 and n. 152.

[68] On hospitality, see for reference J.E.H. Sherry, *The Laws for Innkeepers for Hotels, Motels, Restaurants and Clubs* (Ithaca, London, 1993) esp. pp. 3–8; O.R. Constable, *Housing the stranger in the Mediterranean World: Lodging, Trade and Travel in Late Antiquity and the Middle Ages* (Cambridge, 2003), esp. pp. 68–106; C.D. Pohl, *Making Room: Recovering Hospitality as a Christian Tradition* (Grand Rapide, MI, and Cambridge, 1999), esp. pp. 48–53; K. Reyerson, *The Art of the Deal: Intermediaries of Trade in Medieval Montpellier* (Boston, MA, 2002); pp. 47–77; K. Reyerson, 'Medieval hospitality: innkeepers and the infrastructure of trade in Montpellier during the Middle Ages', *Western Society for French History Proceedings* 24 (1997), 38–51. For our area of France, see 'Cahiers de Fanjeaux' 13 (1978). For Italian communes, see G.G. Merlo (ed.), *Esperienze religiose e opere assistenziali nei secoli XII e XIII* (Turin, 1987); G. Albini, *Città e ospedali nella Lombardia medievale* (Bologna, 1993); *Quaderni di Storia Religiosa* 1 (1994); A.J. Grieco and L. Sandri (eds.), *Ospedali e città. L'Italia del centro-nord, XIII-XIV secolo* (Florence, 1997). I owe this bibliographical information to Marina Gazzini, whom I thank very much.

The assumption that the description of the organisation of hospitality in the records, like other aspects of Catharism, was merely a construct, the intellectual creation of a Cathar identity by the inquisitors, completely rules out the possibility of a natural evolution from individual initiative to planned strategy. However, the evidence we have been discussing suggests that assumptions about the impact of inquisitorial discourse on the records need re-assessment. In fact, the evolution we have encountered is firmly in line with the parallel formation and progressive definition of urban policies of hospitality in Italian and other European cities, which followed an almost identical pattern.

Needless to say, when the movements and the need for safe refuges increased – after the tightening of papal control over dissent – our houses/hospices became even more crucial; their activity had to be safeguarded by secrecy and defined by a higher degree of organisation.

The depositions in the Doat records were not driven by the urge to classify of the sort that could affect the writing of a manual. In fact, during the hearings the descriptions of names and categories were also shaped by the deponents themselves. Something which came from *them* was the fact that they remembered at one point in time a whole bundle of disparate events and details from the past. Further, they both remembered and reported these things not with the mentality and perception they had possessed at various points in the past, but from the outlook they possessed *now*, when deposing. Certainly, there will have been intervention by the notaries or inquisitors in the recording of deponents' wording, yet such intervention will have been very uneven and subjective, depending on the individual cases, inquisitors, notaries, deponents, time of recording and so on. Otherwise there would have been no need for a further labelling, or indeed for 'proper' definition in a manual. In both cases, the sources provide a 'snapshot' of an existing reality, and forward it to us (although subjectively modified) as the author perceived it.

Linguistic and semantic categories aside, what we can understand from both kinds of text is that Cathar 'houses' were not just hospices, they could also be the main foci of community life, places for recovery and also places where preaching and rites were performed:[69] a double feature which appears very frequently in our depositions. In the early days, before the coming of the Crusaders, they also tended to be places where one preferred to receive the *consolamentum* and die 'among the heretics' – as shown, for example, by Guilabert of St Paul, a local lord, who was

---

[69] As pointed out by Bertuzzi, *'Ecclesiarum forma'*, pp. 106–7.

brought ill to the local 'hospice of the said heretics, and there he died, among them, and was buried in the cemetery of the heretics'.[70]

Although each snippet of confession is a case in itself, it seems legitimate to draw general conclusions. People could be hosted in Cathar houses for just a few days, or even a single night, or for periods lasting up to several years. Raymond Arquier, known as Baussan, specifies that in these 'houses' up to fifteen or twenty people could be hosted together at a time.[71] Though the kind of protection offered to friends could be just temporary – food and rest for travelling Cathars – Cathar 'housing policy' could also turn towards longer-term residence. We may suppose that this best suited those who, as newcomers to the area, needed time and a safe environment to establish their own residence; or those who, because of a criminal record, could not use the legal system in order to buy or rent a property; or – again – those who wanted to escape the inquisitors and their spies for a while.

Sometimes witnesses also gave evidence about their hosts' main job. Especially in Italy they often ran their own workshops or commercial activities, as weavers, pharmacists or dealers in leather goods or needles. This should not surprise us. Such craftsmen and traders were the most likely to travel between markets, get in touch with different cultural environments, emigrate to new commercial areas from where skills and goods could be imported, or speak more than one language without arousing suspicion. These individuals were plausibly travelling and hosting new apprentices, new workers brought in from somewhere else. In their workshops, during work hours, ideas could be easily shared between labourers. Equally, their professional skills made them extremely flexible and adaptable when they needed to move on to new places.

A possible outcome of the houses/hospice/workshop structure (especially in Italy in times of persecution) was the formation of little communities of exiles coming from the same area, or heretical clusters, focused around one (or more) centres. These can be considered as further aggregations within areas of high heretical density. Many examples of *loci hereticorum* have been found throughout the north of Italy.[72] In some the presence of French exiles is documented. A famous example is *Strata Levata* [= raised street] in Piacenza, mainly colonised by weavers and their workshops,

---

[70] 'Hospicium dictorum hereticorum, et ibi mortuus fuit inter eos, et sepultus fuit in cimiterio hereticali', D24, f. 112v.
[71] 'Usque ad quindecim vel viginti personas', D25, f. 278v.
[72] Paolini, 'Domus e zona' reviews them at pp. 376–9, and nn. 20–32.

where there is evidence of heretical activities.[73] Lomastro Tognato suggests 'the presence of a group of literate persons' coming from France and living in Vicenza up to the Crusade of 1209–29, whom she connects with heretical environments.[74] Another example is the little community of people from Toulouse encountered by Raymond Baussan in Cuneo.[75] Its existence is confirmed in the deposition of Peter of Beauville, who lived in Cuneo for seven years, and met many heretics from Toulouse 'living openly and working on leather straps in a workshop run by Arnaud Guillelmi Porrerius, who was from Toulouse from the Bourget-Nau';[76] and also by the testimony of brother Lanfranc of Bergamo, inquisitor, who records the 'Toulousans of Cuneo'.[77] In years of persecution these clusters could offer safety and protection to the chief members of the Cathar hierarchy, in fact perpetuating its existence and safe succession, and so safeguarding the very existence of the Cathar church.[78]

Safety was a key issue, but not just in times of active persecution. The commercial routes were not the only ones taken by messengers, travellers and those who escaped. As Dossat has correctly pointed out, pilgrimage routes and pilgrim-like appearance represented another opportunity for disguise and for making one's trips as inconspicuous as possible. Guiraud Gallard met four heretics in his father's house 'who were going around in the guise of the pilgrims';[79] a Cathar deacon disguised himself 'with the clothes of a pilgrim' in Rome;[80] Fabrissa of Limoux hosted a couple of Lombard 'pilgrims' on the way to Santiago, who had met people from Toulouse in Italy, and carried pins and needles: foreigners from Piacenza, in contact with *fugitive* from Toulouse and *agulherii*

---

[73] A woman from Piacenza said to Fabrissa of Limoux that 'many people of the region of Toulouse lived in Piacenza' ('Multe gentes de partibus Tholosanis morabantur in Plasensa', D25, f. 45v), and that 'she had seen many other people from the region of Toulouse in Piacenza' ('multas alias personas de Tholosanis partibus viderat in Plasentia', D25, f. 45v); at D25, f. 141r it is specified that the heretics from Toulouse run a hospice 'in a certain alleyway called Strada Levata' ('in quadam carreria que vocatur Strata Levata'). On the connections between heresy and politics in Piacenza, see my 'Il "Liber Suprastella" (1235), fonte antieraticale piacentina. L'ambiente ed il motivo di produzione', *Archivio Storico per le Province Parmensi*, IV ser., 49 (1997), 405–27, esp. pp. 411–23, and nn. 23–8 and 'Dissenso e presenza ereticale a Piacenza e nelle città padane tra gli anni Cinquanta e Settanta del Duecento' (forthcoming).

[74] F. Lomastro Tognato, *L'eresia a Vicenza nel Duecento* (Vicenza, 1988), p. 18: her suggestion, however, although based on documentary evidence, is rightly cautious.

[75] D25, f. 146v.

[76] 'Publice morantes et operantes de corrigiis in operario conducto ab Arnaldo Guillelmi Porrerio qui fuit de Tholosa de Burgueto Novo', D25, f. 299r.

[77] 'Tholosani de Cuneo', Collectoria 133, in Biscaro, 'Inquistori ed eretici lombardi', p. 483.

[78] Griffe, 'La Languedoc Cathare', p. 133.

[79] 'Item vidit quatuor hereticos in domo patris eius ... qui ibant ad modum pere grinorum', D22, f. 20r.

[80] 'Diaconum hereticorum in habitu peregrini', D23, f. 92r.

('fugitives' and 'pin-men').[81] There is enough here to be highly suspicious of Fabrissa's acquaintances.

The overlapping of pilgrimage routes and those followed by our suspects has been traced by Dossat.[82] This simple disguise, in fact, allowed substantial freedom to move in the open, even over long distances on pre-existing routes. There was no need to think up new ones or to beat new paths. Moreover, even in cases where they were detected as positive suspects or merely suspicious individuals, they could still travel. Often, in fact, it was the inquisitors themselves who condemned heretics to go on pilgrimages – either locally or abroad – as an alternative to other light penances such as fines and wearing crosses.[83] And what about the spies – those who declared to the heretics that they were Cathars, when they were in fact traitors and apostates?

Pilgrims, traders, exiles, suspects, people on the run, spies, messengers, guides, all of these characters, either individually or in little groups were moving up and down the main routes between France, Spain and Italy, but also from village to village, house to house. Behind them, or mingling among them, were the inquisitors' servants and informers, and the inquisitors themselves. This was indeed a lively communication network.

The picture we have been examining suggests that it is simplistic to think of inquisitorial pressure as the sole impetus of Cathar movements. The difference between ordinary movements and emergency measures, those dictated by risk or necessity, is well highlighted in the example of Raymond Baussan of Lagarde of Laurac. Raymond, like Peter of Beauville, was indeed a keen traveller and himself a hospice-holder in Piacenza.[84] He was summoned and auditioned in 1274 and gave testimony about events that occurred in his earlier 'heretical life'. After the 1246 ban on heretics by Manfred of Apulia, he eventually ended up in Alessandria, in Piedmont, where, for reasons unknown, he had to seek shelter for the following seven years 'not in specific hospices, but in taverns, and wherever he found best'.[85] Raymond had experienced and highlights both kinds of movement: 'normal' travelling, where one would be hosted in Cathar houses,

---

[81] 'Dicebant se peregrinos volentes ire apud Sanctum Iacobum' 'ducebant secum quemdam asellum cum quo portabant acus et cibum suum', D25, ff. 44v–45r.

[82] Y. Dossat, 'Types exceptionnels de pèlerins: l'hérétique, le voyageur déguisé, le professionnel', *Cahiers de Fanjeaux* 15 (1980), pp. 207–25, p. 208.

[83] The use of pilgrimages as a form of penance was frequent, for example, in the sentences of Brother William Arnold, collected in D21. Here the inquisitor also releases letters of safe conduct for the pilgrims themselves at ff. 167v–174v.

[84] See above, note n. 65.

[85] 'Non in certis hospitiis, sed per tabernas, et ubi melius inveniebat', D25, f.143r. The example is quoted by Guiraud, *Histoire*, vol. II, p. 260. Guiraud, however, omits to quote the length of time Baussan spent in such a precarious accommodation.

and the exceptional conditions of living in other accommodation, like taverns and inns, that is, where non-Cathar travellers would usually stay.

Below the surface of a statement which is superficially not particularly interesting, Raymond's words are in fact extremely useful, and they suggest two more points. The first is that, as early as the late 1240s, although moving together with traders and pilgrims, Cathars were not completely mixing with them. They would follow existing routes and possibly use fairs and pilgrimages as a pretext for travelling, but preferably would neither interact too closely with others not known to them nor stay at normal hospices. Presumably, again, the situation of relative freedom where 'ideas travelled with people', as argued above, had already come to an end. Suspicion and fear had taken over, and it was necessary to be extra careful about one's movements and one's company. The second point is that Raymond shows how Cathars resorted to lodging in ordinary inns and taverns only in cases of extreme danger; their natural choice would have been to stay at 'known hospices'. Again, the communication and hospitality network cannot be seen exclusively as a response to inquisitorial pressures; instead, it changed under the threat of repression, to look more like non-heretical travelling.

'NEGATIVE' MOVEMENTS

Raymond Baussan's example brings us to the next topic, 'negative' travelling. As indicated above, this includes all movements induced by pressure, fear and persecution.

Although Cathars believed themselves to be bearers of the message of true salvation and part of the true Church, nevertheless they were well aware that to the Catholic Church they were illegal and illegitimate, and therefore liable to persecution. After the brutalities of the Albigensian Crusade of 1209–29, there was certainly no doubt. Despite some years of relative peace afterwards, that episode signalled a turning-point in their perception of themselves as being 'other'. Of course, it did not mean that Cathars felt illegitimate. On the contrary, being persecuted made them even more convinced of their own moral legitimacy. Cathar literature in fact highlights this point as the core of a Cathar sense of belonging and identity. The last chapter of the *Liber de duobus principiis* is devoted to the 'persecuted Church';[86] so is paragraph 10 of the *Gleisa de Dio*.[87]

---

[86] C. Thouzellier (ed.), *Livre des deux principes* (Paris, 1973), pp. 412–55.
[87] *Gleisa de Dio*, in T. Venckeleer, 'Un recueil Cathare: le manuscrit A.6.10 de la "Collection Vaudoise" de Dublin', *Revue Belge de Philologie et d'Histoire* 38 (1960), 815–34, pp. 828–9; on the topic, see also R. Manselli, 'Dolore e morte nella esperienza religiosa catara', in *Il dolore e la morte nella spiritualità*

Cathars knew all too well that they were acting against the dominant religious power; that they were part of a 'counter-system'; and that the two 'systems' were mutually exclusive. In light of this, in a sense all Cathar movements could be classified as 'negative', even in times of relative political stability.

The 'negative' movements to be studied here, however, are those related to a change from the normal practice of communication and travel. The first turning-point is the post-Crusade period, while the second came after the years 1260–5, when papal policies of repression, together with greater efficiency in the inquisitorial system and a significant decline in protection by the local lay lords, made things substantially more dangerous for Cathars and other heretical communities. This led to an increase in mobility, to a rise in the number of fleeing travellers and to a change in the routes they followed. Greater danger meant a higher number of people trying to escape either a condemnation or simply a summons. More people on the run meant that a higher level of organisation was needed in the existing hospitality system and – inevitably – more secrecy and caution when moving around. Especially if travelling long distances (e.g. to and from Lombardy), there was a greater exposure and more risk of being tracked down and captured, as demonstrated by the case of Arnaud Bretos 'the Catalan' and his companion Peter Girberg, who were in fact arrested while travelling to 'Lombardy'.[88] The level of suspicion had grown, so it was no longer enough to disguise oneself among other travellers.

The need for increased security produced two prevalent attitudes. On the one hand, people like Raymond of Baussan tried to hide behind an appearance of conformity; on the other some people worked out a more secretive way of moving around. Probably the second became the safer option. It seems that people started travelling away from the main roads, preferring woods and fields, or shepherds' paths. Many times trips were planned differently: during the winter,[89] when weather conditions were particularly hard for travellers and fewer people moved around; and at night, in order to reach hospices during hours of darkness.[90] D23

---

dei secoli XII e XIII, Atti del V Convegno Internazionale di Studi (Todi, 7–10 Ottobre 1962), (Todi, 1967) pp. 235–59.

[88] 'And while they were travelling towards Lombardy, he the witness Arnaud de Bretos "the Catalan" and the aforesaid Peter Girberg his companion were captured on the way' ('Et dum irent versus Lombardiam, ipse testis Arnaud de Bretos catalanus et dictus Petrus Girberga socius fuerunt capti in via'), D24, f. 192v.

[89] As for example in D25, f. 153r.

[90] As we cannot ascribe to these sources the didactic meaning and modes of publicistic discourse, we have to assume that these nocturnal movements were likely to have occurred in this way. See among the others Peter of Beauville, D25, ff. 297r–331v and D26, ff. 1r–2v..

mentions dozens of occurrences of people meeting heretics in huts (*cabane*) in the woods.[91] It seems likely that in the 1230s and 1240s these more hidden and temporary structures replaced the pre-Crusade 'houses publicly run' (*domus quam tenebat publice*) mentioned in all our records, as they seem to be places of meeting, where 'priests' preached, were visited and honoured, and shared meals with believers. They seem to be either personal possessions, or simply places of temporary shelter.

According to our evidence, however, huts never completely replaced 'houses of heretics'. We may also suppose that, in times of danger, Cathar transfers relied on those houses and communities which were more protected and better integrated into the local environment, perhaps the older, long-established ones, which enjoyed a good reputation in the neighbourhood, or were surrounded by a strong Cathar enclave.

But where were our travellers heading, when escaping the French inquisitors? The destinations most frequently named in our depositions for the post-Crusade years are, unsurprisingly, the Italian ones. Such a pattern in the records could be in part the result of deliberate inquisitorial intervention. Interrogation technique was becoming more refined and officials better trained and more aware of their adversaries' habits. Thus they tended to ask for information from specific individuals, already renowned as messengers or 'conductors', or they enquired about specific locations, as new links between French and Italian communities gradually came to the fore. Certainly, the focus of questioning to some degree shapes these sources. However, the appearance of these destinations in the records is not in itself in question, and there is no reason to doubt the existence of links between them and some French communities.

Within the area often identified as 'Lombardy', witnesses also refer to specific cities and towns. Pavia, Cremona and Piacenza are most frequently mentioned, followed by Genoa, Cuneo and Alessandria. There are also references to Asti, S. Quirico near Genoa, Tortona, Milan, Como, Sirmione, Mantua, Verona, and further south to Bologna, Pisa, Lucca, Pistoia, Rome, Naples, Guardia Lombarda and the region of Apulia. The selection is not surprising, as most of these destinations are also mentioned by the sources as residences of a deacon.[92] There does not seem to have been a preferential sequence of destinations. The preference was indeed for long trips touching several Italian centres, and for cities and towns rather than villages. However, passing through Genoa, which

---

[91] For instance, see the high occurrence of such places in Arnaude of Lamothe's deposition (D23, esp. ff. 24r–27v) and Peter of Fogasset's (D23, esp. ff. 316r–326r).

[92] See Bertuzzi, *Ecclesiarum forma*, pp. 73, 81.

appears very often in these depositions, was more or less unavoidable for those coming from France through the pass of Col di Tenda. Pavia is the most frequently quoted location between other destinations, and it looks as if it was a point of assembly, a kind of sorting centre. Pavia and Piacenza – perhaps not by chance the two cities with the highest number of hospices – were places where people could return several times during their lifetime, at the end of a trip or as a starting point for another one. A sort of 'route' from Genoa to Pavia and Piacenza seems to have been used. Outside this particular journeying pattern, we can see people tending to establish fixed residences or to reside for longer periods in other places.

In some cases deponents go into greater detail about the exact place where meetings were held and people were hosted. Unsurprisingly, the locations are often in line with the (already identified) pattern of establishment near the rivers or canals, where local craftsmen had their workshops.[93] In Pavia, we can draw up a little list of places to stay: 'in a certain alleyway called *de Bruelh*',[94] 'on the riverside of the river *de Thosii*' at Peter of Montagut's place, where people call him 'Berenger',[95] at Peter of Beauville's,[96] Raymond of Caraman's[97] or with Raymond Papier of Avignon.[98] In Piacenza, as already mentioned, there was the well-known area called *Strada Levata*,[99] where some French people ran houses/hospices: Raymond Baussan of Lagarde of Laurac,[100] Steven Donati,[101] Peter Pictavin of Toulouse[102] and Peter of Beauville.[103] The most popular destination in Genoa is 'in the alleyway of the Furriers' where Peter Furrier ran a hospice.[104] There is also mention of an 'archway' in St Lawrence square, 'run' ('conducta') by Bonet of Cuneo;[105] while the house of Henry of Milan was the meeting point of an all-Italian contingent: there Peter of Beauville met the 'perfect' Peter of Prato, Bonella of Florence, James

---

[93] See Paolini, 'Domus e zona', p. 385.
[94] 'In quadam carreria dictam de Bruelh', D25, f. 245r.
[95] 'In rippa fluminis de Thosii (unidentified)', D25, f. 329v.
[96] D25, f. 144r; D26, f.15v.
[97] D26, f. 35r.
[98] D25, f. 247r.
[99] D25, f. 141r, and see above, n. 73.
[100] D25, f. 141r.
[101] D25, ff. 141v, 302r, 329r.
[102] D25, f. 142r.
[103] D25, f. 131v. Possibly also at the house of John Capellan, where Raymond Bruguier, barber of Najac, Stephen Garrigue and William of Elves found shelter (D23, f. 214v).
[104] 'In carreria Pellicciarie', D25, f. 306r, and D25, f. 329r. I prefer using here the English translation 'Furrier' for consistency.
[105] D25, f. 329r.

of Martesana of Cuneo and Henry's wife and son.[106] As mentioned before, a little community had been established in Cuneo, in Piedmont, where many people from Toulouse worked in the workshop run by Arnaud Guillem of Toulouse and his wife Beatrix.[107] In Alessandria there were the hospices run by John Sedacer, where people worked as weavers,[108] Arnold Lombard's home and the one owned by 'the Sedaffers' (probably another name for the first on the list).[109] In Cremona people met at Raymond Sem's place.[110]

The distinction between micro- and macro-movements is not relevant to a discussion of 'enforced' movement. All of the trips recorded have something deeper to teach us: that after the years of harsher inquisitorial policy, there was a shift of focus inside Catharism. Far from being evenly distributed in both France and Italy, communities and individuals looked to Italian cities as the places for a safer Cathar life, a shelter from persecution. Such a significant shift, although involving both believers and hierarchy, meant for the latter the existence of an escape route and, in some cases, safety. Members of the hierarchy were valued as precious 'tools' for the maintenance and perpetuation of Catharism.

Among the various duties of a messenger, it seems that he or she had to act as a conduit for transfers of money between individuals or for the benefit of charitable causes.[111] The existence of common funds and so-called 'money of the heretics' ('pecunia hereticorum') features both in Italian depositions,[112] and in France, and is attested as late as Gui's *Sententie*.[113] It is not surprising to find this frequently mentioned. The records memorialised this practice as it fell into the category of 'suspicious actions'. In fact, it connected people through a communal policy of mutual support.

---

[106] D25, f. 328v.
[107] D25, ff.299r–v.
[108] D25, f. 304v.
[109] 'Dels Sedaffers', D25, ff. 329v, 330r.
[110] D24, f. 97v.
[111] See A. Roach, 'The Cathar Economy', *Reading Medieval Studies* 12 (1986), 51–71; more generally on the links between Cathars and economic issues, Roach, *The Devil's World*, pp. 119–20, and 153–4; on the treasure and funds of the heretics, see Dupré-Theseider, 'Le Catharisme Languedocien', p. 315, n. 41; Duvernoy, *La réligion*, pp. 249–52, who reckons that the necessity of a 'mobilisation' of possession was primarily due to the persecution; Bertuzzi, 'Ecclesiarum forma', p. 107, instead thinks the 'money question' not completely clear; yet; some examples are quoted in Y. Dossat, 'Les Cathares d'après les documents', pp. 89.
[112] See for instance the several occurrences listed in Paolini-Orioli under the headings 'denarii' and 'depositum' (p. 70), 'pecunia' (p. 81), in the Indexes to the *Acta S. Officii Bononie*.
[113] See Ph. Van Limborch (ed.), Bernard Gui, *Liber sententiarum inquisitionis Tholosanae (1307–1323)*, (Amsterdam, 1692), pp. 14, 229.

The examples of money transactions are many. Especially when intended to benefit the 'heretics', or meant for a charitable purpose, this money became in the eyes of the inquisitors a vehicle of contagion and sometimes proof of guilt. We can expect an overall increase in the sheer quantity of money moving during these 'negative' trips. People wanted to get rid of their possessions, transform them into cash and move that cash somewhere safer, seeing that they ran the risk of having it confiscated by the inquisitors if they were condemned. William Rafard explains this system. 'He said that when the same witness wished to go into Lombardy to be hereticated, he went to Montpellier with his cows in the manner of a merchant; and there he sold them. And from there, with his money and Peter Maurel of Auriac or of Toulouse, messenger of the heretics, who was his guide, he went into Lombardy.'[114] Money could be given to somebody who acted as a temporary keeper – though sometimes he would not give it back.[115] It could be handed over temporarily, or for the duration of its owner's detention. And it could be bequeathed to one's offspring as their inheritance, or left to the Cathars, perhaps after a *consolamentum*.[116] The famous Guilabert of Castres spells out to Bernard Otho the reason for this. 'He [Guilabert] said to him, the witness, that he had taken from the Church of the heretics, and received much from them, and that he [Bernard] should restore it to them.' So Bernard made a legacy to them.[117] A very interesting case of money issues sparking a dispute occurs in the deposition of Peter Guillaume of Roquevidal. Stephen Donati, a 'messenger', owed Peter a sum of money which had been entrusted to Stephen by Peter's father. Stephen, however, refused to give it back, because – so he claimed – Peter's father had previously stolen some land from Stephen's brother. Stephen therefore obtained permission from his 'Cathar bishop' to keep the money as repayment for the stolen land.[118] Here the 'bishop' acts as peace-keeper, a wise man who had

---

[114] 'Quando ipse testis voluit ire in Lombardiam ad hereticandum se ivit versum Montem Pessullanum cum vaccis suis ad modum mercatoris; et ibi vendidit eas. Et inde cum peccunia sua et Petro Maurelli de Auriaco vel de Tholosa, nuntio hereticorum, qui erat ductor suus, ivit/in Lombardiam', D26, f. 15r–v.

[115] Aladaix of Montgaillard wanted to go to 'Lombardy', and sent through a 'messenger' the sum of 100 *solidi* of Toulouse to two other 'messengers' based in Italy – Stephen Donati and Peter of Prato – 'so that they keep it for her' ('ut dictam peccuniam servarent dicte Aladaicis'). Then, she changed her mind about the journey, and asked for the money to be transferred to her mother, a *perfecta* who was already in Cremona. The mother died, and Aladaix's money was lost (D25, f. 322v).

[116] Various examples can be quoted, among which are D22, f. 36r; D22, f. 113v; D23, f. 184r; D23, f. 195r; D23, f. 300v.

[117] 'Dixit eidem testi quod ipse testis abstulerat ecclesie hereticorum et receperat ab eis multum, et quod restitueret illud eis', D24, f. 87v.

[118] D25, f. 130v and ff.

the authority to permit or forbid transactions and adjudge controversial issues.[119] Modern scholarship has turned against the common assumption that the Cathar 'clergy' kept themselves above and apart from such worldly things, and this kind of activity supports this reaction.[120]

Moreover, the existence of major 'common funds' or bank-like deposits[121] is clearly demonstrated in the case of Montségur, where the keepers of this money managed to escape 'so that the Church of the heretics should not lose its treasure, which was hidden in the woods'.[122] Elsewhere, Peter Roger of Mirepoix is mentioned as the person responsible for all the *comande* (translated by Duvernoy as 'dépôts des fonds', 'depot of capital resources'[123]) kept in Montségur, and lost after the siege. Peter of Flaire lost 300 *solidi* there.[124]

The messengers acted therefore like 'travelling banks', gathering money from more than one 'customer', and sometimes transferring it to individuals or to a community.[125] Another striking example is offered by the case of Bernard Hugues, who, like his father Raymond,[126] spent almost all of his confession talking about money being moved about. We see him taking sums on commission from one place to another, and learn that the money had to be carried in special linen bags.[127] At times this money could be invested, in order to increase the available cash. However, financial speculation came at a cost, as explained by Peter of Beauville, who received the sum of 100 *imperiales* from his fellow Stephen Donati 'for dealing' ('ad negotiandum'). The arrangement was that Peter could keep for himself half of the money he eventually made ('medietatem

[119] There are occurrences of higher clergy settling disputes between two or more parties, such as in D22, f. 73v; D22, ff. 87r–v; D22, ff. 121r–v; D22, ff. 221r–v; D24, ff. 103v–104r.

[120] See L. Paolini, 'Esiti ereticali della conversione alla povertà', in *La conversione alla povertà nell'Italia dei secoli XII–XIV. Atti del XXVII Convegno storico Internazionale (Tòdi, 14–17 October 1990)*, (Spoleto, 1991), pp. 127–86, pp. 158–9 and n. 76, p. 159; Roach, *The Devil's World*, p. 7, pp. 118–19, pp. 153–4.

[121] 'Infinite money' ('infinita peccunia') in D23, f. 217r; 'many possessions' ('multa bona') in D23, f. 271v; 'gold, silver and infinite money' ('aurum, argentum et peccuniam infinitam') in D24, f. 171v.

[122] 'Ne ecclesia hereticorum posset amittere thesaurum suum, qui erat absconditus in nemoribus', D22, ff. 128r–v; see also the same episode in D24, f. 62r and D24, f. 171v.

[123] Duvernoy, *La réligion*, p. 250.

[124] '[Peter and his sister] asked the witness [Arnaud Roger] whether he knew anything of the "comande" of Montségur, as he Peter of Flaire well lost three hundred *solidi* which he had deposited to the heretics in the said castle, and he the witness said to the said Peter of Flaire that Peter Roger of Mirepoix had all the "comande" of the said castle' ['... quesierunt ab ipso teste si sciebat ali-/quod de comandis Montis Securi, quia ipse P. de Flaira amiserat bene trecentos solidos quos deposuerat hereticis in dicto castro, et ipse testis dixit dicto P. de Flaira quod Petrus Rogerii de Mirapisce habuerat omnes comandas dicti castri'], D22, ff. 153r–v.

[125] See, for example, D25, f. 187v–188r.

[126] D25, f. 116r.

[127] D25, f. 67v and ff.

lucri'). Unfortunately, at some point, he decided to entrust 155 *imperiales* to his son Arnaud, and Arnaud 'took it away and wasted it' ('asportavit et vastavit').[128] Sometimes, when people went on the run, they kept their money with them, although we would have expected it to be safer to travel apart from one's goods.

Money transfers could serve several purposes. Apart from the obvious fear of being deprived of one's property for at least two generations,[129] there was also the need to transform goods into cash, so that it could be carried elsewhere in order to be used to rebuild a life. As seen above, there is also evidence of the existence of 'common funds' for anyone affiliated, a kind of 'kitty'. People could pay into such funds, or borrow from them, either to start a new activity or in order to cover some expenses. Peter *de Romegos* said to Amblard Vassal that 'if he [Amblard] wished … to go into Lombardy, he would take him the witness with him, and he would provide for the expenses which he, the witness [Peter], wished to make'.[130] The heretics were well paid for performing the rites of heretication[131] – possibly such payments were semi-voluntary gifts to them – and made further transactions with the money they accumulated.

Not even the Cathar clergy were immune from the risk of litigation over goods or cash, as shown by the case of Raymond Hugues, knight of Aiguesvives, whose father 'gave lands to the heretics … *ad acapitum*, every now and then, and wrote documents in which he the witness was obliged to praise these *acapiti*'. Raymond was evidently annoyed with the situation, and claimed that he was forced into making such statements,

---

[128] D25, f. 302v. Elsewhere Peter received another sum of 500 Genoese pounds from Peter 'the furrier' of Piacenza, acting in the name of Pons Boer (D25, f. 306r).

[129] Legislation prescribing a 'financial punishment' of heretics (confiscation of goods and disinheritance of offspring) has its conceptual origin in the idea of the heretic as a judicial subject with no right to property. This concept first appeared in both the Theodosian and Justinian codes. It was then refined and fixed into a code of practice around the second half of the twelfth century and transferred – due to its double nature of canon and civil normative – in city statutes and inquisitorial manuals around the second half of the thirteenth century. Innocent III's *Vergentis in senium*, as early as 1199, had established the possibility that a heretic's patrimony might also be requisitioned even if there were Catholic offspring, and it is considered as a turning-point in the juridical definition of the problem. See H. Maisonneuve, *Études sur les origines de l'Inquisition*, (Paris, 1960), pp. 31–6, pp. 36–40; L. Paolini, 'Le finanze dell'Inquisizione in Italia (XIII–XIV sec.)', in *Gli spazi economici della Chiesa nell'Occidente mediterraneo (secc. XII–metà XIV), Atti del XVI Convegno internazionale di studi, (Pistoia, 16–19 May 1997)*, (Pistoia, 1998), pp. 441–81; Idem, 'Inquisizioni medievali, pp. 177–98, esp. pp. 194–8; W.K. Boyd, *The Ecclesiastical Edicts of the Theodosian Code*, (New York, 1905); M.C. Mirow and K.A. Kelly, 'Laws on religion from the Theodosian and Justinianic Codes', in R. Valantasis (ed.), *Religions of Late Antiquity in Practice*, (Princeton, NJ and Oxford, 2000), pp. 263–74, esp. pp. 269–74.

[130] 'Quod si vellet … ire in Lombardiam, ipse duceret ipsum testem secum, et provideret sibi de expensis quod ipse testis voluit facere', D25, f. 185r–v.

[131] Up to a hundred *solidi*, according to a deposition (D24, f. 261r and ff.).

perhaps to obtain favour with the inquisitors, or perhaps simply out of anger with this father for depriving him of his rights to these lands, preferring the heretics to his own son.[132] By contrast, William Rafardi of Roquefort, on his way to Lombardy, 'advised … Marquise to send some sum of money to the church of the heretics in Lombardy'. When she refused to make a donation, claiming that she did not have money available right there, William became sarcastic. 'And he the witness reprimanded her, saying that she would certainly have it prepared for William Unaud, her son, if he wanted to indulge in some frivolity, and she did not have anything for the Church of God.' A woman present consoled him, saying 'to him the witness that he the witness, who was a poor man, was more fortunate than the same ladies who were rich!'[133] Bernard Hugues reclaims money from someone owing money to the heretics in order to pay for a mare bought for them,[134] while the boy Aldric recalled the time when he and Aladaix of Palaisville, planning a trip to Italy, needed someone to 'lend them money for expenses'.[135]

Harsher inquisitorial procedures, therefore, had pushed people and their goods to safer places to live, where they could establish a business, or find work in someone else's workshop without fearing for their own safety. The general expression 'to go to "Lombardy"' ('ire ad Lombardiam') or 'to go to "Lombardy"' to the heretics' ('ire ad Lombardiam ad hereticos') occurs frequently in our records, and appears to be a kind of umbrella phrase. It signifies a wide range of actions. It could mean 'go to "Lombardy" to join somebody else', 'to hear the heretics preaching and teaching', 'to receive the sacraments', 'move to "Lombardy" for good', or 'go on a temporary trip' to 'Lombardy', for unspecified purposes. Why keep it general? Either it was the inquisitors' decision, since deponents' declarations were all the same, or the deponent had not declared more than this – as he or she did not deem it necessary, and nor did the inquisitor for the purpose of the hearing. Whatever the case (most probably a mixture of the two), the practice of moving to 'Lombardy' was so common that it generated its own commonplace phrase.

---

[132] 'Dabat quandoque terras ad acapitum hereticis, qui manebant publice apud Lauranum, et faciebat cartas quas faciebat dicti acapitis laudari ab ipso teste', D23, f. 117v.

[133] 'Ammonuit predictam dominam Marquesiam quod mitteret aliquam summam peccunie ecclesie hereticorum in Lombardiam' … 'Et tunc ipse testis redarguit eam, dicens quod bene haberet paratum pro Guillelmo Unaudi, filio suo, si vellet facere aliquam vanitatem, et non habebat aliquid pro ecclesia Dei' … 'dixit ipsi testi quod melius erat fortunatus ipse testis, qui erat pauper homo, quam ipse domine que divites erant!', D26, ff. 32v–33r.

[134] D25, f. 80r–v.

[135] 'Mutuarent sibi pecuniam pro expensis', D25, f. 17r. Other interesting examples in D25, f. 101r; and D25, f. 190r.

It is now evident that the existing 'Italian connection' became much more crucial every time the level of risk increased.[136] Restricted in freedom by increasing danger, Cathar communities tried to rescue what mattered most to them. For some it was money, for others life or their loved ones, for the whole community it was their clergy. Cathar clergy needed to be taken to safety, as they represented a kind of 'common patrimony' for believers. Moving to 'Lombardy' for good, or an increase in these exchanges between the two countries, inevitably created not merely a change in the way people saw the religious focus of the Cathar church but also − consequently − a dangerous vacuum in French Catharism, where rituals and sacraments were at the core of the group's identity. Believers needed their clergy in order to feel like one brotherhood. For those who could afford it, trips to Italy 'to the heretics' became a kind of pilgrimage to the source of faith. 'There is no Salvation without the "heretics" ', says William Rafardi to a relative, in order to persuade him to migrate to Italy. Then he is himself moved to compassion, considering that the man has two little children, and allows him to stay.[137]

Understandably, decisions to leave or to stay were not so clear-cut for everybody. Some were unsure that running away was the best thing to do, others were against the whole idea. Gardubius, knight of Montgaillard, wondered how it would be possible to maintain his social position, before deciding what to do.[138] Bernard of Roquefort changed his mind halfway through the trip, after hearing that life in Lombardy would be almost as risky as in France, and 'that heretics equally suffered scandal and persecution in "Lombardy" as well as in this land'.[139] Others, like Pierre Autier's son Guillaume, were sceptical about what might be found there, 'nothing good' ('nichil boni'). Or they had absolutely no idea what to expect, like Arnaud Tesseyre of Lordat. Or they were curious about living conditions, like the group of customers of the merchant from Lombardy, who to the question 'what kind of land is that of Lombardy?' replied that 'it is good! ... in Lombardy nobody harms the Jews, the Saracens or the heretics, as long as they want to work hard to gain their necessities'.[140]

---

[136] Dupré, with Manselli, reckons that the crucial date has to be identified as 1244, with the siege of Montségur. Still, this was not a proper migration, according to him, but a temporary movement while waiting 'for the storm to pass'. Dupré-Theseider, 'Le Catharisme Languedocien', p. 305–6.

[137] 'Non erat salvatio nisi cum hereticis', D26, f. 22r. The same phrase recurs also in D24, f. 254v, in the deposition of Raymond of Montlaur, and in the following one: D24, f. 255r.

[138] 'Si posset ibi manere tanquam miles ad honorem suum, et si inveniret ibi dominum cum quo posset habere necessaria, Marquisium de Monteferrato vel alium', D25, f. 324v.

[139] 'Heretici similiter patiebantur scandalum et persecutionem in Lombardia sicut et in terra ista', D26, f. 34r.

[140] J. Duvernoy (ed.), *Le régistre de Jacques Fournir, évêque à Pamiers (1318–1325)* (Toulouse, 1965), vol. III, p. 216 (161b); vol. III, p. 604; 'qualis terra erat Lombardia, qui mercerius respondit quod bona ...

Petronille of Villefranche commented on a man who came back from 'Lombardy', because he met 'bad people' ('malam gentem') who 'had received him badly' ('male receptaverant').[141]

Finally, one case throws interesting new light on Catharism's view of its own structure and identity. It is, once again, a trip dictated by necessity, certainly planned in a time of restrictions, although it could be argued that there is still a strong component of 'positive' will behind it. There are two reports of the episode. During Urban IV's pontificate[142] William *de Capellano* and Peter Guillaume of Roqueville[143] went to the papal curia in Rome, where they met the pope's vice-chancellor, 'magister Michael'.[144] On their way back, they stopped in Piacenza, at Peter of Beauville's 'house', where other Cathars were staying. The two encouraged Beauville's lodgers to return to France, where – they said – they could all enjoy the pardon granted by the inquisitors.[145]

These depositions appear to be the only testimony regarding the Roman trip. Why did William and Peter go? What authority did they have to do this? Was it a political strategy planned by the hierarchy, or simply their personal initiative? Some parallels spring to mind. Papal approval for a new religious order or fraternity was essential to its recognition within Christianity. The Franciscans (1210) and Dominicans (1215) – and also the Waldensians (1179) and Humiliati (1198–9) – all followed the same pattern in order to be officially integrated by the Church. Can we assume that the Cathar pair were on a mission to achieve the same result? Unfortunately, the two records of this episode are very brief. We cannot trace the outcome of the enterprise, nor do we have more information about its main purpose. However, an attempt to regularise their position within the Catholic Church was never part of the Cathars' agenda. Instead, a stark contraposition between the Roman Church and the 'Church of God' was at the heart of Cathar belief and practice. It makes more sense to suggest a kind of 'peace mission', aiming to negotiate a truce in the long-lasting struggle, perhaps a trip to lodge a formal complaint against some inquisitor's excessive persecuting enthusiasm, or

---

[141] in Lombardia nullus homo facit malum Iudeis, Sarracenis vel hereticis, solummodo quod velint bene laborare pro suis necessariis habendis', II, p. 157–8 (149d–150a).

[141] D25, f. 4r.

[142] Probably between 1261 and 1262.

[143] Peter was the son of the lord of Montgaillard, Bertrand of Roqueville, 'perfect'.

[144] Michael appears in the letter *Adiutos morum et* of 16 January 1264 as 'Master Michael, vicechancellor of the Holy Roman Church' ('Magister Michael, Sancte Romane Ecclesie vicecancellarius'), J. Guiraud (ed.), *Les Régistres d'Urbain IV (1261–4)* (Paris, 1904).

[145] The two depositions referring to this episode are that of Peter Guillaume of Roqueville (D25, f. 130v and ff.), and Peter of Beauville (D25, f. 323r).

to obtain a reduction of penalties for condemned believers.[146] Contrary to common procedure, the two Cathars did not plead for it from the local inquisitors, nor had they waited for the local tribunal to proclaim a *tempus gratie*. Instead, they went directly to the source of authority, the papacy, where – perhaps – they obtained a 'discount' on penances for all of those who spontaneously came back to France from their Italian exile. It could have been a clever ploy, potentially allowing safe return for many of those previously on the run. On the other hand, the return of a significant number of men and women on the 'wanted' list would have provided the inquisitors with new information, more pieces in the jig-saw puzzle of their enquiries, and possibly a substantial range of potential bargaining tools to be used later on.

THE INQUISITORS' CHASE[147]

The opening paragraphs of this chapter talked about 'inquisitorial move-ment' as somehow being different from, although contemporary to and overlapping with, Cathar mobility. It has already been convincingly demonstrated by modern scholarship that inquisitors constantly moved around as they pursued the different tasks linked to the search and trial of the suspects.[148] How did they move? What lies behind the question is the fact that although the norms of inquisition, as expressed in papal directives, were uniform, their application and the management of inqui-sition varied greatly from region to region. Paolini has demonstrated the existence of an 'Italian model' in inquisitorial manuals.[149] We also know of a substantial difference in tackling heresy in Italy, so it does not seem invalid to use the idea of the 'models' in order to describe how the Inquisition was run and organised in each individual area.

It is vital to distinguish between our two foci, France and Italy, when discussing the power and management of local inquisitorial tribunals. In the south of France, the local church and those commissioned by the

---

[146] Even without referring to our case, Merlo suggests a series of interesting options for trips to Rome by heretics: the 'attractiveness' of the Roman curia for those who wished to confirm their opposition to the *Ecclesia malignantium*, the thirst for 'adventure' and risk, especially for the more committed to preaching, the contacts with the central Italian communities nearby – church of Florence and the Marca Spoletina – (*Eretici e inquisitori*, p. 94).

[147] I use here the same word as Zanella ('Malessere ereticale', p. 51), although in a different light. My position on the role of inquisitors as 'hunters' is in disagreement with Given's, for instance in 'Factional politics', and in *Inquisition and Medieval Society*, pp. 86–8; opposite perspective in Merlo, *Eretici e inquisitori*, pp. 75–97.

[148] Especially evident in Benedetti's work 'Le finanze', 'Le parole e le opere'.

[149] Paolini, 'Il modello italiano'.

pope (as the inquisitors were) enjoyed a relationship of rather close collaboration; in fact, closer and more fruitful than that between papal officials and political authorities. On that front, the local political elite (still
for the most part organised on patterns of seigneurial authority) always
displayed a benevolent – if not openly supportive – attitude towards
Cathar milieux and other groups of dissenters. Such lack of support from
the lay power, at times even turning into outright opposition, pushed
the Inquisition to act in conjunction with the local church, at parochial
and diocesan levels. Inquisitors, both natives and foreigners, focused their
efforts on specific places or areas, rather than organising a tighter-knit
strategy of collaboration with a specific religious order – as happened
in Italy with the Mendicants – or acting within a structured project,
for example the 1229 'peace mission' of cardinal Ugolino of Ostia to
the Italian cities of the Po valley. In a way the French inquisitors were
mostly acting on their own, although sufficiently supported by ecclesiastical authorities in the area of their inquiry.

In Italy, however, the Inquisition came under attack on both fronts.
Both local lay authorities *and* bishops were reluctant to cooperate, thus
creating a need for more sophisticated organisation.[150] The territorial
structure of the Inquisition in the Italian regions followed the mendicant
pattern, with inquisition 'provinces' overlapping with mendicant ones.
With the Mendicants themselves the Inquisition enjoyed a close and
successful collaboration. Overall, a more difficult political situation gave
birth to a better planned system.[151]

On the ground, there was scope for suspects to play on the relatively
disconnected nature of the tribunals, when they could claim to have been
absolved or condemned by one inquisitor, without the others knowing
of it. During his hearing, Guiraud *de Averro*, of the diocese of Cahors,
a knight, was shown a letter written by the inquisitor William Arnold
with the confirmation of a granted penance: a fee and a pilgrimage to
Rome for Lent. Guiraud denied ever having met the inquisitor 'and he
said that he believed that the said letter was a fake, or that his name had

---

[150] A good synthesis is in P. Diehl, 'Overcoming reluctance to prosecute heresy in thirteenth-century Italy', in *Christendom and its Discontents*, pp. 47–66.
[151] The idea of 'inquisitorial provinces', however, is still unclear. I suspect that this geographical partition was more the result of the control effectively exerted over inquisitorial matters by the Mendicant provinces, than a proper establishment of 'provinces'. Such a territorialisation, ascribed to Innocent IV (*Quia tunc potissime* – 1254), would thus be a consequence of committing to the provinces all responsibilities for the election, control and management of the inquisitors. See my 'Inquisizione francescana in Toscana fino al pontificato di Giovanni XXII', in *Frati minori e inquisizione. Atti del XXXIII Convegno internazionale (Assisi, 6–8 Ottobre 2005)*, (Spoleto, 2006), pp. 287–324, esp. pp. 291–2.

been mistakenly written in it'.[152] Although one might suppose that the inquisitor knew much more than he wanted to disclose about Guiraud's judicial ups and downs, and that his real knowledge lies hidden beneath the surface of the records, it is significant that, even when faced with the written evidence, the knight attempted to divert the course of the trial by denying the existence of a previous hearing.

Guiraud's case is not isolated. Evidently, either William Arnold and Stephen of St Thibéry (the inquisitors) were particularly lax in their handling of the recording procedure, or witnesses attempted to use their own interpretation of the procedure (which effectively created a gap in the communication chain) as a means of escaping further convictions. Otho of Baretges, whom we shall meet later as one of the strongest opponents of inquisitorial authority in the region of Moissac,[153] declared that he had already testified before the famous pair, 'however, he did not depose under oath, as they did not want to receive his oath'.[154] Another witness, Pons Grimoard, had appeared in court in 1236, during the 'general inquisition' ('inquisitio generalis') proclaimed by the two inquisitors in the Toulouse diocese. By so doing, he says, he had avoided death, prison and the confiscation of his possessions. After the hearing and his abjuration, he was given a written permit stating his penance, absolution and the right to be dealt with as an 'honest and Catholic man' ('virum fidelem et catholicum') by the authorities, were he to be stopped again. However, this letter – probably in order to keep it brief – contained only a general statement of his previous conviction, 'that he many and many times and in several places had seen heretics' ('se pluries et in pluribus locis vidisse hereticos'), and Pons could play on this relative vagueness in order to carry on holding Cathar beliefs. The second hearing highlights this procedural 'hiccup' and inserts the missing details into the official record. Pons added that his wife Baretges' deposition had also not been recorded: can we believe them? Did the inquisitor have the means to verify such declarations? It does not seem that he took any action to trace back such documentation.[155] Behind the desire to get themselves out of trouble by minimising their involvement with heresy, the declarations of Guiraud, Otho and Pons do not sound unlikely. Letters like the ones they mentioned had in fact been used since the times of the earliest enquiries. They were probably very similar to the safe-conduct

---

[152] 'Et dixit quod reputat dictam litteram esse falsam, vel per errorem positum nomen suum in ea', D26, f. 63v.
[153] See Chapter 4, p. XVXVXV.
[154] 'Non tamen deposuit iuratus quia ipsi noluerunt (ms. "voluerunt") recipere iuramentum suum', D22, f. 45v.
[155] The case is recorded in D22, ff. 39r–43v.

issued by Dominic of Guzmàn in 1211[156] to Pons Roger after his abjuration, which 'reconciled the person carrying ... [it], Pons Roger, who has converted, by the grace of God, from the sect of the heretics', and defined the penance assigned to Pons in expiation. The concise letter (it had to be carried like a sort of 'orthodoxy licence') ended by stating that 'he will have to show this letter to his chaplain each month. We also order the chaplain to take extreme care of his [Pons'] life. He [Pons] will have to observe carefully these things (= 'prescriptions'), unless the lord legate would otherwise let his will on the issue be known to us [Dominic]'.[157]

Given the relative disconnectedness of the French inquisitorial tribunals, a comparison between the two parties (Catholics and Cathars) and their systems shows clearly that while the inquisitorial strategy gradually took shape as a consequence of pre-existing dynamics, the heretical network of movements and connections itself derived from the nature of the Cathar church. It was a result of its organisation as a church with specific rituals and customs (the 'positive' side), but it also arose from their being an alternative, illegal, organisation (the 'negative' side). With time, both negative and positive forces merged into one, and gave life to the specific identity of the dissident group.

The Inquisition was on a hunt, and needed to catch up with its prey. It did so through two different tactics. On the one hand it put in place a policy of 'zero tolerance', increased its efforts, invested more money, multiplied the number of inquiries and harshened the penances. On the other hand, and more effectively, it sought to infiltrate the heretics' own system, by using informers and spies. Internal accusations were already in use within the framework of a trial, as a method of obtaining information before interrogating a suspect. This must have already loosened the heretics' bonds of loyalty and secrecy, introducing suspicion and fear. Nevertheless, the employment of apostates as permanent informers by the ecclesiastical authorities was probably far more effective and disruptive than a neighbour exposing somebody by mentioning views expressed in a private conversation. After abjuring, many offered information to the

---

[156] The chronology of this letter has been updated by S. Tugwell in 'Notes on the life of St Dominic', *Archivum Fratrum Praedicatorum* 73 (2003), 1–141. Other examples of safe-conducts are recorded in D21, ff. 167v–174v.

[157] 'Reconciliamus presentium latorem, Poncium Rogerium, ab hereticorum secta Deo largiente conversum ... Cartam istam capellano suo per singulos menses ostendat. Capellano etiam precipimus ut de vita eius diligenter adhibeat. Hec omnia diligenter observet, donec alias super hiis dominus legatus suam nobis exprimat voluntatem', V.J. Koudelka (ed.), *Monumenta diplomatica S. Dominici*, vol. 25, (Rome, 1966), n. 8, pp. 16–18.

inquisitors in exchange for money, protection or in order to bargain for a reduction of penance, or they did this following a sincere conversion.[158]

The use of such procedures, the handling of the judicial consequences (above all the anonymity of the informers) and the need for the accused to know the identity of their accusers, had long been debated in canon law – ever since the first execution in Orléans (1022), and especially after 1229, the year of the Peace of Paris and the Council of Toulouse, and of the end of the Albigensian Crusade. Popes and inquisitors agonised over the use of informers and its possible risks, and the legal resolutions achieved varied. Both Gui Foulques and Bernard Gui, for instance, appear sceptical and rather cautious about the use and misuse of 'internal' information.[159]

Manuals and *consilia* stress the need for collaboration, to extort information from those who abjured, doing this through a phrase inserted in their own oath of abjuration. The early *Consultatio* of Pierre d'Albalat (1241–2) suggests the following formula: 'If I shall know or come to know about anyone of the aforementioned [heretics] or about their supporters (*fautores*), anywhere, I shall reveal what I know as soon as I can to a bishop, or a prelate, or a judge, or a lord of that place, as long as they are Catholics and faithful to the Holy Roman Church.'[160] The recommendation, in conformity with Chapter XII of the Council of Toulouse,[161] was reiterated by other famous texts, such as the Council of Béziers (1246). This stated: 'Moreover, make all people, men as well as women, male from fourteen years, female from twelve years of age and above, abjure heresy, and make them swear an oath that they will observe faith and defend the Catholic Church, and that they will persecute heretics, as above, with an oath.'[162] By the fourteenth century, however, the practice was so deeply embedded in the trial procedures that Gui's *Practica* and *Sententiae* include a promise of disclosure in the formula to be pronounced by all those who abjured. 'Therefore, we promise and swear that we shall do our best to look for, find and give to justice all heretics, believers, and their *fautores* [= 'supporters'], defenders, and *receptatores* [= 'receivers'], as well as those

---

[158] Evans, 'Hunting Subversion', with a repertoire of canon law articles and manuals; Benedetti, 'Le parole e le opere', p. 141.

[159] Evans, 'Hunting Subversion', pp. 14–20.

[160] 'Si aliquem vel aliquos de predictis, vel de eorum fautoribus alicubi scivero vel intellexero, revelabo eum quam cito habuero opportunitatem episcopo, vel prelato vel iudici vel rectori illius loci, catholicis tamen et fidem sancte Romane Ecclesie observantibus', Selge (ed.), *Texte*, p. 55.

[161] Ch. XII. *De iuramento a singuils catholicis praestando*, Selge (ed.), *Texte*, pp. 32–3.

[162] 'Preterea universos tam mares, quam feminas, masculos a quatuordecim, feminas a duodecim annis et supra, faciatis abiurare omnem heresim, et iurare quod fidem servent et defendant catholicam ecclesiam, et hereticos persequantur, ut supra in iuramento', Mansi, *Sacrorum conciliorum nova et amplissima collectio* 23 (Graz, 1961), cols. 722–3, chs. 31–3.

who are on the run, with whatever name they are known, wherever and whenever we should know them to be or about any of the aforesaid.'[163] However, there is no mention of the collaborator as an institutionalised figure, called 'spy' or 'explorer', or otherwise, in the manuals.

The *Collectorie*, however, supply evidence of such mercenary collaboration by recording the money paid to men and women who 'did very much for the office ... and revealed many things to the inquisitors', and these are sometimes called 'explorers', or 'spies'.[164] Among them were people who previously had been either convicted or suspected of heretical connections. Nevertheless, it is necessary to remain cautious about the specific involvement of these spies in the framework of the trial. The information taken from the *Collectorie* themselves is blurred and not easily decodable.[165]

Assorted collaborators are also recorded in Doat 21–6. Among them is the case of Pons Faure, knight of Villeneuve, who said he had tried to 'buy' his fellows' trust by giving them 'a marinated eel, so that the said heretics could trust in him the witness, and he the witness could capture them'.[166] Peter Guillaume of Roquevidal, however, had a very personal reason for collaborating with the authorities. He – apparently an ex-'messenger', now in very close contact with the inquisitors, with whose permission he travels to and from Italy – obtained from them a letter with which he could claim back from the heretic Stephen Donati (but also from any other person on Stephen's behalf) the sum of 200 *solidi* of Toulouse owed to him by the heretics.[167] A strange permission indeed, if not seen in the light of a continuing relationship with the inquisitorial officials.

In Doat 21–6 there are four occurrences of the use of real spies. The first is the bare record made by the notary at the end of a document, declaring that he 'here wrote all the aforesaid which the said Bernard of Ceseratz did in the matter of heresy with the agreement of the church, and because of this he caused three women heretics to be taken'.[168] In the

---

[163] See *'Le manuel'*, VII, 5; 'Item promittimus et iuramus quod pro posse nostro persequemur et revelabimus seu detegemus hereticos, credentes, fautores, defensores et receptatores eorum ac pro heresi fugitivos quibusconque nominibus censeantur, quandocumque et ubicumque sciverimus eos esse vel aliquem de predictis', *Liber sententiarum*, p. 295.

[164] 'Multa servicia fecerat officio et aliis inquisitoribus et multa eis revelaverat.' The case is that of Anexia of Piacenza, quoted in Biscaro, 'Inquisitori ed eretici lombardi', p. 515, and one of the many taken from *Collectoria* 133.

[165] Benedetti, 'Le parole e le opere', pp. 146–7.

[166] 'Ipse testis dedit hereticis unam anguillam salsatam, et hac de causa ut dicti heretici crederent in ipso teste, ut quod ipse testis posset hereticos capere', D24, f. 118r.

[167] D25, ff. 131v–133r.

[168] 'Qui hec scripsit omnia predicta que dictus Bernardus de Ceseratz fecit de facto heresis de consensu ecclesie, et proper hoc fecit capi tres hereticas', D23, f. 185r.

second instance, noted during the trial against Bernard Otho (first half of the 1240s),[169] the archbishop of Toulouse wanted to enquire further into the existence of a 'house' of heretics allegedly inhabited by two Good Women and thirty believers. So – said the bishop – 'in order to know this, we have sent our explorers'. Were these 'explorers' true spies? Thirdly, testimony relating to events of 1233–5 mentions collaborators using the same terminology and in a similar context, and gives us a better under-standing of the practice. Here, Marquise of Prouille, previously a Good Woman, admitted that she had made contact with some suspects 'because she was an explorer of heretics for *magister* Radulph of Narbonne, and that she the witness 'explored' the aforesaid heretics, but did not cap-ture them, although she did go to the aforementioned house'.[170] Later on, she also admitted that she had brought them some fish, for which she had paid 'with the money given by *magister* Radulph, for whom she "explored" those heretics. And for this reason the same *magister* Radulph of Narbonne went there, and captured one of the aforesaid heretics, and the others fled through the wood, yet he took what they left and their things'.[171] So, Marquise's task was that of getting in touch with the her-etics, thanks to her knowledge of people and habits, then holding on to them – as she did not have the power to proceed to the capture (or decided not to) – in order to allow the inquisitor to step in and arrest the suspects. She was clearly a spy employed on a regular basis, as proved by another episode, where, after having meticulously named all those present at a heretical meeting, she 'added that she the witness "explored" all these heretics on behalf of the above mentioned *magister* Radulph'.[172] What is not clear is the reason why she was then called again to give a deposition to a different tribunal. It seems likely that the identities of spies were not disclosed by inquisitors to their colleagues. After all, a spy had to be hidden behind his or her secret identity, while at the same time remaining credible to his or her 'fellow heretics'. Whatever the case,

---

[169] D21, f. 35r (without date, but it is a *c*. XIII document, following an oath from 1209, and preceed-ing letters from 1228) 'ad quod sciendum hoc anno misimus exploratores nostros'.

[170] 'Eo quia erat exploratrix hereticorum pro magistro Radulpho, qui (!) ipsa testis exploravit ipsos hereticos, non tamen cepit eos, licet venisset in domum dictam', D23, f. 98r. The deposition refers back to the years 1234–5. This *magister* Radulphe could be the episcopal inquisitor for the bishop of Carcassonne quoted in Douais, *Documents*, vol. I, p. cxxxi (1251–4), also known to be one of the authors of ms. Clermont-Ferrand 160 (1250s). Douais also quotes William Radulphe (or simply, 'Radulphe'), bishop of Carcassonne from 1255 to 1264, (Douais, *Documents*, vol. I, p. cclxxxv).

[171] 'Et ibi ipsa testis dedit eisdem here-/ticis pisces quos emerat ipsa testis de denariis magistri Radulfi cui ipsa testis exploravit ipsos hereticos, propter quod idem magister Radulfus de Narbona venit ibi et cepit unum de prefatis hereticis, et alii fugerunt per nemus, tamen spolia eorum et raubam occupavit (ms. "occupabit")', D23, f. 98v.

[172] 'Adiecit etiam quod ipsa testis exploravit dictos hereticos prefato magistro Radulpho', D23, f. 98v.

Marquise had to reveal her identity during the hearing, and the notary recorded it as an important element of her statement. Clearly, in this respect also, the exchange of information between tribunals and inquisitors was not completely effective.

The last example is that of Amblard Vassal of Arifat, who sheds some light both on the employment of spies, and on the lack of coordination between the tribunals. He was involved in an obscure sequence of abjurations and interrogations. A fugitive, Amblard was first of all interrogated by the Dominican William Bernard and his companion, inquisitors at Castres in the Albigeois, who – apparently – did not grant him a penance. Amblard did not remember whether he had ever abjured before William Bernard or had been reconciled by him. Later, he was captured by the inquisitor Stephen of Gâtine, who brought him to Lombers, and released him on bail. Once again he did not remember whether he had abjured. After this second hearing Amblard made the decision to collaborate with the inquisitorial tribunal. In fact, there must have been a bargain behind the conditions for his release to start with, as the record says that he was freed 'on a security of forty pounds, in the hope that he the witness would hand over the heretics'.[173] So, even in 1264–5 Amblard was not obliged to collaborate; rather, the tribunal was hoping for his aid once he had been released. But the story goes on. 'Item, he said that he the witness then had the intention of capturing the heretics and handing them over to the inquisitors if he could, but he could not, because after that they were wary of him.'[174] Later on, Amblard specified more clearly the relationship between himself and the authorities.

He also said that he the witness had permission at that time to see heretics and to draw them in so that he could capture them, as Pestilhac and William Textor, servants of the inquisition, had told him the witness; and because he could not capture the heretics and hand them over, he did not dare return to the inquisitor, but fled. And then brother Stephen, the aforesaid inquisitor, demanded and extorted the aforesaid penalty from his guarantors. And from that time on he the witness was a fugitive, until now.[175]

---

[173] 'Sub cautione quadraginta librarum, et spe quod ipse testis redderet hereticos', D25, f. 185r and ff. (1274).

[174] 'Item dixit quod tunc ipse testis fuit in proposito capiendi hereticos et reddendi inquisitoribus si posset, sed non potuit quia ex tunc cavebant sibi ab eo', D25, f. 185r.

[175] 'Dixit etiam quod ipse testis habebat tunc licentiam videndi hereticos et atrahendi eos ut eos posset capere prout dixerant ipsi testi Pestilhe(u)s et Guillelmus textor servientes inquisitionis, et quia non potuit hereticos capere, et reddere, non fuit ausus redire ad inquisitor [sic] sed fugit, et tunc frater Stephanus inquisitor predictus exigit et extorsit predictam penam a fideiussoribus suis, et ex tunc ipse testis fuit profugus usque modo', D25, f. 186r.

Amblard's deposition is problematic. What emerges *prima facie* from his declaration is his unofficial recruitment as a spy by the servants of the inquisition, a weaver and another unspecified individual. The term 'explorator' is not used; rather, he described in detail the duties connected to his new status, presumably as they had been explained to him at that time. Then, there is the admission of scant success in his task. 'He could not capture heretics' due to the lack of trust people had in him. A feeble excuse? Perhaps. However, because of his failure, Amblard feared to appear again before the inquisitor without any prey. And what about brother Stephen? He 'demanded and extorted' ('exigit and extorsit') a penance from Amblard's guarantors, in the witness's absence. This is hardly a flattering representation of this inquisitor who, once his collaborator has apparently broken the agreement, does not hesitate to seize – as declared – his penalty from the guarantors, making life for Amblard even more difficult. Since then Amblard had been on the run – this time a fugitive – until his recapture and trial. Did he tell the truth during this second trial? Did he really try to capture heretics? Did he have a licence to do so in the first place? All these are, regrettably, open-ended questions.

Amblard probably knew that he was not the only one expected – more or less officially – to betray his former companions. Another very famous case is that of Raymond Baussan of Lagarde of Laurac, already seen running hospices in Italy, travelling and trying to hide 'in common inns'.[176] His deposition is rich in information about the life of one who was a *receptator*, a *fugitivus*, runner of a hostel and a spy. Apparently, in fact, Raymond – who was a 'spontaneous witness' – had already abjured before the inquisitor, and had therefore obtained legal recognition of his new status.[177] The inquisitor provided him with *littere*, and a *licentia*, a permit to travel without being summoned again. His contribution to the tribunal was, in fact, crucial. The capture of both Peter of Beauville and Raymond Papier, two among the most-wanted messengers and *receptatores* of the time, was mainly due to his intervention. The meaning of written permits is clear enough: through them Raymond could carry on with his normal activities without being persecuted by other inquisitors. Presumably he also carried the letters with him at the hearing where he appeared spontaneously, in order to prove his status as collaborator.

While Marquise and Raymond appear to have been employed through a thorough procedure of appointment (as it might be called), Amblard's deposition is murkier. Why? It could be that, while giving evidence,

---

[176] See above, n. 85.
[177] D25, f. 146r ff. The date is not precisely stated here, but elements in the deposition suggest that it could be placed around 1264.

either he or the notary focussed on the one aspect of his life which made him liable: the reason for him being on the run. After all, among the three cases, his is the only instance of a failed collaboration with the inquisitors: 'he could not capture heretics'. However, the reconstruction, albeit partial and distorted by Amblard's personal condition, appears at the very least suspicious. The relationship between spies and inquisitors as it appears from Marquise's and Raymond's depositions, is more in line with that which emerges from the *Collectorie*. There, collaborators are portrayed as tightly linked with their employers. They are rewarded with a payment for their services, although it is not always clear whether this money is meant to be something like a proper wage, a one-off payment, or a refund of expenses. Possibly different inquisitors applied different techniques, and we can assume the existence of a mix of all three possibilities. When they fall ill, the inquisitors provide for their needs, buying them food, blankets and wood for the fire. Sometimes the spies' living expenses, rent for example, are covered by the inquisitorial tribunal.[178]

As already noted, collaboration could be offered either on a regular basis, or in order to help the inquisitor and cast oneself in a good light – or perhaps to divert attention from one's misdeeds. To do that, however, official status as a collaborator was not a prerequisite. William Feraut, for instance, had voluntarily appeared before the inquisitors with a pretext, confessed and finally abjured. He used a little ploy to win over his judge. He declared that he had 'found some sort of letters on the road after the aforementioned William Faure, written for the heretics, and took them to brother Bernard of Caux, and then abjured'.[179] Although the recording of Feraut's speech is not clear, even this snippet tells us the following: first of all, that Feraut was previously in contact with some sort of heresy or heretics; second, that he was for some reason behind William Faure in some sort of move from one place to another; third, that whatever the content of these letters was, they were important for the inquisitor; and, finally, that communication among the heretics could use written documents. Most importantly, this case shows that any assistance to the enquiry stood a good chance of being rewarded, even if this meant simply that the inquisitor adopted a cosier attitude towards a cooperative witness.

Another glimpse on the matter is offered by a couple of documents included in the register of Jacques Fournier, which record a 'pact' between Arnaud Sicre of Ax and the bishop of Pamiers (1319–22) for the capture of

---

[178] Collectoria 133 reports numerous cases, Biscaro 'Inquisitori ed eretici lombardi'.

[179] 'Invenit quasdam litteras in via post W. Fabri predictum, que erant scripte pro hereticis, et has tradidit fratri B. de Cautio, et abiuravit', D22, f. 27r – I have not found confirmation for this evidence in other records.

the heretic Belibaste. While the first document details the strategy followed by Arnaud during his mission, the second one is the more official recognition that inquisitors 'understood through experience that these [heretics] cannot be easily found ... unless they are detected either through their accomplices, or through those who know otherwise their devious ways'.[180]

'Therefore, we ... sent Arnaud Sicre ... to explore and enquire cautiously, discreetly and promptly some fugitives for heresy ... and allowed Arnaud to act with them on the outside pretending and simulating similarity and conformity in his rites (= in the way he professed his faith), especially in the presence of a heretic or heretics, because otherwise they would not trust him, although in his heart he did not believe or agree with their errors.'[181]

Official literature, the manuals, is silent on the practice of a 'professional' collaboration, as well as on the judicial status of *exploratores*. However, Pseudo-David of Augsburg in his *Tractatus de inquisitione hereticorum*, without mentioning an already institutionalised figure, throws light on an existing practice and on the requirements made of the explorers. The following is a deliberately loose translation:

And there may be some shrewd and capable individuals who would be willing to watch what they are up to; people who, with episcopal permission, could present themselves as being pro the heretics and in touch with them, people who could talk to them carefully but without lying; people about whom there would be no worry that they might be infected by the heretics. If such individuals are available, they could investigate the secrets of the heretics and get to know their habits and words, and investigate them and their supporters, and search out their hiding places and cells. They could take note and put down in writing, harmoniously [perhaps meaning 'in a way that allows cross-reference'?] the elements on the basis of which each of them could be found guilty of heresy. And these persons could find out when the heretics' teachers are going to be present or when many are going to be gathered in one place, so that they can report this and other info about the heretics in good time to the inquisitors and bring about their arrest. And they could be employed as witnesses of some of these facts against these heretics, doing this according to legal form. And this could greatly help the Church in the extirpation of heretical wickedness.[182]

---

[180] The documents are also commented upon by Molinier in his *Rapport*, 'experiencia magistrante didicimus, non possunt de facili reperiri, ... nisi detecti fuerint aut per eorum complices aut per tales qui vias eorum devias alias cognoverint', Molinier, *Rapport*, pp. 305–7, p. 306.

[181] 'Idcirco, nos ... misimus Arnaldum Cicredi, ... ad explorandum et perquirendum caute, discrete et sollicite fugitivos quosdam pro heresi ... permisimus ut se exterius posset eisdem fingere et simulare in suis ritibus consimilem et conformem, maxime coram heretico vel hereticis, ex eo quia aliter non confiderent de eodem, ita dumtaxat ne corde eorum erroribus crederet aut consentiret', Fournier, *Register*, II, p. 80; Molinier, *Rapport*, pp. 306–7.

[182] 'Et si haberentur aliqui qui sagaciter scirent et vellent eos in huiusmodi observare vel qui de licencia episcoporum se ipsis hereticis favorabiles et familiares ostenderent, qui caute scirent loqui cum eis sine mendacio, et de quibus non esset timor quod inficerentur ab eis, isti possent secreta

The *De inquisitione* confirms our impression that the practice of employing people as spies was not itself clandestine. As it was freely acknowledged in the trial records when required by the inquiry, so it was explained to the inquisitors, although no formal recognition of a status of 'explorers' is made. Yet, with the sole exception of this source, the manuals (still, internal sources written for professionals) do not dwell on, explain or get into detail about the use of spies, among the methods of inquiry. Is this a 'strategic' silence? It does not appear so. Certainly, there is a substantial difference in the intended purpose of the two kinds of sources. While the records – either trial or expense ones – list facts and names, connections and words retrospectively, the manuals are official teaching aids to train professionals, and look forward, in a proactive manner.[183] It seems, however, that the answer lies not so much in the absence of comment in the manuals, as in its presence both in trial records and registers of expenses. Although not officially recognised, the costs of the employment of informers could not be deleted from the tribunals' expenses. This would have made the accounts uneven and caused discrepancies in the inquisitor's financial balance. Equally, the reason for mentioning informers and spies in the trial records is the added value such evidence could give to the depositions. Notaries and inquisitors chose to keep this element in the official record as it strengthened their accusations. What accusation or statement could, indeed, be stronger than one made by the system's recognised and authorised collaborators?

Both inquisitorial tactics, the more traditional one based on enquiries and collaboration with the local clergy (made more intense by a new need for increased efforts), and the 'underground' tactic which relied on the help of spies, informers and occasional tip-offs, show that inquisitors operated on two levels. Together with the 'official' procedure, whose legitimacy derived from the recognised authorities of the pope, canon law and manuals, a new methodology gradually came to the fore: the employment of spies and explorers was a well-known

---

eorum perscrutari et mores et verba agnoscere et personas ipsorum et fautores investigare et latibula et conventicula perquirere, et ea, per que singuli eorum possent convinci de heresi, concorditer notare et in scripto redigere, et, quando magistri eorum presentes essent vel plures in unum convenirent, explorare, ut suo tempore hec et alia inquisitoribus hereticorum indicarent, et comprehendi eos facerent, et horum contra eos testes existerent secundum formam iuris, et hoc multum conferret ecclesie ad extirpationem heretice pravitatis', Pseudo-David of Augsburg, *Tractatus de inquisitione*, p. 222.

[183] The proactive feature of manuals is particularly highlighted by those who believe in the actual weight they had in 'shaping', or 'creating' heresy in its literate and institutional aspects. See, for instance, G. Zanella, *Itinerari ereticali: Patari e Catari tra Rimini e Verona*, ('Studi Storici' 153), (Rome, 1986), p. 30.

practice among the inquisitors and their adversaries. Both strategies bear witness to an Inquisition that is far from the images of 'repressive system' and 'investigative machine'.[184] Arguably, they describe instead the steps leading to and gradually building up a new system which sometimes awkwardly, and certainly tentatively, finds its own way over time.

In the same perspective one can also see the long-standing dialectic between manuals and *consilia sapientium*. Because the *consilia* were produced, copied into inquisitors' anthologies and used over a considerable period, they cannot be merely regarded as the prototypes of more structured manuals. They answered a constant need for clarification and the *ad hoc* availability of pieces of legislation.[185] Manuals never eliminated *consilia* from everyday enquiries, as the wider outlook required by a general code of practice could not respond to all the variations and specific cases inquisitors had to face day by day, and which were specifically addressed by *consilia*. Also, the wide scope for interpretation and (possibly) misuse offered by any law was too great a risk to take, and could lead to serious mistakes and inconsistencies by individual tribunals.

On this double track inquisitors handled their everyday duties. Evidently, they made an effort to regulate the continuing practice, the use of spies, through the issue of letters to the individual collaborators to protect their identities and their activities. However, there is no evidence that these methods were regularised or supervised. Other inquisitors did not know of their identity, and nothing suggests that copies were taken of such documents, or that they were considered official documents at all. They were, it seems, treated as passports in case the collaborator needed or wanted to contact the inquisitors again. But they became absolutely useless if in the hands of those on the run. In other words, the only way by which inquisitors managed to obtain inside information on the organisation of their 'prey' was patchy. As this practice seems to have relied on individual initiative, perhaps there was less need for it to be regulated, codified, or indeed clarified to the practitioners.

---

[184] See above, n. 4.

[185] See, for instance, the case outlined in my 'Decostruzione testuale nel *consi lium* agli inquisitori di Carcassonne del 1330 (Paris, Bibliothèque Nationale de France, *Collection Doat*, vol. 32)', in M.C. De Matteis (ed.), *Ovidio Capitani: quaranta anni per la storia medioevale* (Bologna, 2003), vol. II, pp. 137–50, where a *consilium* is required well after (1330) what is considered to be the 'end of the prolific season of *consilia*', seen by Parmeggiani around the very beginning of the fourteenth century ('Un secolo di manualistica', p. 249). See also Paolini, *L'eresia Catara*, pp. 18–29; Benedetti, 'Le parole e le opere', p. 130.

CONCLUSIONS

The picture presented here of the movements of Cathars and their adversaries offers a new perspective. Behind the filters and the linguistic constriction of the discourse, which have been tackled by stages as they emerged from the texts, these records do indeed give a colourful and extremely lively depiction of Cathar life and thought. We have to assume a planned and organised institution, while at the same time detaching ourselves from any need to impose precise names on functions and structures. In other words, we must avoid the polemicists' temptation to reduce a very fluid and variable situation into an intellectually coherent scheme, and instead follow the inquisitors' example and, like them, remain open to inconsistencies and linguistic anachronisms.

What are we left with? We seem to be dealing with a Cathar church which relies strongly on interpersonal relationships, links and connections between its clergy and believers, as is plainly stated in the *Gleisa de Dio*. 'This Church is not made of stones, or wood, or of anything made by hand ... But this holy Church is the assembly of the faithful and of holy men.'[186] This church structured itself according to such principles, yet at the same time it had to compromise with everyday necessities by building on pre-existing models and vocabulary for its own internal management. Although the Cathars were strongly opposed to the notion of dedicated buildings, in the end it was difficult entirely to avoid them. The network of hospices, the private residences, the huts, all inevitably ended up looking similar to non-Cathar hostels and Catholic places of cult and preaching. In Montségur in 1240, where the Cathar hierarchy sought shelter and the protection needed in order to efficiently run the network of proselytism and administration of the sacraments, the bishop Bertrand Martin 'very often ... preached in some house which was designated for giving a sermon'.[187] This happened in an exceptional situation, at an exceptionally dangerous time, but still in a safe enough environment for leading a 'normal' community life.

However, whether messengers, guides and collaborators, fake pilgrims or 'priests', all these people constituted the living church, a true travelling institution which reached believers and people in need of words and rites through a capillary distribution of the holy. All of these circuits effectively *made* the church of the Cathars, in such a manner that only by tuning in to the same frame of mind and adapting their strategy to their

---

[186] *Gleisa de Dio*, ch. 1; Wakefield and Evans, p. 596.

[187] 'Sepissime Bertrandus Martini espicopus hereticus predicabat in quadam domo que erat deputata ad faciendum sermonem', D23, f. 202r.

adversaries' could inquisitors undermine and eventually break the resistance in Languedoc. Only by using insiders and by physically following their quarry could they get hold of them.

The relationship between French and Italian communities, although made much closer in times of more intense inquisitorial activities and persecution, relied on pre-existing friendly contacts between 'ecclesiastical cells', but it was built upon itineraries, links and habits that were neither necessarily religious, nor necessarily Cathar. While witness to the existence of a structured church, of its ways and beliefs, the depositions are also testimony to the constant intertwining of dissent and order, normality and exceptionality, of the tensions faced by individuals and the struggle between being 'alternative' believers and ordinary human beings. Thus, an investigation of the topic of 'Catharism and its mobility' needs to be conducted on two parallel grounds. On the one hand, by referring to statements made in anti-heretical and Cathar official texts, both with their own idealised vision of mobility and travel. On the other hand, by taking into account the hundreds of descriptions of concrete practice, made for the purpose of the hearings, but certainly more nuanced and less stereotyped than the first ones.

Chapter 3

HERETICAL ITINERANCY

REMISE

As we have seen, travelling Cathars were not the only heretics on the roads of Europe; nor were they the only target of Catholic strategic countermoves. Extreme heretical mobility is highlighted in all Catholic sources, both theoretical and judicial, and this mirrors the actual movements of individuals and groups. It also contributed to the creation of the *topos* of the wandering heretic in public opinion and collective mindset. In order to set our evidence on Cathar mobility in perspective and to make sense of it, therefore, we need to locate it in the wider panorama of heretical movements. In order to obtain a good overview of the problem of itinerancy (including itinerancy as the basis for an accusation of heresy), we must analyse these groups' own views of the meaning of travelling and set these alongside the Catholic sources' depiction of the 'illegitimate preacher'.

Ever since the twelfth century the presence of wandering preachers, both individuals and groups, had been recorded throughout Europe. All scholars agree on the unprepared and inconsistent attitude displayed by the Church before this unprecedented challenge to its monopoly of preaching. Some even detect the same ambiguity in Catholic writers' depictions of approved wandering preachers, for example, Bernard of Tiron, Norbert of Xanten, Peter the Hermit and Robert of Arbrissel.[1]

---

[1] See R.I. Moore, *The Origins of European Dissent* (London, 1977), pp. 70, 90, 106–7; B.M. Kienzle, *Cistercians, Heresy and the Crusade in Occitania 1145–1229* (York, 2001), p. 43; G. Dickson, 'Encounters in medieval revivalism: monks, friars and popular enthusiasts', *Church History* 68/2 (1999), 265–93, esp. pp. 268–9, 284–5, 292–3. The author lists among the possible reactions: 'negation, including mockery, derision, denunciation, accusations of heresy; affirmation, including praise, endorsement, support, an evident desire to take part, and outright participation, with its contradictions and consequences, and charismatic dominance' (p. 268); C. Dereine, 'Les prédicateurs "apostoliques" dans les diocèses de Thérouanne, Tournai et Cambrai Arras durant les années 1075–1125', *Analecta Praemonstratensia* 59 (1983), 171–89, esp. pp. 172, 179, 180–1. On the natural follow-up of these

The roots of this sudden and widespread growth of *preaching*, which made it difficult to discriminate between non-authorised and authorised preachers, are still a matter of controversy.[2] It seems, however, that they can be traced back to the late eleventh to early twelfth centuries, when several factors intersected, influencing each other, and coming together to shape the new religiosity of post-millennial Europe. These factors converged in that turning-point in the history of the Church, the Gregorian reform. The papacy, challenged by the laity, reacted through a deep process of self-analysis and the development of new forms of religiosity. The most highly developed of these lay challenges were the Milanese Patarenes. They exemplified the lay movements of this period: criticism of the clergy, open defiance of the Church authorities in the name of the Gospels, an increasingly important role for the laity, the self-awareness of believers and the presence of charismatic leaders. At its core there lay a deep, sometimes violent, criticism of the clergy, accused of *being* corrupted, and therefore of *having* corrupted the original message of the Gospels.

As a consequence, the urge to reaffirm the true inheritance from the apostles became overwhelming. A common believer was upgraded into a credible follower of Christ, so long as he or she was inspired by and conformed to the apostolic lifestyle. Such *apostolicity* came to be taken as *the* indicator of the piety and trustworthiness of both religious and lay people.

groups in the following century, with particular emphasis on the reaction of the Church, see B. Bolton, 'Poverty as protest: some inspirational groups at the turn of the twelfth century', in *The Church in a Changing Society: Conflict, Reconciliation or Adjustment?* (Uppsala, 1978), pp. 28–32 [now repr. in B. Bolton, *Innocent III: Studies on Papal Authority and Pastoral Care*, Variorum Collected Studies 490, (Ashgate, 1995), XIII, pp. 1–11].

[2] For Roach it was the inevitable consequence of the wreckage of a church monopoly, when wandering preachers and dissenters 'filled a vacuum in pastoral care', 'gave a role to the laity' and displayed an undeniable awareness of new, compelling preaching methods. In doing so, they contributed to expand the possibilities for a religious life (Roach, *The Devil's World*, pp. 11–12, 27–33, 66). Moore, more widely, highlights the disintegration of a conceptual world, where preachers acted as charismatic leaders, and therefore could gain such widespread popular support. For Dickson the emphasis has to be placed upon collective religious enthusiasm, and within a bottom-up mechanism of reform of the Church. Such enthusiasm, if not initiated, authorised and – if necessary – curbed by religious authorities, could spark divisions among the populace and between the populace and the clergy ('Encounters in medieval revivalism', p. 265). Dereine sees the papacy of Gregory VII, 'action aussi novatrice qu'intransigeante', at the core of an ambiguous time, when these men could be named either as 'hommes providentiels' or 'dangereux novateurs', and when each party could claim to possess the truth; ultimately, the situation was inevitably generated by the incommunicability between a hierocratic papacy and the promoters of an 'apostolic' lifestyle (*Les Prédicateurs 'apostoliques'*, pp. 172, 180–1). For Lambert, it is a common feature of most popular movements arising before the age of the printing press, which started with a spontaneous period of wandering preachers [M. Lambert, *Medieval Heresy: Popular Movements from the Gregorian Reform to the Reformation*, 3rd edn. (Oxford and Malden, 2002), p. 40]. Kienzle notes that this phenomenon sparked widespread reflection and scholarly debate on preaching itself ('Preaching as touchstone of orthodoxy and dissent', *Medieval Sermon Studies* 42 (1999), pp. 18–53, esp. p. 21).

Two main features are of interest here, first of all the Church's response to this unexpected phenomenon. It was inevitably mixed and uneven, since it consisted of the varying reactions of the individual bishops or Church authorities who happened to have to face these criticisms. The second feature was the unmistakably conscious nature of these challenges. Whether it was a matter of deliberate provocation of the Church authorities or simply the desire for strong reaffirmation of the values and modes of a lost apostolic inheritance, the individuals and groups in question were far from unaware of what they were doing. Examples can be found in R.I. Moore's fine analysis of the first emergence of 'European Dissent'. The roll-call of famous names in his and other modern accounts of the period include Leutard, a peasant from Vertus in the diocese of Châlons around the year 1000, a group reported to the bishop of Arras-Cambrai in 1025, Ariald's Patarenes in Milan, Tanchelm of Antwerp, Ramihrdus, Eon of l'Étoile, and Henry of Lausanne.[3] Apostolicity went hand in hand with preaching and mission, where mission meant both authorisation (by the ecclesiastical authorities and by God, that is, the act of sending [*missio*]) and travel for the purpose of spreading the 'good tidings'. Talking about the heretics of Arras, Moore stresses their mobility, in words which not only suit most of the early groups of dissenters but also define well some of the features of the travellers recounted in our Doat depositions.

> They were mobile, many of them detached from family and countryside to seek their future in crowded and precarious townships and as members of growing communities poorly served by the church and wholly at the mercy of chance employments and ambitious employers, the victims of the process which was creating new wealth and new privilege for a minority of the many who pursued them.[4]

During the thirteenth and fourteenth centuries the model developed and widened, moving from what it had been – the imitation of the apostles (*imitatio apostolorum*) as inheritors of the true and uncorrupted message of salvation – and now involving the imitation of Christ himself (*imitatio Christi*). Religious people aiming at carrying out Christ's teachings in the Gospels adopted a lifestyle of continuous movement along short- and long-distance routes. These people and these routes constitute the core of our interest. The lifestyle necessarily involved lodging in many different residences, which could be both religious houses and private hostels. Effectively, people leading this sort of life were wanderers with no fixed abode.

---

[3] Moore, *The Origins of European Dissent*, pp. 23–81. See also R.I. Moore, *The Birth of Popular Heresy* (Toronto, Buffalo and London, 1995), pp. 9–71, for sources on the same period.
[4] Moore, *The Origins of European Dissent*, pp. 65–6.

Historiography has relegated the topic of heretical itinerancy to the sidelines. This aspect of heretical life has nearly always been seen as simply an inevitable 'physical' by-product of preaching, something to be related to the issues of apostolicism and evangelism.[5] Itinerancy *per se* has been neglected in historical analysis.

The evangelical precept to 'go and preach' implies that both movement and preaching are requirements of true followers of Christ. In fact, preaching had not always entailed movement. It had been done prior to this period – and still was done – within the enclosure of cloisters and parish churches. But now, movement had become necessary, in the more complex perspective that now prevailed of imitation of the apostles and of Christ. Mobility was considered a prerequisite for reaching higher degrees of spiritual perfection, or even as a duty in itself for the truly religious person.

Heretical groups likewise claimed, of course, to refer back to the words of the Gospel, and they aimed at reaching a way of life in conformity with 'the apostolic way', *forma apostolorum*. This shared ideological drive kept bringing into the streets and marketplaces various lay people whose abilities, knowledge and, most of all, right to carry on this way aroused suspicion among Church authorities. In the case of dissenters, adopting the methods of the apostles meant being able to go against the corrupt and evil teachings of the Roman Church, and promoting a new and revolutionary 'plan of life', *propositum vitae*. The combination of missionary zeal, sincere commitment and visibly 'evangelical' appearance, often combined with their detachment from worldly possessions, was extraordinarily effective, and it created a formidable strategy of communication, equal to that of the later friars and approved wandering preachers.

---

[5] The only exception, as far as I know, is T. Scharff, 'Eterodossia come "variante" dell'evangelizzazione nella prospettiva delle fonti dell'Inquisizione', in *Alle frontiere della Cristianità. I frati Mendicanti e l'evangelizzazione tra '200 e '300. Atti del XXVIII Convegno Internazionale (Assisi, 12–14 October 2000)*, Spoleto, 2001, pp. 41–59. For the mainstream historiographical trend, see for instance: K.V. Selge, 'Discussions sur l'apostolicité entre Vaudois, Catholiques et Cathares', *Cahiers de Fanjeaux* 2 (1967), pp. 143–62; T. Manteuffel, *Naissance d'une hérésie: Les adeptes de la pauvreté volontaire au Moyen Âge* (Paris and La Haye, 1970) [orig. edn. Warsaw, 1974]; Ilarino da Milano, 'Vita evangelica e vita apostolica nell'adesione dei riformisti sul papato del secolo XII', in *Problemi di Storia della Chiesa: Il Medioevo dei secoli XII–XV* (Milan, 1976), pp. 21–72; S. Trawkowski, 'Entre l'orthodoxie et l'hérésie: "vita apostolica" et le problème de la désobéissance', in *The Concept of Heresy in the Middle Ages (11th–13th c.), Proceedings of the International Conference (Louvain, May 1973)*, (Leuven, 1976), pp. 157–66; R. Rusconi, '"Forma Apostolorum": l'immagine del predicatore nei movimenti religiosi francesi e italiani dei secoli XII e XIII', *Cristianesimo nella storia* 6, 6.3 (1985), 513–42; E. Pasztor, 'Predicazione itinerante ed evangelizzazione nei secoli XI–XII', in *Evangelizzazione e culture, Atti del Congresso Internazionale scientifico di Missionologia (Rome, 5–12 December 1975)*, (Rome, 1976), vol. II, pp. 169–74; E. Lupieri, 'Modelli scritturistici di comportamento ereticale. Alcuni esempi dei primi tre secoli', *Atti dell'Accademia Nazionale dei Lincei, Memorie. Classe di Scienze morali, storiche e filosofiche*, 383 (1986), ser. VIII, XXVIII, 7, 403–50. See also Chapter 2 above.

This parallel can be taken further. The link with the imitation of Christ and the apostles and the connection with preaching were in fact shared by both heretical and non-heretical groups. When looking at both sides of this coin, therefore, historians face an almost identical situation. It was the same general religious conditions that brought into existence both the legitimate and illegitimate preachers of this period: both sets of preachers had broadly similar aims and adopted similar means to achieve them. Orthodox and heterodox groups referred to the same scriptural authorities, and were rooted in the same ideology. All heretics quoted the Gospel in their defence; all claimed to be its true and exclusive inheritors.[6]

A common textual and ideological patrimony, a common ideal and similar means of achieving it: the insistence on the 'truly apostolic life' responded to a widespread urge and sentiment affecting Western Christianity just after the turn of the millennium. In general, a changing mindset explains the extreme success enjoyed by the preachers and missionaries whose reliability, theoretical competence and aims could of course vary greatly. Such a situation inevitably created confusion about the boundaries of legitimacy among these people, and called for clarification and disciplinary intervention. Its outcomes, therefore, were at the heart of the concerns of the Gregorian and post-Gregorian reformers. It was they who were responsible for the ultimate transformation of the earlier correspondence between apostolic life and evangelism or itinerancy into a new formulation, one which – as we would expect – identified the apostolic life with obedience to the pope as the successor of the apostles and *the* keeper of their inheritance.[7]

When looked at from this perspective – the view that the new religious movements of this period were generically similar – the ambivalence of the Church authorities supports the idea that it was 'inventing' heterodoxy. It was they who determined what could and could not be accepted as legitimate, and it was they who decided the inclusion or

---

[6] Kienzle has pointed out the ambiguity and ambivalence of such common goals: the possibility of opposite points of view on a shared cultural patrimony meant that preaching could be used as a 'touchstone' to establish right from wrong (Kienzle, 'Preaching as a touchstone', esp. pp. 23–5).

[7] See H. Grundmann, *Religious Movements in the Middle Ages* (Notre Dame and London, 1995), pp. 219–26; Manselli, *L'eresia del male*, pp. 138–49; Idem, 'Évangélisme et mythe dans la foi Cathare', *Heresis* 5 (1985), 5–17; Selge ('Discussions sur l'apostolicité'); and Ilarino da Milano ('Vita evangelica e vita apostolica'), stress the transformation into a 'life of obedience'; Trawkowski ('Entre l'orthodoxie et l'hérésie') and Manteuffel (*Naissance d'une hérésie*) have pointed out the relevance of the local clergy and part of the hierarchy in opposing the freedom of the itinerant preachers; on the desire to limit potential social disruption see also G.G. Merlo, 'Controllo ed emarginazione della dissidenza religiosa', in *Francescanesimo e vita religiosa dei laici nel '200, Atti del VII Convegno Internazionale (Assisi, 16–18 October 1980)*, (Assisi, 1981), pp. 367–88, esp. p. 376; Kienzle, 'Preaching as a touchstone'.

exclusion of such groups in or from the body of Christianity – directly through excommunication, or indirectly, through the creation of norms in theology and canon law. Those who disagreed with or disobeyed these norms were therefore guilty of *hairesis*, the 'choice' of dissent.

One aspect of this interpretation, however, is less than convincing. Here historiography has perhaps sinned through excessive scepticism, in its deconstruction of medieval religious dissenting groups. Its weakness is that it plays down the weight and importance of their religious challenge, by grossly undervaluing the awareness and free will displayed by these 'new religions' (*religiones novae*).[8] Currently, modern scholarship usually tackles the heresy or orthodoxy of this period in two ways. Either it uses a 'political' angle, arguing that the Church applied the label of 'heresy' in order to establish a political and theoretical basis for its monarchical exclusiveness; Moore is the most famous exponent of this. Or it refuses to attribute any agency to the 'heretics' or reformers, insisting that, through preaching without the permission of the Church and its ministers, they posed a threat to the uniformity of doctrinal interpretation and the papacy's claims to primacy. Both approaches overlook these groups' *will* to challenge, reject or change authority. And they treat beliefs and believers as merely instrumental and incidental to those entities to which they do attribute agency, and therefore schemes, projects and policies: feudal lords, Italian communes with their complex political life, religious orders with their influential 'production of ideas', and the papacy as the ultimate and prime mover of all Christendom.

Without denying the existence of a complex pattern of political interactions influencing the definition of heresy and its treatment, one should recognise that the basic approach is extremely reductive. It derives from an overly rigid application of mental categories which themselves derive from orthodox sources. These include the concept of 'legitimacy' (derived from the idea of preachers 'being sent'), with its immediate derivative of 'orthodoxy', and the idea of heresy as 'functional', as somehow necessary in order to justify the complex dynamics of Christianity.

---

[8] In the Middle Ages, the word *religio* principally meant 'religious Order', as in Orders of Carthusians, etc. or 'monasticism', in a sense that survives in modern English only in the usage 'the religious', a collective noun meaning friars, monks and nuns. Later on, in the high Middle Ages, the meaning of *religio* shifts significantly, from 'religious movements' to a more modern concept. It comes to denote the movements of individuals and people who abandoned the world and followed the Gospel precepts in actions that resembled monastic renunciation. Some of them acquired structured forms within the Church as new religious houses (e.g. Fontevrault) or Orders in the Church (e.g. Premonstratensians), some were kept outside the Church (e.g. Waldensians). For a fuller discussion on this topic, see P. Biller, 'Words and the medieval notion of "religion" ', *Journal of Ecclesiastical History* 36 (1985), 351–69.

In fact, most new religious groups campaigning for the introduction of reforming ideas were quite consciously introducing a challenging Christian message, embodying a dissenting 'otherness', sometimes with a rebellious attitude, sometimes open to discussion. They even succeeded – in the case of the Cathars – in effecting the complete and utter replacement of the existing hierarchy by one of their own. All these groups strongly believed in the legitimacy of their own ambition. By criticising or opposing the existing hierarchy, they did two things. In the first place, they recognised that hierarchy's central and leading role within Christianity, and sought reform to make it 'as it should be'. Secondly, by alleging perversion of the original evangelical message, they de-legitimised the Church's role. The Church of Rome, in other words, was indeed viewed as the head of Christianity. Its perverse behaviour and corrupt clergy, had however made it an impostor, as declared by the Pseudo-Apostle, Rolandino *de Ollis* of Modena: he preached that 'the Roman Church was good and holy, while its shepherds were evil'.[9] The Cathar Pons of Gameville rejects the similitude between apostles and clergy, saying that 'it can be well understood that clerics do not hold to the way of the apostles, because the apostles did not kill nor did they put people to death, as these do'.[10]

Catharism represents a further stage in this pattern: Cathars put themselves forward as the *only* Church. Having denied any legitimacy to Peter's see, they overturned the categories for a definition of orthodoxy and heresy. They used the same weapons as their opponents by erecting an alternative hierarchy which to some extent mirrored that of the Catholics; they fought using the same methods as their rivals. Moreover, the Cathars' missionary structure had two aspects. On the one hand it responded to the need for internal organisation (as seen in Chapter 2), and on the other it established a new ecclesiological pattern.

A reconsideration of the problem is therefore needed. A more searching analysis will distinguish between the different groups of reformers, treating preaching and itinerancy as two separate elements, each of which must be treated individually. We shall focus on the thirteenth and fourteenth centuries, continuing to confine the investigation to our Doat sources, bearing in mind the earlier examples, surveyed earlier, that paved the way for this later stage.

---

[9] 'Ecclesia Romana erat bona et sancta, set pastores eiusdem erant mali', in *Acta Sancti Officii Bononie*, vol. II, p. 431.

[10] 'Sed bene potest cognosci quod clerici non tenent viam apostolorum, quia apostoli non occidebant nec morti homines exponebant sicut ipsi faciunt', D25, f. 47r.

DOCTRINE

All reformers refer back to the 'Gospel model', although doing so to different degrees and from different angles. Whether this means a general model of behaviour, acceptance of the Gospels as textual authorities, or is merely a starting point, an inheritance, all the reformers assume a genesis in the words of this common textual patrimony. The enormous influence of the Gospels at the core of the Mendicant lifestyle, as well as of the so-called *Wanderprädiger* (wandering preachers) and the Waldensians, for example, is also visible in the 'models of sanctity' developed and advertised by the Church during the twelfth and thirteenth centuries. It has in fact been shown that in this period sanctity was shaped by the 'Gospel model', which prevailed over all previous models and was strongly promoted by papal policy, especially under Innocent III. [11]

Roberto Rusconi has studied in remarkable depth the connections between preaching and preachers, their manuscripts and the modes of popularisation of the Word; he has concentrated on their doctrinal origins. [12] From the twelfth century, a 'truly apostolic life' ('vita vere apostolica'), structured upon preaching, poverty and itinerancy, referred back to certain key passages of the synoptic Gospels: Matthew 10:7–16; [13] Mark 6:7–13 [14] and Luke 10:1–12, [15] with a few variations. Following the

---

[11] See A. Vauchez, *La sainteté en Occident aux derniers siècles du Moyen Age*, ('Bibliothèque des Écoles Françaises d'Athènes et de Rome', 241), (Rome, 1988), pp. 450 and ff.; Trawkowski, *Entre l'Orthodoxie et l'Hérésie;* Pasztor, 'Predicazione itinerante'; Ilarino da Milano, 'Vita evangelica', esp. pp. 22, 30.

[12] Rusconi, ' "Forma apostolorum" '.

[13] 'And proclaim as you go, saying, "The kingdom of heaven is at hand." Heal the sick, raise the dead, cleanse lepers, cast out demons. You received without paying; give without pay. Acquire no gold nor silver nor copper for your belts, no bag for your journey nor two tunics nor sandals nor a staff, for the labourer deserves his food. And whatever town or village you enter, find out who is worthy in it and stay there until you depart. As you enter the house, greet it. And if the house is worthy, let your peace come upon it, but if it is not worthy, let your peace return to you. And if anyone will not receive you or listen to your words, shake off the dust from your feet when you leave that house or town. Truly, I say to you, it will be more bearable on the day of judgement for the land of Sodom and Gomorrah than for that town. Behold, I am sending you out as sheep in the midst of wolves, so be wise as serpents and innocent as doves.' Matthew 10:7–16.

[14] 'And he called the twelve and began to send them out two by two, and gave them authority over the unclean spirits. He charged them to take nothing for their journey except a staff: no bread, no bag, no money in their belts, but to wear sandals and not put on two tunics. And he said to them: "Whenever you enter a house, stay there until you depart from there. And if any place will not receive you and they will not listen to you, when you leave, shake off the dust that is on your feet as a testimony against them." So they went out and proclaimed that people should repent. And they cast out many demons and anointed with oil many who were sick and healed them.' Mark 6:7–13.

[15] 'After this the Lord appointed seventy-two others and sent them on ahead of him, two by two, into every town and place where he himself was about to go. And he said to them, "The harvest is plentiful, but the labourers are few. Therefore pray earnestly to the Lord of the harvest to send

teaching of Diego of Osma, the Dominicans added Romans 10:15[16] to support their ideal of poor preachers; the Franciscans, on the other hand, preferred to cite Luke 9:3[17] and Matthew 19:21[18] and 16:24.[19]

The first three passages focus on the missionary aim behind preaching. They underline how mission *per se* is a necessary consequence, a sign of obedience to Christ's words, while defining the appropriate behaviour of the true preacher. The passage from St Paul's epistle to the Romans links the two actions, preaching and itinerancy, in a 'functional' relationship: 'how will they preach without being sent?' ('quomodo vero predicabunt nisi mittantur?'). According to St Paul, itinerancy is subordinate, although necessary, to the most important mandate of preaching.

For Franciscan preachers, the perspective is slightly different. Clearly, their focus is on passages which highlight poverty as a life option, the core of a believer's vocation. Poverty is considered to be of a piece with preaching and the 'imitation of Christ'. Here, itinerancy is merely an instrument to reach this perfect state of Christian life. A true believer is an itinerant, either because he or she imitates Christ, or because he or she imitates the apostles, or because as a follower of poverty he or she is a wanderer, a nomad despising the ordinary conventions of living in the world, as 'fools of God' should do.

The numerous preachers and wanderers travelling on the roads of medieval Europe, therefore, were referring back to this common textual patrimony, each group highlighting one or another aspect of the complex pattern of functions and aspects of the 'following of Christ' (*sequela Christi*). Heretics and reformers were among them.

---

out labourers into his harvest. Go your way; behold, I am sending you out as lambs in the midst of wolves. Carry no moneybag, no knapsack, no sandals, and greet no one on the road. Whatever house you enter, first say, 'Peace be to this house!' And if a son of peace is there, your peace will rest upon him. But if not, it will return to you. And remain in the same house, eating and drinking what they provide, for the labourer deserves his wages. Do not go from house to house. Whenever you enter a town and they receive you, eat what is set before you. Heal the sick in it and say to them, 'The kingdom of God has come near to you.' But whenever you enter a town and they do not receive you, go into its streets and say, 'even the dust of your town that clings to our feet we wipe off against you. Nevertheless know this, that the kingdom of God has come near.' I tell you, it will be more bearable on that day for Sodom that for that town.'' Luke 10:1–12.

[16] 'And how are they to preach unless they are sent? As it is written, "How beautiful are the feet of those who preach the good news!"' Romans 10:15.

[17] 'And he said to them, "Take nothing for your journey, no staff, nor bag, nor bread, nor money; and do not have two tunics."' Luke 9:3.

[18] 'Jesus said to him, "If you would be perfect, go, sell what you possess and give it to the poor, and you will have treasure in heaven; and come, follow me."' Matthew 19:21.

[19] 'Then Jesus told his disciples, "If anyone would come after me, let him deny himself and take up to his cross and follow me."' Matthew 16:24.

In what follows, our analysis will be limited to the Waldensians, Cathars and Pseudo-Apostles, touching only briefly upon other groups, such as the Humiliati. It is extremely difficult, in fact, to establish general features in their case, as the several Humiliati fraternities did not conform to a common institutional framework and textual patrimony. Although all of the chosen groups differ substantially from one other, within themselves they are sufficiently structured and alike to provide the basis for a good case-study.

SOURCES

When dealing with heresy, the hermeneutic approach to the available sources is *the* essential preliminary. That is to say, how are we to deal with these texts and with their vision of things? On the one side there are Catholic texts, driven by the attempt to justify their theoretical condemnation and practical persecution. Their aim is to codify and oppose any dissent, in some cases we might even say to 'construct' it in a textual form, and use it in a political perspective. On the other side there are sources derived from the heretics, whose aim is purely the definition of precepts, the codification of a *propositum vitae* [a form of life] and an identity for themselves. These are more oriented towards an active and practical goal. At the same time, however, we should not make our definitions too rigid. And we must be aware that – however indirectly – there is an underlying mechanism in operation by which any process of self-justification implies automatically some degree of self-definition, and vice versa. The different perspectives and biases within both kinds of texts should make us extremely cautious when seeking to define the issue of itinerancy in heretical groups. We must be aware of these limitations, and avoid taking the texts at face value.

The Catholics

The starting point for Catholic writers is an agreed definition of heretical behaviour. They depict the heretic as someone who preaches without licence, spending his life as a vagrant, in an uncontrolled and illegitimate condition of mobility. Such behaviour places the individual in a theoretically grey area, where lack of direction by a recognised religious structure immediately identifies potential danger. The sources also focus on the heretics' 'fake apostolicity': the assumed air of sanctity which derives from a deliberate intention to pervert the Gospel message, or from a dubious interpretation of the text, or even from simplicity of mind.[20]

In a study in 1979, Maria Corti discussed the reasons for the medieval condemnation of unlicensed wandering and placed the turning-point – once again – in the eleventh century.[21] Prior to this period, a ternary semantic model (also called 'trinitarian': the famous 'three orders' of those who fight, those who pray and those who work) still co-existed with a number of others. These could be dualist (such as laypeople/religious people), or hybrid (for example, the different status for believers: married, celibate, consecrated). From the eleventh century the ternary model prevailed: contemporary scholars set more rigid boundaries between its three worlds. A correspondence with the Holy Trinity, of which the model was an earthly reflection, made it exemplary and unique. From then on, what went beyond the model 'does not exist at a level of signs ... it lives at existential level as error, discord, an element that is negative and entropic (i.e. pluralising and centrifugal)'.[22] The meaning of the word *ordo* itself (as both the abstract result of 'ordering', 'putting in place', and 'order' as a congregation of people living together by rules) reflects this rigidity. The medieval, post-Gregorian reform mindset became static and inflexible. 'The healthy Christian ought to feel tied to his surroundings, his authentic *locus deputatus* in the divine model.'[23] Among the binary opposites generated by this semantic mechanism – opposites which cast light on our later discussion – are 'high/low', 'immobile/mobile', 'ordered/disordered', 'closed/open'. The last one is of particular interest here. The opposition between closed space (the cloister, the church) and open space (the square, the roads) contravened 'rigid spatial and modal oppositions', and generated the further one, 'immobile/mobile', from which stemmed the preachers' rejection of wanderers, 'all those who leave the place assigned by God for their dwelling, unless pilgrimage or the orders of a superior are involved'.[24] In this light the double meaning of the word 'mission' can be clarified with reference to the medieval obsession with authorisation. Only when considering its ambivalent significance as 'being sent' and 'the action of going to spread the word of salvation', can we understand the importance of authorisation. Wandering to spread the 'good tidings' was regarded as licit only

---

[20] Many examples are quoted in G. Gonnet, 'Le cheminement de Vaudois vers le schisme et l'hérésie (1174–1218)', *Cahiers de Civilisation Medievale* 19 (1976), 309–45, pp. 315–29 (about Waldensians' behaviour); Kienzle, 'Preaching as a touchstone', in several places.

[21] M. Corti, 'Models and antimodels in medieval culture', *New Literary History* 10/2 (1979), 339–66.

[22] Corti, 'Models and antimodels', p. 341.

[23] *Ibid.*

[24] Corti, 'Models and Antimodels', p. 348.

when stemming from the authority which sent, and thus gave meaning to, an action that otherwise would have transgressed the boundaries of the cultural models of reference.[25] Anti-heretical writers do not normally draw subtle distinctions between heretical groups, and they utilise a common repository of images to structure their accusations. Raoul Ardens, Eckbert of Schönau, Hugo of Rouen, Bernard of Clairvaux, Stephen of Bourbon, Geoffrey of Auxerre and Walter Map,[26] together with Durand of Huesca, Peter of Vaux-de Cernai, Ebrard of Béthune, Richard of Poitiers and Anselm of Alessandria all focus strongly on the false similarity to the apostles displayed by the dissenting groups; a falsity which, it is claimed, is demonstrated by their erroneous or simplistic doctrine, and by their disobedient behaviour.[27]

A powerful invective was launched against wandering preachers by Joachim of Fiore. In his work *De articulis fidei* Joachim condemns those who choose to follow their religious vocation outside a regular monastery, and defines them laconically as 'pseudo-monks, who are named wanderers and *sarabaite*'.[28] Joachim was particularly concerned (following the teaching of St Bernard of Clairvaux) about the lack of discipline and control of those monks who chose to seek their own personal fulfilment without submitting to the direction of an established institution.

Another well-known example is the description of the founder of the Pseudo-Apostles, Gerald Segarelli, by Salimbene of Adam, who wrote about him and his rise to popularity in Parma in the 1280s. Segarelli is accused by the Franciscan writer of 'going about the world as a pilgrim and a pauper'. Like their founder, his followers pervert the true apostolic ideal, hence the name given to them by their opponents, the Pseudo-Apostles. The Pseudo-Apostles allegedly mock the modes and

---

[25] See the thoughts in Kienzle, 'Preaching as a touchstone', pp. 25, 29–36; R. I. Moore *The Formation of a Persecuting Society: Power and Deviance in Western Europe* (Oxford, 1987), p. 140; B.M. Kienzle, 'Holiness and obedience: denouncement of twelfth-century Waldensian lay preaching', in Ferreiro, A. (ed.), *The Devil, Heresy and Witchcraft in the Middle Ages: Essays in Honor of J.B. Russell* (Leiden, 1998), pp. 259–78, esp. pp. 263–4.
[26] See Grundmann, *Religious Movements*, pp. 221–2 and ff.
[27] Scharff, 'Eterodossia come variante', pp. 49–50, 58–9.
[28] 'Pseudomonachi qui dicuntur girovagi et sarabaite' quoted in R. Manselli, 'Testimonianze minori sulle eresie: Gioacchino da Fiore di fronte a catari e valdesi, *Studi Medievali*, III ser., 18/2 (1977), 567–83, p. 572. 'Sarabaite' is used here to indicate monks who do not belong to any recognised rule, as described in Cassian's *Collatio* 18, ch. 7. This is reminiscent of Hamilton's description of hermits and others as 'indistinguishable from tramps' – see *Religion in the Medieval West*, (London, 1986), p. 117. The reference is to the first chapter of the Benedictine Rule, recording the description of the 'sarabaites' as those 'living in two's and three's, or even singly, without a shepherd, enclosed, not in the Lord's sheepfold, but in their own, the gratification of their desires is law unto them; because what they choose to do they call holy, but what they dislike they hold to be unlawful'.

meanings of being an apostle.[29] Angelo Clareno, one of the strongest
supporters of the purist line of behaviour in the Franciscan Order, the
Spiritual Franciscans, gave a sharp description of the followers of Dolcino
of Novara (preaching between 1300 and 1307). The Dolciniani were in
a direct line of descent from the Pseudo-Apostles. They lived in idleness
as though they were animals. 'They roam about without a destination;
they take their own, fallible will, their own *voluntas*, as the sole guide'.[30]
One modern scholar, Orioli, has talked about an obsession with potential
uncontrolled itinerancy which is shown by the authorities; they tried to
impose permanent employment as the appropriate penance for individuals belonging to this group in order to limit their missionary mobility,
rather than tackling their socially annoying and excessive begging.[31]

When describing the Pseudo-Apostles in his *Practica*, Bernard Gui was
highly concerned about two main features: they were irregular and they
did not submit to any rule. In particular their founder Segarelli 'established that the Order was named "order of the Apostles", who wandered
around the world like poor mendicants, living on alms, and preaching to
the people, everywhere'[32] ... 'At times they walked wearing soles, at other
times barefoot. They abandoned the usual behaviour of the faithful, both
in style of life and habits, and outwardly simulated a perfect and apostolic
life to their audiences by their clothing, gestures and evangelical doctrine,
and to the people by their rites'.[33]

---

[29] Salimbene de Adam, *Chronicle*, ed. J.L. Baird, G. Baglivi and J.R. Kane, ('Medieval and Renaissance
Texts and Studies' 40), (Binghamton, 1986), p. 269. Salimbene points out three reasons for them
being outside the 'state of salvation' ('status salvationis'): being disrespectful of authority, not
observing chastity and usurping the habit of the apostles (1208–27); and eight reasons for their
foolishness: not having a chief, wandering in the world on their own, being purposeless and
useless, lacking a discipline, lacking a proper religious instruction, wandering from house to
house, leaving their jobs and usurping the preaching vocation (1230–8). On the itinerancy of the
Pseudo-Apostles, see R. Orioli, *'Venit perfidus heresiarcha'. Il movimento apostolico-dolciniano dal 1260
al 1307* (Rome, 1988), pp. 169–87.

[30] Angelo Clareno, *Historia septem tribolationum ordinis minorum*, in F. Ehrle, 'Die Spiritualen, ihr
Verhältniss zum Franciscanerorden und zu den Fraticellen', *Archiv für Literatur und Kirchengeschichte
des Mittelalters* 2 (1886), p. 131, quoted in 'Controllo ed emarginazione della dissidenza religiosa',
in *Francescanesimo e vita religiosa dei laici nel '200, Atti del VII Convegno Internazionale (Assisi, 16–18
October 1980)*, (Assisi, 1981), pp. 367–88, pp. 385–6.

[31] Orioli, *Venit perfidus*, p. 171, where he quotes several examples taken from the trials recorded in the
Acta S. Officii Bononie; for further examples, see also the *Index* to the same work at p. 76 ('labor/
laborare'), 81 ('peregrinus ire per mundum'), 82 ('predicatio/predicare') and 88 ('vagabundus/
vagari').

[32] 'Instituit Apostolorum ordinem nominari qui per mundum discurrerent sicut pauperes mendi-
cantes et de elemosinis viventes et predicarent populis ubique', Bernard Gui, *Le Manuel*, p. 68.

[33] 'Aliquando utentes solis, aliquando nudis pedibus incedebant, a communi conversatione fidelium
vita et moribus dissidentes, vitam perfectam et apostolicam in se ipsis exterius tali habitu tali gestu
et doctrinam evangelicam auditoribus tali ritu populis simulabant.' *Ibid.*, pp. 68–9.

Walter Map gives us a subtler and more precise description, this time of the Waldensian brothers and sisters. 'They have no fixed habitations. They go about two by two, barefoot, clad in woollen garments, owning nothing, holding all things in common like the apostles, naked, following a naked Christ.'[34] Gui provides further information on the Waldensian brothers, describing their missionary organisation during the general 'chapters'. 'And during those chapters, he who is the greatest of all ordains and arranges with regard to priests and deacons: how they are to be sent to different parts and regions to their believers and friends in order to listen to confessions and collect alms; and he hears and receives the reckoning of collections and expenses.'[35] Gui displays, as ever, sharp observation in highlighting the strong link between itinerancy, administration of the sacraments and financial organisation. Then, he moves on to report on the Waldensians' own self-description: 'They call themselves successors of the apostles, and act as teachers and confessors to others, and go about the territories visiting and confirming their disciples in error ... Also, they carry out their preaching in the houses of their believers, as is discussed above, or sometimes while travelling, or in the streets.'[36]

As Brian Stock noted, talking specifically of this group, Catholic controversialists were writing for an audience who could make appropriate sense of an 'already contextualised set of previous thoughts and actions'.[37] In other words, by criticising habits and misdeeds of Waldensian brothers and sisters, they could utilise a patrimony of standard accusations, shaped at an earlier time – again, the time of the Gregorian reform – which, in the eyes of a reader, would immediately recall the unlicensed, illegitimate behaviour of heretics. The Waldensians were not chosen by Stock at random. They embodied well his idea of 'textual communities', as 'types of micro-societies organised around the common understanding of a text ... not entirely composed of literates. The minimum requirement

---

[34] 'Hii certa nusquam habent domicilia, bini et bini circueunt nudipedes, laneis induti, nihil habentes, omni sibi communia tanquam apostoli, nudi nudum Christum sequentes', *De nugis curialium*, in G. Gonnet (ed.), *Enchiridion fontium Valdensium* (Torre Pellice, 1958), pp. 122–4, p. 123; Wakefield and Evans, p. 204.

[35] 'Et in illis capitulis maior omnium ordinat et disponit de presbiteris et dyachonibus et de mittendis ad diversas partes et regiones ad credentes et amicos suos pro confessionibus audiendis et elemosinis colligendis et audit et recepit rationem de collectis et de expensis factis', *Ibid.*, pp. 50–2.

[36] 'Hii dicunt se esse apostolorum successores et sunt magistri aliorum et confessores et circumeunt per terras visitando et confirmando discipulos in errore ... Item, predicationem suam faciunt in domibus credentium suorum, sicut pretactum est supra, aliquando in itinere seu in via', *Ibid.*, pp. 61–2.

[37] B. Stock, 'History, literature and medieval textuality', *Yale French Studies* 70 (1986), 7–17, pp. 15–16.

was just one literate, the *interpres*, who understood a set of texts and was able to pass this message on verbally to others.'[38]

The chief and most dangerous trait of these heretical groups, according to Catholic polemicists, is their habit of wandering as vagrants without the strong support of a profound knowledge and correct interpretation of the Scriptures. They claim to have freely chosen this lifestyle, because it allows freedom from excessive rules, but as such it inevitably leads to a complete lack of organisation and planning. The image depicted by these Catholic sources is one of a 'conscious vagrant'; his fault lies in his misinterpretation of the Gospel message. The response of the Church authorities is shaped by this stereotypical image. The Bolognese *Acta Sancti Officii* offer a clear example of determination to punish individual dissenters' dangerous itinerancy. The sentences pronounced by Bolognese inquisitors frequently state that Pseudo-Apostles 'ought not to wander around in the world, or to quit the city of Bologna or its district'.[39]

Gui was a fine psychologist, always sharp in discerning between subtleties: other inquisitorial writers do not display the same understanding of the problem of itinerancy related to heretical behaviour. Nearly all manuals are silent about this issue. The 1255 *consilium* by Gui Foulques, one of the most popular didactic texts and included in most inquisitorial manuals, makes explicit reference to those who move around in order to escape punishment or trial, connecting movement not so much with the doctrine and ideal of 'truly apostolic life', as with inquisitorial practice and fugitives. For him it is a problem of a judicial nature, rather than one of doctrine. In pointing out this aspect, Foulques shows how the identification between 'truly apostolic life' and obedience to the Church authorities is already in place. Although it is evident that the mental association between movement and danger is not completely clear in Foulques' mind – he suggests pilgrimage as a possible punishment – the insistence on imprisonment as a possible penance is justified 'not so much as a penalty for the crime, but as a prevention, lest they [the heretics] taint or contaminate others'.[40]

The *propositum vitae* of the so-called Poor Catholics of 1208, touches upon the issue of itinerancy, making it part of the fraternity's recommended lifestyle. It is particularly suggestive, as the Poor Catholics began

---

[38] Stock, 'History, literature', p. 12; see also G. Audisio, *The Waldensian Dissent; Persecution and Survival c. 1170–c. 1570*, (Cambridge, 1999), p. 11.

[39] 'Item quod non debeat vagari per mundum nec egredi civitatem Bononie nec districtu', *Acta Sancti Officii Bononie*, pp. 317, 369, and ff.

[40] '[Et carceris illa reclusio] non est tam ad penam criminis quam ad cautelam ne noceant, ne alios inficiant,' Gui Folques, *Consultatio*, in Lomastro Tognato, *L'eresia a Vicenza*, p. 200 – Carena (ed.), p. 474.

as a recognised, legitimate order professing poverty, and its very institution marked conscious distancing between itself and the now illegitimate Waldensians, their former confrères. The *propositum* states that 'If a layperson wishes to conform to our suggestions, we recommend that, other than those suitable for preaching and disputing with the heretics, the rest should remain in the[ir] houses, leading a religious and well-ordered life, distributing their own goods with justice and mercy, and working with their hands.'[41]

The clear prescription of a life led 'in houses', 'religious' but also 'well-ordered' makes specific sense within our perspective. It is an orthodox response to the existing worries about new religious groupings. The Poor Catholics can in fact be considered as a reactionary movement, set up to counteract heterodox groups, and for this purpose designed with the very features the heretics did not have. It is papal anti-heretical policy that is being affirmed in the Poor Catholics' *propositum vite*.

The same pattern can be seen at a later date in the rules for the Parmesan 'Militia of the Virgin', which in 1261 stipulated for novices: 'That nobody goes without a brother as companion or a religious person of that order, nor presumes to go from place to place or suddenly leaves his monastery in any way without the licence of the prior.'[42]

Behind the general uniformity in accusations and regulations, however, some signs of differentiation appear in the anti-heretical sources themselves. The slight variations introduced by some authors become extremely significant, precisely because they are variations within generally agreed stereotypes. Eberwin of Steinfeld, writing around 1143–4, says the following: 'Of themselves, they say. "We, the poor of Christ, who have no fixed abode, and flee from city to city like sheep amidst wolves, are persecuted as were the apostles and the martyrs".'[43] Eberwin is here referring to the heretics of Cologne, probably Cathars, and does so particularly accurately – as we shall see later – highlighting their view of incessant persecution as forcing mobility upon them. What we have here are not vagrant heretics, not mere rebels of no fixed abode, rather they

---

[41] 'Si quis vero secularium in nostro voluerit consilio permanere consulimus, ut exceptis idoneis ad exhortandum et contra hereticos disputandum, ceteri in domibus [suis] religiose et ordinate vivendo permaneant, res suas in iustitia et misericordia dispensando, manibus laborando', G.G. Meersemann *Dossier de l'ordre de la Pénitence au XIIIe siècle*, ('Spicilegium Friburgense' 7), (Fribourg, 1961), pp. 282–4. Also quoted in Rusconi, 'Forma apostolorum', pp. 250–1.

[42] 'Non vadat aliquis sine socio fratre vel religiosa persona, videlicet ipsius ordinis, de loco ad locum neque sponte a monasterii sui absque licentia sui prioris egredi quoquo modo presumat', in Meersemann, *Dossier*, p. 296, ch. 'De vita fratrum in conventibus commorantium'.

[43] 'De se dicunt: nos pauperes Christi, instabiles, de civitate in civitatem fugientes, sicut oves in medio luporum, cum apostolis et martyribus persecutionem patimur', Eberwin of Steinfeld, *Letter CDLXXII*, PL 182, cols. 67–78; Wakefield and Evans, p. 129.

are fugitives persecuted as the apostles and the martyrs were, and, just like the apostles and martyrs, the holders of the Truth. It is the reverse of our heretical stereotype. The *topos* of the 'fugitive heretic', a negative image of someone moving from place to place at night, and preaching in hidden places ('in latibulis'), is turned round. Cathars suffer persecution in exactly the same way as the Christian martyrs had before them. Their condition becomes legitimate, the condition of the martyrs; they are confronting an illegitimate power which seeks to crush a legitimate creed with violence. Their situation forces them into a hidden life, one without certainty and fixed residence.

The *Liber Suprastella* was an anti-heretical treatise written in 1235 and mainly addressed to the two Cathar churches of the Concorezzenses and Albanenses, which were separated by doctrinal issues and by differing interpretations of the Scriptures. Its author, the lay notary Salvo Burci, recounts that 'for this reason, so that they should be brought back to a single creed, they wasted very many resources by travelling to many different places, wandering here and there on the face of the earth'.[44] It is a particularly interesting description, as it presents a third kind of itinerancy. Here the wandering heretic becomes someone who tries to manage and solve problems internal to his own congregation by means of travelling. No longer a persecuted lamb, or a dangerous individual, according to this passage the traveller is someone who attempts to manage internal issues by resolving a schism within his own church, and he does so by moving from one community to another, perhaps to organise meetings or carry messages and gifts. This traveller spends large sums of money, 'temporal goods', driven by his church's needs, presumably embarking on trips organised by the hierarchy as part of a broader political strategy. It is a picture which matches the image of the 'living church', as outlined in the previous chapter. Later on the *Liber Suprastella* shifts back to the stereotypical image of the preaching heretic, lacking any rule or residence. 'It is a habit of the heretic to scurry here and there "blaspheming", that is preaching. He should be handed to Satan, that is put in prison ... so that he learns not to blaspheme, that is so that he cannot go hither and thither preaching to the people, or "blaspheming"!'[45]

---

[44] 'Et propter hoc, ut reducerentur ad unam fidem, multum de temporalibus rebus consumpserunt in diversis et multis itineribus euntes, huc atque illuc vagantes per orbem terrarum', C. Bruschi (ed.), Salvus Burcius, *Liber Suprastella*, ('Fonti per la storia dell'Italia Medievale – Antiquitates' 15), (Rome, 2002), p. 5.

[45] 'Consuetudo est erretici quod discurit huc atque illuc blasphemando, id est predicando: detur ergo Sathane, id est ponatur in carcere, sicut predixi de Catholico, ut discat non blasphemare, hoc est ut non possit ire huc atque illuc predicando populum vel blasphemando', *Ibid.*, p. 275.

The cases of Robert of Arbrissel, Norbert of Xanten, Henry of Lausanne, Arnold of Brescia, Bernard of Tiron and Vidal of Savigny have been presented as examples of the intensity of the controversy and debate generated in this period by the issues of itinerancy and wandering preaching.[46] Papal policy veered between pastoral encouragement (as in the case of Robert of Arbrissel, for example) and excommunication, struggling to settle upon theoretical and, consequently, judicial limits for wandering preachers.[47] On the one hand the ideal types portrayed by the saints' lives stress the cathartic passage from an eremitical life in the woods, led in solitude among uncivilised people, and the saint's response to God's call through founding a regular community, where 'regularity' identifies the core of the mission. Bernard of Tiron 'with great purity of life, was ruling regularly and wisely the monastery entrusted to him' ('In magna puritate vite, monasterium sibi commissum sapienter ac regulariter gubernabat'). Similarly, Robert of Arbrissel gathers and rules over 'those regulars, who worked incessantly to live regularly [= according to a Rule], in the way of the primitive church' ('illi, regulares, qui more primitive ecclesie vivere satagebant regulariter').[48] Civilisation over wilderness, organisation over freedom and safety over a life of risk and poverty. Yet, on the other hand, writers and their readership – presumably their respective monastic communities – do not draw such a clear-cut distinction. In the lives of Robert of Arbrissel and Bernard of Tiron the eremitical phase is rather seen as a preparation for a more perfect stage, where the saint, made stronger by a period of prayer and reflection, is now ready to carry the burden of heavier responsibilities when founding and leading the newly constituted community. This is a sort of evangelical preparation that somehow recalls the forty days spent by Jesus in the desert, prior to the Passion. Where – as in the case of Robert of Arbrissel – the saint is seen leaving his community to preach and travel all over the world, this is done after the constitution of the 'regular' monastery, at the express invitation by the pope, in an attempt to civilise new regions and peoples, and with the support of existing religious institutions.[49]

To sum up, Catholic controversialists and writers present (heretical) itinerancy as a distinctive characteristic of these dissenting groups. It is strictly dependent on their preaching activities and on the ideal of imitation of the apostles and therefore – from a Catholic point of view – on

---

[46] Pasztor, '*Predicazione itinerante*': on Robert of Arbrissel, see PL 162, cols. 1017–57; for Vidal of Savigny, see the *Vita* by Stephen of Fougères published by E.P. Sauvage (ed.) *Analecta Bollandiana* 1 (1882), 357–90; for Bernard of Tiron, PL 172, cols. 1363–446.
[47] See Manteuffel, *Naissance d'une hérésie*, pp. 31–46.
[48] PL 162, col. 1396.
[49] PL 162, cols. 1050D–1051C.

the perversion of a role model. All of these characteristics feature in the Catholic accusations of vagrancy, non-conformity to orthodox rules and structures, and irregular preaching: essentially, accusations of irregularity and lack of organisation.

The heretics

Very different is the rival perspective, that of the dissenting individuals and groups. As said before, there is obviously one point of origin, the strong conviction that theirs was the correct interpretation of the Scriptures and of Christian practice.

To start with, let us consider one fraternity – later a recognised Order – for which preaching and itinerancy were the bone of contention, and constituted grounds for temporary exclusion from the official Church: the Humiliati. There is no mention whatsoever of preaching or itinerancy in the Humiliati *proposita*. This silence is telling. In 1184 Pope Lucius III, in his decretal *Ad abolendam*, had specifically condemned the Humiliati for their refusal to accept an ecclesiastical authority's control over their preaching. It would have been surprising if the Order had wanted to dwell, within the renewed 'programme of life', on the issue that had led to them being accused of heterodoxy. Understandably, the reconstruction of the Order focused instead on the Humiliati's lifestyle as being ordered, legitimate and in accordance with the Gospels.[50] There was no mention of preaching. Instead, a whole chapter was devoted to the modes and principles of silence (*Omnis boni principium*, ch. XXV – *De silentio*[51]). There was also consistent insistence on the Rule of St Benedict as a well-structured and rigid code of practice for all communities, and upon discipline (chs. XXIV, XXXV, XXXVII[52]) and exterior signs of conformity (such as the times and modes for prayer, and type of clothing).

---

[50] On the centrality of the Rule within the Humiliati's new programme, see D. Castagnetti, 'La regola del primo e secondo ordine dall'approvazione alla "Regula Benedicti"', in M.P. Alberzoni, A. Ambrosioni, and A. Lucioni (eds.), *Sulle tracce degli Umiliati*, ('Bibliotheca Erudita. Studi e documenti di storia e filologia' 13), (Milan, 1997), pp. 163–250; on the problems regarding the Rule in a longer perspective, see C. Bruschi, 'La memoria dall'eresia alla riammissione. Le cronache quattrocentesche degli Umiliati', *Mélanges de l'École Française de Rome* 115 (2003), vol. I, pp. 325–40; on the beginning of the order, see M.P. Alberzoni, 'San Bernardo e gli Umiliati', in P. Zerbi, *San Bernardo e l'Italia, Atti del Convegno di Studi (Milan, 24–26 May 1990)* (Milan, 1993), pp. 101–29; M.P. Alberzoni, 'Gli inizi degli Umiliati: una riconsiderazione', in *La conversione alla povertà nell'Italia dei secoli XII–XIV, Atti del XXVII Convegno Storico Internazionale, (Todi, 14–17 October 1990)*, (Spoleto, 1991), pp. 187–237; F. Andrews, *The Early Humiliati* (Cambridge, 1998), pp. 38–63, 99–135.

[51] In Zanoni, *Gli Umiliati*, p. 362. The role of silence in Cluniac and Cistercian spirituality has been recently enquired by S.G. Bruce, *Silence and Sign Language in Medieval Monasticism: The Cluniac Tradition, c. 900–1200*, (Cambridge, 2007).

[52] Zanoni, *Gli Umiliati*, pp. 365–6.

The political strategy of re-integration into the body of Christianity set by the Humiliati hierarchy highlighted what the authorities wanted to hear from them: a declaration of good will, of the existence of a solid internal structure, of conformity to approved role models and papal policy. While the Rule of the Humiliati devotes only a couple of lines to outdoor activities, and derives them (yet again) from the authority of the Benedictine rule (ch. XXXII – *De fratribus in via dirigendis*[53]), other documents – still official ones, such as private transactions concerning land and goods, records of commercial partnerships and money transfers – reveal a pattern of constant itinerancy, both 'internal' (between houses) and 'external' (in relation to private or public lay partnerships). Such movement was mainly dictated by individual communities' business affairs and organisation, and responded to the demands for frequent and steady cooperation with existing lay bodies, such as the communes, private enterprises and guilds.[54]

Although they are of differing natures, both the Order's private acts and the *proposita* (the Order's Rule) are official documents. The latter, however, can be seen as producing a 'life plan' for the renewed order, a public declaration of integrity and conformity. As we have seen, itinerancy had constituted for the Humiliati the essence of their disobedience, the original reason for excommunication and de-legitimisation of the whole community which (even if only for a brief span of time) had had for this reason to bear the infamy of heresy. Nevertheless, it is obvious that none of the condemned activities were ever halted. The Order was reintegrated into the body of the Church by Innocent III in 1201. There is evidence of a shifting of the Humiliati's preaching vocation into renewed anti-heretical activity, begun as early as 1211.[55] Equally, as has been noted, the vigorous mobility of the Orders' members emerges from the private records. It followed from internal, organisational needs, and was closely linked with the Order's 'open' aspect, which put it in direct contact with the communal environment.

The silence of Cathar sources on itinerancy is quite different. What is left of the original *corpus* of their texts refers only indirectly to itinerancy.

---

[53] *Ibid.*, p. 364. The chapter is the shortest one, and states, 'If the brothers who are on the road wish to come back on the very day in which they left, they should not dare to eat out, unless allowed to them by the prelate' ('Directi in via fratres, si ea die qua exeunt redire sperant, non presumant foris manducare, nisi forte a prelato his concedatur').

[54] The examples are many. A particularly interesting case, especially for the links between houses of different regions, is the one of Bologna: I. Francica, 'Gli Umiliati a Bologna nel '200: forme e significati di una "religio attiva" ', *Atti e Memorie della Deputazione di Storia Patria per le Province di Romagna* 45 (1994), 271–93.

[55] See Castagnetti, 'La regola del primo e secondo ordine', pp. 183–4.

However, as we have already seen, travelling was one of the most common activities for both high clergy and ordinary believers. Yet Cathar theoretical aims (the very foundation of their ecclesiastical structure), as outlined in the *Gleisa de Dio*, include only marginal references to this issue.

The theological starting point, in Cathar belief, is the insignificance of any physical structure for the True Church. Together with icons and statues and all material artefacts, a physical structure is the work of the Other, the evil principle, Satan. From this theoretical standpoint stems the idea of a Church which has to be 'the assembly of the faithful and of holy men'.[56] Because it is divorced from any physical meeting place, this Church and its members can completely and satisfactorily fulfil the evangelical precepts of Matthew 28:19[57] and Mark 16:15–16.[58] The *Gleisa de Dio* goes further. It is the very lack of a physical location *per se* which creates the necessary conditions to put Cathar theoretical precepts into practice.'But the Church of Christ could not do all these things if it were a house of the sort men call a "church", for such houses cannot walk, or hear, or speak.'[59]

It is clear from this text that to 'walk', 'listen' and 'talk' are perceived as fundamental elements and duties in a Cathar's activity and lifestyle. The sources, however, do not dwell extensively and directly on them. They focus instead on the extreme importance of the 'sacraments' and their administration (the remission of sins through ritual prayer in chapter II, and the administration of spiritual baptism in chapter XI).[60] Sacraments must be performed by the higher clergy, and it is crucial that they are consistently administered in the extensive area of influence of the Cathar churches.

Such priority demonstrates the Cathar interpretation of the 'imitation of the apostles'. Of course, drawing one's inspiration from the followers of Christ meant to go and preach, but in Cathar theology it meant even

---

[56] 'Aquesta sancta gleisa es ajostament de fidels e de saint homes' *Gleisa de Dio*, Venckeleer (ed.), p. 820; Wakefield and Evans, p. 596.

[57] 'Go therefore and make disciples of all nations, baptizing them in the name of the Father and of the Son and of the Holy Spirit', Matthew 28:19.

[58] 'And he said to them, "Go into all the world and proclaim the gospel to the whole creation. Whoever believes and is baptized will be saved, but whoever does not believe will be condemned" ', Mark 16:15–16.

[59] 'Mas totas aquestas cosas no poiria far la gleisa de Christ si ela fos aital maison com la gent apelan gleisa: car aquelas tals maisos no podon andar, ni aovir, ni parlar' *Gleisa de Dio*, Venckeleer (ed.), p. 821; Wakefield and Evans, p. 587.

[60] I shall perform a little 'catholicisation' of terms, here, and call the principal Cathar rites 'sacraments', though this was not, of course, the Cathars' term for them, and I sometimes use the word 'baptism' for the Cathar *consolamentum*. For an account of terminology, see Duvernoy, *Religion*, pp. 151–2.

more the duty of administering the essential sacraments to all believers. According to dualistic doctrine, only a few rituals were to be performed: the *melioramentum*, that is, the prayer by intercession of the 'clergy'; the breaking of blessed bread; the imposition of hands – *consolamentum* – celebrated on a believer's deathbed; and the *servitium*, or *apparellamentum*, the monthly rite of confession of sins to the deacon, reserved for the 'clergy'.[61] In the *Gleisa de Dio* the citation of Matthew 28:19 and Mark 16:15–16 appears in the chapter on baptism, and is merely incidental to the discussion of this rite. The same stance appears in the *Occitan Ritual*. The *Latin Ritual* comments that 'the disciples of Jesus Christ left and stood with the Lord Jesus Christ, and they received from Him the authority to baptise and to forgive sins, in the same way as today do true Christians, who, as heirs of the disciples, in due order received from the Church of God the power actually to perform this baptism of the laying-on of hands and to forgive sins'.[62]

Trials of Waldensian brothers, theological polemics against Waldensians and a handful of texts written by and for Waldensians, among them sermons, refer to the necessity of travel in line with the apostles and their mission. Biller has analysed a large number of Waldensian depositions from France, Italy and the Germanophone area of Europe, and concluded that 'the [inquisitor's] question produced half-memories of sermons by the Waldensian brothers in which they presented their apostolic mission, following Christ's instruction to the apostles to preach *in universum mundum*'.[63] The Waldensians, more than other groups, found their own textual identity in the precept 'go and preach'. So much so that, when confronted by the ecclesiastical authorities over the legitimacy of their mission and consequent vagrancy, they preferred to stick to their apostolic vocation and to 'obey God rather than men', thus incurring papal condemnation and the label of heretics.[64]

Apart from the conscious reference to an apostolic genesis, even in their case we find a significant silence. There is no mention of itinerancy in Valdes's *Profession of Faith*, which does not even mention preaching, nor in the 'minutes' of the 1218 meeting at Bergamo, where French and

---

[61] See Lambert, *The Cathars*, pp. 141–2.

[62] *Latin Ritual*, in A. Dondaine (ed.), *Un traité manichéen du XIIIe siècle, le 'Liber de duobus principiis' suivi d'un fragment de rituel cathare* (Rome, 1939), pp. 64–78, p. 159; Wakefield and Evans, p. 477 (here the translation is 'went forth and stood').

[63] P. Biller, 'Heretics and Long Journeys', in *Freedom of Movement in the Middle Ages: Proceedings of the 2003 Harlaxton Conference*, ed. P. Horden, Harlaxton Medieval Studies 15 (Donnington, 2007), pp. 86–103, p. 9 of the typescript.

[64] See Scharff, 'Eterodossia come variante', pp. 44–5; Audisio, *The Waldensian Dissent*, pp. 143–55; Lambert, *Medieval Heresy*, pp. 74–5, 80–2.

Italian Waldensians debated contentious doctrinal issues, such as marriage, baptism, oaths and their hierarchy.[65] As in the case of the Humiliati, preaching and apostolic movement were issues of contention with the Catholic Church, issues upon which Waldensians were not prepared to compromise. The *Profession* deliberately highlighted areas of common ground with the Church, rather than stressing differences. The text quotes dogmas, sacraments (baptism, confirmation, marriage, communion and ordination), hierarchy (episcopate and priesthood) and pious practices (alms and prayer). It ends with the proposal for a lifestyle of poverty and obedience, all in accordance with the existing precepts and creeds of the Roman Church.[66]

The programmatic texts of Valdes and his followers, therefore, avoid the contentious issue of itinerancy which lay at the heart of the accusation of heterodoxy levelled by Catholic writers. Many learned Catholic controversialists wrote about Waldensian itinerancy[67] and they were inevitably prone to stereotyping their opponents. Another interesting source adds to our picture of the itinerant preachers, the anonymous *De vita et actibus* (thirteenth century), at the point where it deals with their general chapters. 'Item, the chapter appoints and deputes visitors of their friends and believers, who have to visit that year, and two are sent into each region or province in which some of their creed live.'[68] And again, talking about their congregations, 'Up to now, they do not have great gatherings. But they visit the said believers from hospice to hospice, that is to say, whomsoever in their hospices, and there, in each hospice they stay for two or three or four days, sometimes for more, sometimes for less.'[69] This text is interesting in that it goes beyond making the equation 'itinerancy = heresy'. It is a description of the Waldensians' system of pastoral care, which is based on Catholic practices. However, it provides

---

[65] Edited in Gonnet (ed.), *Enchiridion*, pp. 169–83.

[66] A. Dondaine (ed.), *Profession of faith of Valdes*, in 'Aux origines du Valdeisme. Une profession de foix de Valdès', *Archivum Fratrum Praedicatorum* XVI (1946), 191–235 [repr. in A. Dondaine, *Les hérésies et l'Inquisition XII–XIII siècles*, Variorum Collected Studies 314, (Aldershot, 1990), V, pp. 191–235]. This is the opinion of E. Cameron, for whom 'The confession tells us more about the worries of the prelates, and about the essential orthodoxy of Valdesius and his followers, than it does about any distinctive beliefs they may have had' (*Waldenses: Rejections of Holy Church in Medieval Europe* (Oxford, 2000), p. 19; also Audisio, *The Waldensian Dissent*, pp. 14–15.

[67] Survey in Gonnet, 'Le cheminement de Vaudois'.

[68] 'Item, in dicto capitulo deputantur et constituuntur visitatores amicorum suorum et credencium qui visitare debeant illo anno, et mittuntur duo in qualibet regione seu provincia in qua aliqui de eorum credencia conversantur.' *De vita et actibus*, in P. Biller, 'Fingerprinting an anonymous description of the Waldensians', in *Texts and the repression of Medieval Heresy*, pp. 163–207, esp. pp. 202–3.

[69] 'Non faciunt quoad presens congregaciones magnas, sed dictos credentes visitant de hospicio in hospicium, videlicet quoslibet in hospiciis eorundem et ibi in quolibet hospicio manent per duos vel tres vel quatuor dies, aliquociens plus, aliquociens minus.' *Ibid.*, pp. 204–5.

an account of a different kind of mobility, comparable to that of our Languedocian Cathars. The anonymous writer was describing what usually happened, with the simple purpose of noting which features could help in the identification of Waldensians. There is no apologetic agenda behind this description, nor is it a series of standard accusations. Rather, it is a neutral depiction. And it confirms our view of highly mobile structures and communities, for which travel did not simply mean imitation of the apostles, but also – more practically – management of clusters of brethren. It was a means of exerting some sort of control over them, and of fulfilling pastoral duties.

Humbert of Romans

An interesting and unusual insight into the issue of itinerancy is provided in the writings of Humbert of Romans.[70] He was Dominican Master General for a decade (1254–64), and in his encyclical letters to the members of the Order[71] he focused insistently on this theme. He urged his brothers to become missionaries, spreading and defending the Word and the memory of Christ among the people. His exhortations are particularly revealing if read within the specific context of Dominican inquisitorial history and the textual development of its procedure. It was in these years that the Dominican inquisition returned to Languedoc, after the 'crisis' of the period 1249–55, when southern French tribunals were run by local officials. The proliferation of manuals and *consilia* reached a climax between 1243 and the end of the 1250s. Inevitably, the views of Humbert of Romans proved crucial for a definition and perception of itinerancy which was at once up-to-date and prescriptive for his Order and the inquisition. The officials were Dominicans before they were inquisitors, and the words of their Master General must have been very influential, shaping at least their personal opinions on the matter, if nothing else. Because Humbert's words were directed at Dominicans and dealt with Dominican itinerancy, they provide a view of itinerancy that is for once free of any concern with orthodoxy versus unorthodoxy.

Let us look at his comments in detail. One of his first letters, sent from Milan in 1255, is a powerful exhortation to his Dominican brothers to volunteer for missions far from their homeland. The need to convert various peoples – 'the schismatics, the Saracens, the pagan idolaters,

---

[70] I owe thanks to Saverio Amadori for suggesting this connection to me.
[71] B.M. Reichert (ed.), *Litterae Encyclicae Magistrorum Generalium ordinis Praedicatorum ab anno 1233 usque ad annum 1376* (Rome, 1900), pp. 15–63.

barbarians and all the peoples' ('scismatici, Sarraceni, pagani ydolatri, barbari et universe gentes') – requires a body of brave and daring friars, who were not necessarily available in Dominican houses and convents. According to Humbert, this lack of volunteers, which undermines the feasibility of a 'strategy of movement', is a result of two factors that were clearly visible and worrying in Dominican communities.

One reason is the lack of languages: it is very rare for any friar to want to devote himself to learning, and many of them put curiosity in several things ahead of utility in their studies. The other reason is love for their native soil, whose sweetness has entangled many of them to such an extent – their nature not having been transformed yet through the action of divine grace – that they do not want to leave their land or kinfolk, or forget their own people. Rather, they want to live and die among their relatives and those known to them, and they do not fear that even the Saviour could not have been discovered by his own mother, were he to do as they do.[72]

Humbert does not mince his words. His attack is clear and direct, while at the same time paternal and understanding. His approach brings to the fore a hidden attitude towards monastic itinerancy. According to Humbert most Dominicans – whose role models are and should be the apostles – had put intellectual activities, or rather their personal intellectual development, before their preaching, their duty to the Order. To be a full-time preacher, in fact, meant being prepared for an uncomfortable estrangement from one's homeland, as well as the drain of intellectual energy needed for learning foreign languages, a necessary feature of foreign missions. Humbert heard his brothers calling these obstacles 'heavy' ('gravia'), and although he recognised their weight, he was convinced that they had to be overcome in the name of the Order's particular vocation. 'Woe betide us, if we wish to be preachers and then deviate from the characteristics of a preacher's life!'[73] A good Dominican must be prepared to learn all languages, to leave his own country, to suffer every kind of persecution 'for the Order, for his own faith, even for the salvation of souls and in the name of our Lord Jesus Christ'.[74]

---

[72] 'Unum est defectus linguarum, quibus addiscendis vix ullus frater vult vacare, multis curiositatem multimodam utilitati preponentibus in studendo. Aliud est amor soli natalis, cuius dulcedo sic multos illaqueavit, natura nondum in eis per graciam transformata, quod de terra et cognacione sua nolunt egredi nec oblivisci populum suum, sed vivere volunt et mori inter cognatos et notos suos, non expavescentes, quod inter huiusmodi salvator, eciam a matre propria non potuit inveniri.' *Ibid.*, p. 19.

[73] 'Ve nobis, si predicatores esse volumus et a talium praedicatorum vestigiis deviare.' *Ibid.*

[74] 'Pro ordine, pro fide, pro animarum eciam salute et propter nomen domini nostri Ihesu Christi.' *Ibid.*

One striking feature emerges from this letter: a clear polarisation of Dominicans – the Preachers *par excellence*[75] – and heretics/reformers. Imitation of the apostles through missionary travelling, which was the banner of the latter (and at the same time the measure of their heterodoxy in the eyes of the Roman Church) did not exert the same kind of attraction for the former. Yet the Dominicans were called specifically to fight heresy throughout the Christian world, both by ideological vocation and by the specific character of their Order. These defenders of Roman orthodoxy, however, seem to struggle to fight their adversaries on their adversaries' level. Most surprisingly, we are not dealing here with a time of decadence, but with the high point of the Dominican monopoly over the inquisition in Languedoc, when the inquisitorial structure was already firmly structured, heavily engaged on several fronts (the local tribunals), and almost completely run by the Order.

Clearly, this insight into the life of the Order highlights a crucial issue in the Order's life and management. In the following year (1256) Humbert, writing from Paris, insists on it again, but from a different perspective.

O, how much your charity would rejoice with me over the holy fervour of our brothers, if you knew how many of them, from assorted provinces, offered themselves with most fervent desire to the hardships of this task, even despising the fear of death! Also, we should not despair of some improvement even in those who are seduced by various errors, for they are already showing copious fruits. Certainly those brothers who are working in various provinces to root out heretical depravity have given benefit and are giving benefit. And they do this so fervently that only a little ago it would have seemed incredible. God has in fact freely worked in them over the last two years ago and more.[76]

Humbert then points out that the foreign missions here referred to obtained visible results among the Cumans, Maronites, Tartars, Georgians, Saracens and Prussians. Surprisingly, no explicit reference is made to dualist heretics, at a time when, as we have noted, the Dominican inquisition was at its peak.

Humbert then goes on to address his order. 'Do not worry if you should hear that in the meantime somewhere our brothers are suffering

---

[75] 'Dominicans' was a later term for friars whose name in our period was *Praedicatores*, Preachers.

[76] 'O quantum vestra caritas una mecum gauderet super fratrum sancto fervore, si sciretis quot et quantis de diversis provinciis ad labores huiusmodi ardentissimo desiderio se obtulerunt, mortis eciam pavore contempto! Neque eciam desperandum est de profectu in hiis, qui variis seducuntur erroribus, cum fructus plurimus iam in eis appareat manifeste. Profecerunt siquidem et proficiunt fratres, qui laborant in diversis provinciis ad extirpacionem heretice pravitatis, in tantum ut paulo ante incredibile videbatur id posse fieri, quod per eos iam dominus dignatus est operari a duobus annis et citra.' *Ibid.*, p. 40.

tribulations. You in fact know well that through such things an opportunity to display greater virtue is offered, and that we are put in this situation if we wish to be disciples of the Saviour.'[77] 'New persecutions' ('persecutiones nove') and 'unknown tribulations' ('tribulationes inconsuete') appear again in a letter of the following year. Persecutions and tribulations are called by Humbert 'statements of apostolicity and evangelical promises; they are here the oracles of the prophets and the examples of all the saints' ('asserciones apostolice et evangelice promissiones; hec sunt plane oracula prophetarum et omnium exempla sanctorum'), and – he concludes – 'the faithful had to pass through many tribulations'.[78]

The testimony of Humbert of Romans is important, yet at the same time difficult to measure and understand. Let us return to the main points made so far. We have seen that Catholic sources depict undisciplined itinerancy as the cause of havoc, subversion and irregularity. In contrast, heterodox sources show it as either a free choice or a forced one. In both cases, however, it is an essential feature of the reformist groups which want to return to the Gospels, or to the apostles, or which simply aim to oppose and keep at a distance from the established authorities. All things considered, itinerancy is a positive feature for heretical writers and believers.

What about Humbert of Romans? His letters stem from the same ideological assumption, that is the notion that mobility is part of imitation of the apostles. Yet they also show that the perception of that duty by the Order's members is different. Dominicans have to be pushed into it, while heretics are very keen. To use our usual metaphor, the 'quarry' are well ahead of their 'hunters': heretical groups fulfil the apostolic ideal of itinerancy more successfully than the 'lazy' Preachers. Although in 1256 Humbert talked about the unexpected – and quick – success of his call to arms, his very insistence on the issue and his willingness to highlight the achievements in the framework of a public Paris letter show that there was in fact still a problem, and that it was quite urgent and widespread. Curiously, yet not surprisingly, he uses the same words and images as the Cathar *Liber de duobus principiis*. 'The followers of Christ in times to come will have to endure many scandals and tribulations and persecutions and passion and pains, and even death by the pseudo-Christians and pseudo-prophets, and by evil men and seducers.'[79] And again, 'our Lord

---

[77] 'Non conturbet vobis, si audieritis fratres nostros tribulacionem interdum alicubi sustinere. Ipsi enim scitis, quod in hiis maiorum virtutum occasio ministratur et in hoc positi sumus, si volumus esse discipuli salvatoris.' *Ibid.*, p. 41.

[78] 'Per multas tribulaciones transierunt fideles.' *Ibid.*, p. 44. In this text, *exempla* might mean 'stories with exemplary messages' rather than 'examples'.

[79] 'Sequaces Christi in novissimis temporibus sustinere debent multa scandala et tribulationes et persecutiones et passiones et dolores et etiam mortes per pseudochristos et pseudoprophetas et per

Jesus Christ showed in his words that his disciples will have to endure tribulations and persecutions and even death in time to come, for his name'.[80]

This tardiness on the part of the authorities is not new to us. As we have seen previously, the Doat depositions also indirectly show awareness that the heretical system worked better and faster than the Catholic one. The employment of spies and collaborators is the best evidence of inquisitorial efforts to catch up with the dissident groups. In the depositions there is no sign, however, of a clear demonisation of mobility by the authorities, to match that seen with the Pseudo-Apostles and Waldensians. Moreover, the widespread inquisitorial practice of condemning minor offenders to go on pilgrimages did indeed encourage Cathar movements, and shows an apparent ignorance of the problem in relation to the French Good Men and Women.

Yet inquisitors were not blind to the issue. If Raymond Baussan was able to 'return to the Toulouse area ... with letters and permission from the said inquisitor',[81] as presumably did all the other collaborators and people travelling under the protection of a safe conduct, this means that the papal officials grasped the importance of mobility within the Cathar church. It also means that they understood how the Inquisition could win over its adversaries only through the employment of spies, that is by transforming this disadvantage into an advantage, and using the same structure.

Another interesting element emerging from the writings of Humbert of Romans is the existence of an almost complete separation between the Dominican hierarchy (represented by Humbert) and inquisitorial activities. This is no surprise, and indeed confirms the impressions already outlined in our previous chapter. Evidently, anti-heretical inquiries and the Order's life ran on parallel tracks, and the management of the former does not seem to have depended at all on the Master General's instructions and policies. Rather, he shows more interest in mission and the conversion of foreign peoples. Humbert notes the Order's anti-heretical commitment, and uses it as a measure of success and efficiency. However, it is clear from his words that such activities are seen as distinct from the Order's own priorities, as if the heretical emergency touched on the lives of particular Dominican communities only indirectly, or even as if it was someone else's business, rather than the Order's prime concern, preaching and teaching.

---

[80] malos homines et seductores', C. Thouzellier (ed.), *Livre des deux principes*, (Paris, 1973), p. 408.
[81] 'Dominus noster Ihesus Christus hostendit in suis verbis debere suos discipulos substinere tribulationes et persecutiones et etiam mortem tempore venturo pro nomine eius', *Ibid.*, p. 438.
'Cum litteris et licentia dicti inquisitoris ... rediit ad partes Tholose', D25, f. 146r.

Humbert claimed that, following his exhortations, the attitude of his brothers towards travelling and learning foreign languages had radically changed in a strikingly short time, and that only two years after his first letter a large number of volunteers were embarking on missionary enterprises to foreign peoples. Could such a transformation really have occurred? Could the initial opposition to leaving one's homeland and beloved scholarly activities – which seemed both long-standing and well rooted – turn into a mania for travel in such a short time? Could it not be that the Paris letter was yet another attempt to encourage his brothers, who were still too attached to their own habits and places?[82]

Whatever the final answer, this source again suggests that the question of itinerancy was indeed at the heart of the Order's missionary activities. Through Humbert's words the Order, as an orthodox Order, is questioning its own role, both as a preaching and an itinerant religious group. Not only was itinerancy a crucial indicator of the distinction between heresy and orthodoxy; it was also crucial to the Order's identity, in the context of its organisation and the management of its ideological aims. The challenge of the new groups appealing to the apostles threw up fresh doubts about the approved religious groups, calling into question their specific vocation and the legitimacy of their collaboration with the pope and Church authorities in anti-heretical activities. The reformers/ heretics reshuffled the cards of an already established game. Thanks to the letters of Humbert of Romans we can see how the distinction between orthodox and heterodox parameters for the 'correct' imitation of Christ and the apostles was far from clear-cut. Consequently, the need to re-interpret those parameters triggered introspection within the Orders themselves, itself evidence of the ideological confusion generated within the established Church.

SOME THOUGHTS

It is time to reflect. Heretical itinerancy is multifaceted. Although all these facets refer back to the same theological authorities and are inspired by the same role models as the Catholics used, each highlights different aspects of the dialogue or opposition between orthodoxy and heterodoxy. By isolating common aspects, the following four types of itinerancy can be established, depending on which of these aspects is dominant.

(a) Itinerancy as imitation of the apostles, or 'apostolic' itinerancy. This is the most obvious and widespread of the four. It stems from the concept that true followers of Christ and those who heed his teaching must imitate

---

[82] See above.

both him – the Master – and his first followers, the apostles. This kind of itinerancy is guided by Gospel principles, particularly those which assert the need for a missionary diffusion of the message of salvation. However, although often paired with preaching, such itinerancy does not necessarily imply a focus on preaching as the main aim of the missions. Rather, the focus is on living as the apostles did, that is, wandering without a precise destination and residence, giving up possessions and all that might tie one to places and people, begging when in need of food, and seeking shelter from Christians of good will. The association with preaching is a consequence of this lifestyle, and not its stimulus. Zacharias of St Agata, one of the most famous of the Pseudo-Apostles, synthesised this approach in his confession:

Asked what doctrine and lifestyle he follows and observes, he replied: prayer, reflection about the lives and passions of the saints, and – when the hour of need to eat comes – begging and asking for alms. And the foundation of the life and state of such apostles is to observe poverty and sell all and give it to the poor, and not to have or possess any goods of one's own. Also, he said that their doctrine is to preach and urge all believers and non-believers to believe in one God and the trinity in unity, and that He had suffered for mankind, and had descended to hell and rose from the dead on the third day.[83]

Translated by Salimbene's hostile pen, this attitude becomes a bitter 'going around in the world on their own', 'spending the whole day wandering in idleness, travelling the world without an aim' and 'wandering around the city to look at the women'.[84]

An initial phase of 'apostolic' itinerancy featured in all of the new reformist groups which were later approved by the ecclesiastical authorities. For all of them, however, after official recognition a second, legitimate phase necessarily involved a redefinition of their vocation to itinerancy, reshaping it to comply with existing legislation and papal control. As we have seen, in fact, for most Catholic writers it is because of its itinerancy that a group or an individual can be labelled heretical, or at least suspect. In their eyes, heresy is an 'external' factor, a powerful

---

[83] 'Interrogatus qualem vitam et doctrinam facit et servat, respondit orare, contemplari vitas et passiones sanctorum et, cum est hora necessitatis comedendi, mendicari et petere ellemosinas et fundamentum vite et status dictorum apostolorum est servare paupertatem et omnia vendere et dare pauperibus et bona propria non habere nec possidere. Item dixit quod doctrina eius est predicare et ortari omnes fideles et infideles ut credant in unum Deum et trinum in unitate et ipsum passum fore pro genere humano, et descendisse ad infernum et resurresisse a mortuis tercia die.' *Acta S. Officii Bononie*, pp. 389–90.

[84] 'Ibant igitur ambo tota die per civitatem et mirabantur Parmenses', 'tota die discurrebant per civitatem mulieres videndo, reliquum tempus expendebant in ocio et nichil operabantur' *Chronica*, Scalia (ed.), pp. 392, 393.

virus that can contaminate the whole body of the Church. As such, any potential attack on the body of Christianity must necessarily come from the outside, from something which is difficult to define, to understand and to regulate. Who fitted this ideological picture better than religious vagrants? In this perspective the sudden choice of vagrancy as a lifestyle by individuals or groups, jobless, without the defined aim of – say – a pilgrimage, and living on alms or preaching without license, posed a serious risk to society and the Church. It was suspect and destabilising.

All the movements which aim at reformation, which criticise or openly oppose the Church, are faced with a *conditio sine qua non*. Either they opt for the form of a religious Order, ruled and disciplined by established authority, where communities and their lifestyles are clearly defined and approved by the competent bodies, or they automatically fall into the category of outsiders. If the latter, they will be considered as true outcasts because they *chose* not to be part of an existing community, and because of this choice they will be persecuted as antisocial entities. The clearest example of this attitude are the so-called Pseudo-Apostles and followers of Dolcino of Novara. The focus is on itinerant life as a deliberate expression of non-conformity.

(b) Itinerancy as a consequence of preaching, or 'missionary' itinerancy. Whereas the first category is essentially driven by the desire to imitate Christ and the apostles, this one is its immediate consequence. In other words, the widespread desire to follow the role models of Christianity leads to the symbiosis of itinerancy and preaching; but for some the core of such imitation is preaching. For such groups, first among them the Waldensians, preaching becomes the main vocational activity. Their first aim and *raison d'être* is the dissemination of the word of Christ. The main prerequisite for this task is a profound and firm knowledge of the Scriptures, pursued through their availability and popularisation in vernacular translation.

Within this context, to be missionaries therefore becomes an obligation, an indispensable condition for the true followers of Christ. All members of the group are bound to be missionaries but, above all, to be preachers. The practice of preaching is deemed essential to the group's being. Spreading the word of salvation is the core task of these fraternities – open critics of the Roman Church for its erroneous interpretation of the Scriptures – and they avoid committing themselves to anything which would tie them to a fixed location. Together with this opposition often goes a rebellious attitude. In the specific case of the Waldensians, it has been rightly pointed out that mission work was considered to be an indispensable feature of one's personal training and a necessary basis for individual salvation. In fact, Waldensians were determined to extend the authorisation to preach to all their affiliates.[85] On the opposing side, the condemnation of Waldensians by the Church, as pointed out earlier, was promulgated in 1184 on the basis of their determination to preach. 'They assume for themselves the authority to preach.'[86]

Here again, Catholic sources depict the heretic as socially disturbing, guilty of disruptive behaviour which affected both society and the Church. Uncontrolled mobility had to be banned precisely because this would curb their preaching. Once again the equation underlining our sources is that of the vagrant as heretic.

(c) Itinerancy as escape. This type is implicitly associated with the heretics' awareness of themselves as being irregular, outside the official system. Even more, it is associated with the consequence of such irregularity, persecution. It is utterly beyond any ideological programme and remote from any attempt at imitation, but it ends up in the identification of the persecuted with the true followers of Christ, as in the ideal line traced by the *Liber de duobus principiis* between the prophets, Christ, the apostles and saints, and the 'true Christians' of the present age. As a type of escape, this third kind of mobility is a consequence of the very existence of a dissident group and of their activities, which are illegal in the eyes of the Church; a result of the individual's and the group's pertinacity in and attachment to error.

Inevitably, all heretical groups exhibit this kind of 'obligatory movement'. A way of life is forced upon them, when the authority they reject forbids freedom of belief and preaching. At the same time, there is an implicit recognition that it is their own status of otherness which determines their 'fugitive nature': it is only because they refuse to conform to the rules set by the Roman Church that the Roman Church pushes them into a life on the run. Yet, from the opposite perspective, it is because they are on the run that they are liable to be persecuted.

As anticipated above, Cathars manage to take this further. Somehow they sublimate the imposition of a fugitive identity into the highest form of imitation of Christ. Seeing themselves as persecuted victims, they are allowed to call themselves saints; going even further, they transform their situation into the most perfect form of sanctity, martyrdom. By becoming martyrs for freedom and justice they reach a condition closest to that of the apostles, and so approach perfection. When we look at them

---

[85] See Selge, 'Discussions sur l'apostolicité', p. 158; A. Molnàr, *Storia dei Valdesi, I, Dalle origini all'adesione alla Riforma* (Turin, 1974), p. 145 and ff., 263 and ff.; Rusconi, 'Forma apostolorum', p. 517; Bertuzzi, *Ecclesiarum forma*, pp. 20–8, 173–95.

[86] 'Auctoritatem sibi vendicant predicandi', *Ad abolendam*, in Friedberg (ed.) *Corpus iuris canonici. Decretalium collectiones*, 2nd edn. (Leipzig, 1955), cols. 780–2.

more closely we can see that they successfully and completely subvert the semantics of this area. What the Catholics call 'escape' they call 'persecution', or 'martyrdom'; and as 'persecution' or 'martyrdom' they mostly accept it willingly and gladly, at times even seek it. 'There was no death so beautiful as that by fire', says brother Bernard/Gerald Bonuspanis.[87]

Undeniably, the ideological ground for this transformation of meaning is embedded in the Cathars' belief that they represented the True Church. Incessant movement to escape the threat of spies and collaborators and to evade trials, prison and execution is – according to this inverse logic – itself a warranty of the group's legitimacy. To live and most of all to die as Christ and the apostles lived and died guarantees the thread of continuity between the role models and the believers. It is the ultimate and complete identification, far surpassing any ideal of imitation. Cathars *are* the true disciples, and as such are legitimate heirs of the apostolic tradition. Their preaching and way of life become more than a good example and a powerful homily: by becoming martyrs they divert the line of continuity from Christ and his first followers away from the Church of Rome and on to themselves.[88]

It comes as no surprise to find a whole chapter in the *Liber de duobus principiis* dedicated to this issue.[89] Here a line of succession is drawn chronologically from the prophets to the apostles and the saints. Its justification and commentary is taken from the Letter of St Paul to the Hebrews (11:32–40), which was now radically interpreted and became the manifesto of the 'wandering Cathars':

And what more shall I say? I do not have time to tell about Gideon, Barak, Samson, Jephthah, David, Samuel and the prophets, who through faith conquered kingdoms, administered justice, and gained what was promised; who shut the mouths of lions, quenched the fury of the flames, and escaped the edge of the sword; whose weakness was turned to strength; and who became powerful in battle and routed foreign armies. Women received back their dead, raised to life again. Others were tortured and refused to be released, so that they might

---

[87] 'Non erat ita pulchra mors nisi per ignem', D25, f. 3r.

[88] For a discussion of the connection between the idea of martyrdom and the cult of relics, see above, Chapter 2, n. 14. The sources do not give evidence of an established cult of the martyrs, parallel to the Catholic belief (*martyrum memoria*), and the obsession with the destruction of any physical remains of executions of Cathars was only displayed by the Catholic authorities. This could reasonably be ascribed to the Cathars' total rejection of the body: as soon as the souls became free through death, their body would be discarded and forgotten by the living as a 'surplus'. It must be remembered, however, that this explanation is acceptable only in the case of programmatic texts. There is no sufficient evidence to believe that such an extreme and radical position was in fact accepted in practice by the majority of believers.

[89] 'De persecutione prophetarum et Christi et Apostolorum et aliorum qui secuntur eos', *Livre des deux principes*, pp. 405–55. Wakefield and Evans, pp. 578–91.

gain a better resurrection. Some faced jeers and flogging, while still others were chained and put in prison. They were stoned; they were sawed in two; they were put to death by the sword. They went about in sheepskins and goatskins, destitute, persecuted and mistreated: the world was not worthy of them. They wandered in deserts and mountains, and in caves and holes in the ground. These were all commended for their faith, yet none of them received what had been promised. God had planned something better for us so that only together with us would they be made perfect.

The *topos* of the 'fugitive heretic', which lay at the core of all Catholic anti-heretical polemics, is transformed when considered from the Cathar point of view. The shift from the escape for persecution experienced as a negative dynamic in itself, to the idea of escape as positive manifesto provides a strong reaffirmation of the group's identity as a legitimate religious institution.

(d) Itinerancy as a tool, or 'sacramental' itinerancy. As with the preceding categories, this last one again represents an itinerancy which is 'functional' to a group's identity. However, this fourth type adds a new feature to the functionality. Itinerancy here becomes an organisational matter. Appearing only among the groups of dualist *Boni Christiani*, it represents the true essence of the Cathar church, as outlined in the previous chapter. Because of its prominence in the depositions recorded in the Doat volumes, it merits further and more detailed consideration.

ONCE AGAIN, DOAT 21−6

When dealing with the fourth category, we have to step back from theory. In order to understand the relationship between movement and its diverse functions within Catharism, its links with the sacramental life of the communities, it is necessary to contextualise them, once again, within the organisation of the Cathar church.

... as he the witness [Peter of Beauville] was in Lombardy for the first time, he returned secretly to the town of Avignon, to his own hospice which [in the meantime] was run by his wife, Guillelme, as her own dowry. She, in fact, had not been able to follow him, yet. She kept and hid him for ten to fifteen days or so, and [while he was there] Athon of Artigat and his wife Galharde came to know that he was there, and saw him and talked to him. He, the witness, said also that later he made his return known through Guillelme, his wife, to Stephen Donati of Montgaillard, a kinsman of the witness, who at the order of the witness came to Toulouse and bought for him a *sarcina* of goods to take to Lombardy. [Stephen] brought them to the witness' house in Avignon, and one night Guillaume Dauzet of Avignon came to the witness's house with whom the witness, having received the aforesaid goods and said farewell to his wife, left his own aforesaid home, and they both went to a certain wood between Les Cassès and Folcarde, where they found Hugues Dominic, Pons Arnaud and Arnaud Amard.[90]

This long excerpt is taken from the deposition of a man who can be considered the Cathar 'messenger' *par excellence*, Peter of Beauville. Even at a glance there is a notable occurrence of nouns and verbs connected to the idea of movement and travel.[91] Here the impact of filters superimposed by notaries or inquisitors is not relevant, nor is the selection of events that Peter is recounting. Peter is known as a messenger; the legal enquiry obviously concentrates on his connections within France and between France and Lombardy. He isolates a portion of events, probably only a very small part of what he knows, and recounts them *in some way* to the inquisitor's officials. Even if this is only a summary of his tale or the barest transcription of it, the facts are recited. And despite the assortment of words in the Latin we are forced to use – a choice made by the notary who recorded and translated Peter's vernacular – these extant words do refer to travels and movements. I have studied elsewhere the peculiarities of this particular enquiry,[92] and noticed how, within the same register, the inquisitors Raoul of Plassac and Pons of Parnac used a rather flexible style both in interrogation and also in the recording of question and answer. When compared to other highly narrative accounts contained in Doat 25, the style in Peter's deposition stands out as very dry and 'functional'. His story sounds like a cartographer's tale: from one place to another, on to the next, and then to another again … without going into too much detail.

Peter of Beauville can be taken as an overt and 'concentrated' case; nevertheless, he is not alone. As the previous chapter showed, there are hundreds of testimonies about travel and movements in general. Some general features emerge clearly from a survey of all of the Doat volumes

---

[90] 'Cum ipse testis [Petrus de Beauvilla] prima vice fuisset in Lombardia, rediit latenter ad castrum Avinionis ad hospitium proprium quod tenebat Guillelma uxor ipsius testis pro dote sua, que nondum secuta fuerat ipsum testem, quod tenuit et celavit eum ibi X vel quindecim dies vel circa, et sciverunt eum ibi, et viderunt, et loquti fuerunt cum eo Atho de Artigat, et Galharda uxor eius. Dixit etiam quod deinde significavit ipse testis adventum suum per Guillelmam uxorem ipsius testis Stephano Donati de Montegalhardo consanguineo ipsius testis qui de mandato ipsius testis venit Tholosam et emit pro ipso teste unam sarcinam de mercibus portandis in Lombardiam, et portavit eas in Avinionem in domum ipsius testis, et quadam nocte venit ad ipsum testem Guillelmus Dauzet de Avinione, cum quo ipse testis, acceptis predictis mercibus, dato etiam comeato uxori sue, recessit de domo sua predicta, et ambo iverunt ad quoddam nemus inter Cassers et Folcardam ubi invenerunt Hugonem Dominici et Pontium Arnaldi et Arnaldum Amardi', D25, ff. 310v–311v.

[91] Similar situation in the example of Maria of Vicenza, in *Acta S. Officii Bononie*, Indici, p. 177.

[92] C. Bruschi, 'Gli inquisitori Raoul de Plassac e Pons de Parnac e l'inchiesta tolosana degli anni 1273–80', in *Praedicatores Inquisitores*, pp. 471–93.

21–6. The Cathar organisation – whether considered a church or something else – is completely and intentionally one with no fixed abodes. In it preaching activity – which is the clergy's responsibility – is closely associated with the need to administer sacraments. The priests' commitments are in fact planned in stages. As they go to where sacraments are needed, and while blessing a believer on his deathbed with the *consolamentum*, they meet other believers who have gathered there in response to the priest's presence, to hear his or her words. It is very difficult to determine which takes priority, the sacramental or the didactic purpose. It seems, however, that both are fitted into the priest's busy schedule, and that the system of announcing the priest's presence to the known believers of the area through 'messengers' did indeed work very effectively.

Sacraments, preaching and movements are therefore tied together with a double knot. However, we must not forget the specificity of each inquiry. Each Doat volume – if not each deposition – has its own modes of recording, and each inquiry had its own purposes. It is very clear that different modes of registration have shaped the text which is the end result. While the first chapter has already established this, we need to recall some of the consequences. For example, deponents whose words are registered in some of the volumes are found guilty of listening to the 'perfects' preaching in some noble household, or in the clergy's houses, which (prior to the coming of the crusaders) were 'held publicly', as the depositions often indicate. And as preaching is at the core of the inquisitors' concern, it becomes the focus of the depositions. Yet, a reading restricted to these volumes alone would give an erroneous picture of Catharism, all centred on elitist groups, strictly connected with the local political framework, courtly life and the preaching activities of some of the most renowned 'priests': Bertrand Martin, Guilabert of Castres and Guillaume Vidal.

Equally, limiting the reading only to other registers would result in something just as partial, but biased in another direction: a totally rural picture, where Catharism is depicted through the eyes of traders and peasants. Here the *perfectus* is a completely different character from the highly literate, slightly mundane court-goer: he or she appears more as a passive object, moved here and there by the messengers and guides, a 'sacrament-machine' passed along from household to household, to where somebody had expressed the need for a ceremony. The famous image of the 'priest' reported in D24, for instance, shows him as something both solemn and terrible: 'as a monster sitting there in his seat like a motionless log'.[93] Here the leading clergy, visiting houses where their

---

[93] 'Sicut monstrum qui sedebat ibi in sella sua sicut truncus immobilis', D24, f. 137v.

skills are needed, appear indifferent and detached. It seems sometimes from the depositions that the 'priests" presence is a silent one, at other times withdrawn, or non-communicative, and that all they do is pronounce repetitive and ritualistic formulae. My point is, therefore, that these images are created by filters. The most likely representation of an 'ideal type' of a Good Man or Woman travelling to administer sacraments – were it at all possible to find one – would probably display a mixture of all of these characteristics.[94]

Differences aside, however, one may still arrive at a more balanced picture of Catharism, something which – whatever the limitations – still remains the main goal of our research. Essentially, it seems that both components, ritual and preaching, are portrayed equally in the depositions. This is not an attempt to 'average out' the data in our texts in any statistical manner, but to pick out the features which they have in common.

The picture which emerges is of a very busy community, in which 'priests' frantically move from one destination to the next; their activities are varied and their schedules rather tight. Exhaustion must have taken its toll, especially because, together with a presumably tiring level of activity, risk was ever present, and increased over time. The Cathar meeting of Pieusse has already been mentioned. It offers vivid evidence that Cathar organisation had expanded significantly, and now required substantial reassessment. Evidently the hierarchy, under pressure from the believers, felt that the old 'ecclesial districts' were not catering sufficiently for increasing demand, and that a new structure was needed. This would have eased the pressures on the active 'priesthood'. The Cathars of Razès asked for a bishop of their own, saying that 'heretics' were required to meet the believers' needs, and that unless a new 'district' was established, they were uncertain where they should turn to, either the hierarchy of Toulouse or that of Carcassonne.[95]

Whether the focus of such activity lay in open preaching in houses or village squares, or in the hidden private ritualism witnessed in some of the records, both activities represented the two main duties of the clergy. The intensification of inquiries and interrogations had limited

---

[94] See the discussion of how talks of travel make it into the 'club of historical facts' in P. Biller, 'Heretics and Long Journeys', in *Freedom of Movement in the Middle Ages: Proceedings of the 2003 Harlaxton Conference*, ed. P. Horden, Harlaxton Medieval Studies 15 (Donnington, 2007), pp. 86-103.

[95] 'It was inconvenient for them that for their necessities the heretics either had to go [to places] or were not available ... A bishopric should be granted to the same heretics of Redèz' ('Non erat expediens eis quod pro necessitatibus suis adirent vel vacarent heretici ... episcopatus concederetur eisdem hereticis de Redesio'), D23, ff. 269v–270r.

preaching and ritualism to private venues, sometimes to the huts in the woods, where believers could perhaps make the most of the presence of a Good Man or Woman without excessive risk. However, even behind this difference in location, the perseverance shown by the whole Cathar community in maintaining such collective habits highlights the extreme importance of both activities.

There were two main occasions when believers and hierarchy convened: preaching, and the administration of sacraments. Although both identify the Church as a community, they are perceived as separate activities, and their importance is substantially different. On the one hand, preaching can target a very mixed audience: people who already believe and attend Cathar communities, who have come to the meeting only to hear a good sermon from somebody they cherish and respect as a spiritual guide; and also those not yet converted, and who were simply interested in and curious about new religious ideas. On the other hand, in the case of sacramental gatherings, those present had already accepted and agreed on a leading role for the clergy and hierarchy, and were therefore personally more deeply involved in the less public life of the Cathar church. Their transgression was all the greater in the eyes of the Catholics. The distinction between attending a sermon and attending a rite was recognised as crucial both by inquisitors and deponents. The records show special care when asking about or confessing to attendance at only one of them, as against both. One can almost feel the anxiety of those who were present only at the sermons when they protested their absence from the second phase of the meeting: 'but I was not present when they hereticated the sick person'; 'I went out of the room'; 'then I left after the sermon and I did not adore the heretics'.

In this comparison, not only is preaching or listening to sermons a less compromising activity, it remains, at all events, a controlled diffusion of knowledge: not everything can be preached, and not to everyone. It does not create a real exchange between believers and preachers. On the contrary, it is a strategy of intellectual control where only one of the parties knows the score. The gap between hierarchy and common believers is still there, and there does not seem to have been an effort or desire to bargain for a more egalitarian management of the Church. The existence of a strategy – and, consequently, the existence of a structure or Church – is evident through the case of Pieusse. When the structure came under pressure, or experienced increasing demand, the members of its hierarchy responded with concrete remedies. They agreed to a rational and practical expansion of the existing system. Another passage shows a comparable response in the face of necessity. At the beginning of the 1240s a group of high Cathar clergy begged Raymond Pereille, lord of

Montségur, for leave to lodge in his *castrum* 'so that in that castle the church of the heretics could have its domicile, and headquarters, and from there it could send out and defend its preachers'.[96]

Within such an ecclesiastical structure, what kind of mobility do we encounter? First of all, we must draw a distinction between clergy and believers. Sacramental and preaching activities obliged the individual cleric to engage in continuous movement, either in the open or in the secrecy of hidden meetings. The needs of an ever-increasing and demanding Church forced the hierarchy to adapt and expand the existing structure of evangelisation and pastoral care. However, there was still a clear determination to keep control over the subjects of preaching, both for security and – chiefly – for doctrinal motives.

What of believers' itinerancy? Its purpose is not the imitation of Christ or a missionary ideal: believers travel as part of the existing ecclesial structure. They go to meet the priests, to revere them and receive blessings from them, to listen to their sermons. They meet where the priests are lodged, in hospices or private residences, and they often bring gifts or money to them, simple *fogacias*, loafs of flat bread, fish pies or marinated eels. Sometimes they have meals with the priests, and these become another ritual moment as believers can attend a *fractio panis* (breaking of bread), the semi-Eucharistic sharing of blessed bread. This incessant movement to and from the hospices, day and night, has the forms and modes of pilgrimage, and at the same time overtones of a feudal *homage*. Once the priest reaches a new destination the 'messenger' somehow advertises his presence to known sympathisers or to the members of the local church. They seem glad to take advantage of his presence, and go willingly to meet him.

We are not concerned here to establish a 'tachometer' of Cathar mobility. But the extraordinary frequency of travels, both by the believers and by the clergy, shows that movement was essential in keeping the Cathar church alive. It was indispensable to support a structure that consisted of both the hierarchy and the faithful, collaborating in mutual support. This living Cathar church acquired its substance from these continuous travel-linked activities. The numbers involved are sometime striking: Philippa, wife of Roger of Mirepoix, admits to having hosted in her house in Montségur fifty knights, who had gathered there to venerate the heretics.[97] This is the case especially if one considers that those recorded are

---

[96] 'Ad hoc ut in ipso castro posset ecclesia hereticorum habere domicilium et caput et inde posset transmittere et deffendere predicatores suos', D24, f. 44r.

[97] D24, f. 196v; also, D25, f. 278v witnesses the presence of 15–20 people at a time in heretical hospices.

only scant remnants of a practice which was only partially recorded in people's depositions.

CONCLUSIONS

A survey of heretical itinerancy and mobility shows that they were instrumental in polarising orthodoxy and heterodoxy. They reaffirmed the first, and defined the second; they are indispensable even for the definition of such a distinction. Legitimate and illegitimate groups used their shared scriptural roots as a warrant of their link with the inheritance of the Gospels and the apostles. Equally, both parties used this scriptural substratum to discredit and de-legitimise their rivals, by accusing them of perversion of the true message, and misinterpretation of textual authorities. A mobile and fluid lifestyle clashed openly with the Roman Church, which relied on fixed places of residence, careful territorial delimitation, stable regulations, precise definitions and rigorous control by recognised authorities – control which was only centralised at the beginning of the thirteenth century. In their contrasts the two worlds clashed visibly: in the eyes of the Roman hierarchy stability versus instability was the point of differentiation between legal preaching activities and illegal wandering. A truly obsessive insistence on the dangers of heretical mobility features in all Catholic polemical writings and preaching.

However, an exception to this general attitude to heretical mobility is represented by attitudes to Cathar mobility. Even inquisitors were not too worried about this aspect of the heretical lifestyle *per se*. Instead, they ended up using it as a weapon in a more effective method of inquiry. 'Explorers' and spies were inserted into the heretical structure, and by betraying it served as a powerful tool for the authorities.

While heretics willingly embraced a life of movement, it seems that the Dominicans did not share the same enthusiasm – we must limit our comparison to the Preachers, yet it does not seem too far-fetched to suggest that a similar situation must also have occurred within other contemporary Orders. Why spend time and effort in learning foreign languages, why risk one's life and face multifarious problems and setbacks, while travelling all over the world? The Dominicans to whom Humbert of Romans addressed his powerful exhortation would rather live a sheltered life of routine in their own community. Such a tendency was of course very worrying for the new Master General, who foresaw in this increasingly common attitude the danger of losing the Order's original vocation. In encouraging his brothers to volunteer for foreign missions he reminded them of their special vows, and set before them the image of their founder, the role model of perfection and sanctity.

The tone in the writings of Humbert of Romans is very far from the traditional exhortation found in treatises and moralising anti-heretical texts. It is more familiar and paternal, encouraging his flock to fulfil their own promises. This approach is far from literary exaggeration. It is in response to Humbert's realistic picture of lazy Preachers, whose reasons for not embarking on foreign missions are wholly understandable. Within this dialogue between father and sons, frozen in time through Humbert's letters, insistence on the necessity of an itinerant way of life is utterly detached from mention of the 'heretical problem'. For once mobility is merely a tool, and this in itself highlights the absence of a link between the Order's everyday concerns and inquisitorial activities.

If our distinction between the four categories of heretical mobility makes sense, it is noticeable that only the 'apostolic' and 'missionary' aspects of heretical itinerancy are connected with the definition of what 'heresy' is. It is on the basis of self-styled imitation of Christ and the apostles, and on the imperative to spread the message of salvation that the two opposing parties define themselves as orthodox and attack their rivals as dissenters, or illegitimate. Also, it is on the same two components that the *topos* of the 'fugitive heretic' (*hereticus fugitivus*) is formed. This is an ambivalent image (as always in this dialectic between legitimacy and illegitimacy), which heretical groups see as guaranteeing their own righteousness, as persecuted and martyrs. The Catholics, on the other hand, use it to define their archetypal dissenter. While he does not touch upon the problem of heresy, Humbert of Romans confirms this reading: for him, too, a positive characterisation of movement rests on a call to mission and imitation of the apostles.

What is it that makes this feature – itinerancy – so fluid and ambivalent both in the eyes of contemporaries and in our present analysis? What gives it such an essential and (at the same time) malleable character? Once again, the issue is part of the common heritage of the two parties: they both revert to the same textual corpus, the Scriptures. In a cultural framework where textual authorities are *the* guarantee of truth and correspondingly, the proof of error is provided by demonstrating misinterpretation and perversion of those same Scriptures, this assumes enormous relevance.

Catharism represents here again a special case, as it envisages also a 'sacramental' itinerancy with all its organisational implications. Its anomaly lies in the fact that mobility is not so much valued as an end in itself; it is a means. Clearly, 'sacramental' itinerancy is not devoid of ideological reference to a model, but it is not amount to a fully elaborated ideology. Rather, we could say that it is the consequence of a *gap* in Cathar ideology, that is, its lack of a material infrastructure for its own church. Unlike the Pseudo-Apostles and all groups centred on ideals of poverty, who consciously opt for an itinerant church in line with those ideals, and in rejection of the materialistic aspects of the Roman Church, Catharism shows no trace of such an ideological or rebellious drive. An itinerant organisation the 'living church'; mobility generates their community and overcomes the lack of places for cult and prayer. The 'living church' is structured in terms of hospitality (the private houses, the 'hospices') where specific individuals (the 'messengers') act as living connections between the hierarchy and the believers and sympathisers. Itinerancy is protected and disciplined. The Cathar church is also a highly personal church, where human contacts make up the body of the communities: cases of expansion, such as Montségur and Pieusse, do not represent deliberate imitation of the Catholic territorial structure; they arise from the practical need to provide effective management of the sacraments, and preaching and spreading of the message of salvation. The southern French Cathar churches are not just territorial units. They are areas within which personal links and contacts can be effectively carried on; and as such they form a living ecclesial structure.

Were heretical groups aware of these differences and subtle aims? Did Cathars have any perception of the creation of a structure in movement, a structure which could be attacked and threatened by Catholic authorities only from within? And even from a Catholic point of view, is there any real perception of the value of itinerancy both as a means of defining themselves and of determining the deviancy of others? The answer to all of these questions is: not completely. An endemic lack of sources, together with the scant attention paid to this problem in those sources which are available, demonstrates how *preaching* was the central point at issue. It is therefore legitimate to conclude that not even contemporaries could fully understand the relevance of itinerancy as an issue. Here the overall aim has been to construct a preliminary model as a basis for later research. Analysis of the problem could certainly be taken much further than this: more sources need to be studied in this light, in order to assess the impact of the four categories of itinerancy on each of them. Only then will the problem be given the attention it deserves.

Chapter 4

PATTERNS OF FEAR AND RISK[1]

for Bernard of Rival

STATE OF THE QUESTION (*STATUS QUAESTIONIS*)

When tackling the definition and study of emotions, it is normal to seek answers from the social sciences, psychology and economics, all of which are disciplines that have successfully engaged in a long-standing debate over this issue. Historical analysis has been always rather cautious about entering this theoretical arena, even hostile. The hostility owes much to the ideologically 'heavy' attitude of Marc Bloch. By labelling medieval emotions as 'instable' and 'impulsive acts', which are difficult for historians to categorise, Bloch effectively discouraged the study of emotions in the medieval world. They came to be dismissed as incompatible with a rational theoretical approach.[2] Nevertheless, there is a thread linking early methodological approaches to current historical debates. Particularly in France, the tradition of studying emotions in a historical perspective goes back to the publication of a famous article by Lucien Fevbre in 1941.[3] This formed part of the ground-breaking historical approaches promoted by the early *Annales* school. From then onwards, however, while many of these *Annales* ideas enjoyed a huge and fruitful popularity, the same cannot be said of the study of emotions. For some time this was confined to the field of 'psycho-history', or relegated to other non-historical

---

[1] I am most grateful to all my students on the 2000–03 *Reading and Reviewing History* course at Birmingham, for their suggestions and the interesting points made during the seminars on 'The concept of Fear'.
[2] M. Bloch, *Feudal Society* (London, 1961), ch. 5, pp. 72–87, esp. pp. 72–4 and 81–7.
[3] L. Febvre, 'Comment reconstituer la vie affective d'autrefois? La sensibilité et l'histoire', *Annales d'histoire sociale* 3 (1941), 5–20.

disciplines. Such almost total rejection was challenged only in the late 1970s, when Jean Delumeau published his monumental work on the history of fear, a fine overview based almost wholly on highly literary medieval and early modern sources.[4] And for quite a while this initiative did not inspire many imitators. In Italy only Vito Fumagalli and Piero Camporesi,[5] pursuing very different ideological aims and guided by diverse historical perspectives, have to some extent followed Delumeau's path.

Since the early 1990s, however, the history of emotions has gained more attention, driven by fresh interest in interdisciplinarity, and by the need for 'sellable' medieval topics. This is currently very successful, particularly in the USA.[6] Past ideas on and symbolic representations of anger, sorrow and other emotions are now believed to be portrayed – albeit behind textual and cultural filters – in medieval sources. Doing the history of these emotions is not thought so impossible as it was in the past. A new awareness of textuality and the importance of power relationships in literary discourse has provided historians with the tools to enable them to gauge feelings in their sources.

Historians have taken on board the suggestion made by sociologists that no study of emotions – either *per se* or within a historical perspective – can be detached from an accurate and thorough analysis of the

---

[4] J. Delumeau, *La peur en Occident une cité assiegée (XIV*-*XVIII* siècles)* (Paris, 1978); followed by *Le peché et la peur: la culpabilisation en Occident (XVIII*-*XIX* siècles)* (Paris, 1983) [Engl. edn. *Sin and Fear: The Emergence of a Western Guilt Culture 13th–18th Centuries* (New York, 1990)].

[5] V. Fumagalli, *Quando il cielo s'oscura* (Bologna, 1987), now published in English together with two later studies, *Solitudo carnis* and *La pietra viva*, with the title *Landscapes of Fear: Perceptions of Nature and the City in the Middle Ages* (Cambridge, 1994); G. Camporesi, *The Fear of Hell: Images of Damnation and Salvation in Early Medieval Europe* (University Park, PA, 1991).

[6] The leading authority on this issue is undoubtedly Barbara Rosenwein. See for instance, *Introduction* to B. Rosenwein (ed.), *Anger's Past: The Social Uses of an Emotion in the Middle Ages* (Ithaca and New York, 1998); see also other works by the same author: 'Eros and Clio: Emotional Paradigms in Medieval Historiography', in H.-W. Goetz and J. Jarnut (eds.), *Mediävistik im 21. Jahrhundert: Stand und Perspektiven der internationalen und interdisziplinären Mittelalterforschung* (Munich, 2003), pp. 427–41; 'I sentimenti', in D. Romagnoli (ed.), *Il Medioevo Europeo di Jacques Le Goff* (Milan, 2003), pp. 347–53; 'Emotional Space', in C.S. Jaeger and I. Kasten (eds.), *Emotions and Sensibilities in the Middle Ages* (Berlin, 2003), pp. 287–303; 'The places and spaces of emotion', in *Uomo e spazio nell'Alto Medioevo: Settimane di Studio del Centro Italiano di Studi sull'Alto Medioevo* 50 (Spoleto, 2003), pp. 505–36; 'Emotions in History', *Bulletin du Centre d'Études Médiévales*, (2001–2) (Auxerre, 2002), 87–97; 'Worrying about emotions in history', *American Historical Review* 107 (2002), 821–45; *Emotional Communities in the Early Middle Ages* (Ithaca, 2006). Most recent publications regarding the issue of feelings are S. Knuuttila, *Emotions in Early Medieval Philosophy* (Oxford, 2006); W.I. Miller, *The Anatomy of Disgust* (Harvard, 1998); W. I. Miller, *The Mystery of Courage* (Harvard, 2000); P. Hyams, *Rancour and Reconciliation in Medieval England* (Ithaca, 2003). For methodological approaches, see the discussions in the issue n. 10–12 (2001) of *Early Medieval Europe*, esp. the articles by M. Garrison, C. Cubitt, S. Airlie and C. Larryington.

general cultural and political context in which they developed.[7] Only by following that approach can such study be detached from the evanescent and perhaps potentially all-inclusive category of the irrational, something ultimately unascertainable from a historical point of view.

Such a complex perspective has not so far been extended to the history of medieval heresy and the inquisition, where the sources are rich and suggestive.[8] Here, at the outset, the confrontation between orthodoxy and heterodoxy as two political, religious and textual systems necessarily demands a complete re-assessment of the categories of fear and risk in this specific context. After all, behind the difficulties in detecting filters and biases, these records are among the very few *technical* sources which can provide an understanding of common people's feelings and emotions, of which a few examples have already been given in the first chapter of this book.

Here, however, it is not just a matter of isolating snippets of depositions bearing on fear. The intention in this chapter is to approach the issue more systematically; and in order to do that, a few methodological guidelines must be set out.

First of all, studying emotions brings us up against even more acute problems of a textual nature; that is, problems of language and definitions. Secondly, there is the problem of perceptions, plural. Not only is there the need to set medieval perceptions of fear against our own, modern, perceptions, but also, within the medieval mental framework, there is the need to balance the perceptions of the individual and of the group, and, going further, those of the powerful against those of the powerless. It is undoubtedly hard to determine which perceptions come first and shape the others, and this ultimately proves a rather complex question. Nevertheless, it is an urgent question. For, on this issue, a widespread and unproblematised application of modern evaluative criteria to the inquisitorial sources has again produced among historians an unbalanced image of the emotional relationship between inquisitors and deponents.

Once these starting points have been established, it is important to keep in mind that even the finest historical analysis of a society cannot take for granted a 'general' attitude in it towards emotions. This further limits our understanding of fear. As Yi-Fu Tuan neatly puts it, 'Even when a society seems hedged in by superstitious fears, we cannot assume that the

---

[7] D.L. Scruton, 'Introduction' to D.L. Scruton (ed.), *Sociophobics: The Anthropology of Fear* (Boulder, CO, and London, 1986), pp. 1–42.

[8] For instance, Grado Merlo, when tackling the 'consciousness and risks of a Christian choice' in Waldensian depositions, does not attempt to read the sources in the light of an emotional response, but only as texts offering 'the opportunity to grasp the net and intersection of different cultural levels' (*Valdesi e Valdismi*, pp. 75–86, p. 78 – translations are mine); see also pp. 121–9.

people, individually, live in dread most of the time.'[9] Behind our attempt
to reconstruct, say, a 'medieval, average, perception of fear and risk by a
deponent', there will lie all the individual cases, perceptions and strategies.
It has been a struggle to mould these into my general statements about
fear, and in the moulding much will have been lost. Moreover, we should
always keep in mind that, even in an individual, feelings and emotions
respond to specific situations, either external (that is, influencing their
perception from the outside) or internal (that is, coming from their own
attitude to the events, or their emotional state, at that specific moment).
We cannot assume that one person would have reacted in the same way
to similar situations encountered at different times. The mercurial nature
of emotions should always be kept in mind. These points will be evident
in the last section of this chapter, which provides examples of various
individual fears and risk-taking decisions.

I do not intend to undermine or dismiss the idea that, in the confrontation between inquisitors and deponents, the pressure exerted by
the inquisitorial side was much higher, or that the perception of fear
induced by such an experience must have strongly influenced the dialogue between the parties. However, as in previous chapters, I aim to
re-examine this balance and to restore to the deponents the dignity, individuality and importance they deserve. In the Doat depositions, behind
what is immediately obvious – the top-down direction of the proceedings and the formalisation of the dialogue performance of the trial –
some indications of individuals' reactions are clearly visible,[10] alongside
some that are harder to see. A complex and not fully discernible game
of reciprocal secrecy, a sort of psychological hide-and-seek, was being
played out. There were lies, plots and angry outbursts. What went on
was much less predictable than people have thought. The perception of
risk and fear that heresiologists have so bluntly assumed is in need of
re-assessment.

We may see deponents reacting to the all-powerful ecclesiastical institution, knowing what they *risked* – that it could mark them forever with
the signs of outcasts, confine them to life imprisonment, subject them to
torture or ultimately condemn them to the stake. The question is this. If
they reacted – varyingly – then what for these deponents was the limit
of acceptability of risk? A range of subsidiary questions follows. How

---

[9] Y.-F. Tuan, *Landscapes of Fear* (Oxford, 1979), p. 9.
[10] Very interesting examples are outlined and discussed in ch. 6 of Given, *Inquisition and Medieval society*, ('Manipulation'), probably the first to attempt an evaluation of this reaction to the institutions.
Another recent contribution following Given's steps has appeared by D. Laurendeau, 'Des "voix"
villageois dans les régistres d'Inquisition', *Cahiers de Fanjeaux* 32 (2006), pp. 283–306.

far were they prepared to take that risk, before judging the situation too compromising or unacceptable *for them*? How much could they contemplate enduring, in their challenge to that omnipotent institution? What were the priorities against which they measured any risk? What were the things they feared? Ultimately, the question I have in mind here is the same as the one which lies behind the last declaration of a relapsed heretic. 'Despite knowing what you know, why did you do it?'

We need to bear in mind one general attitude that can be confidently ascribed to all the people who were investigated by the inquisitors for their involvement with heresy and heretics: criticism and rejection of the Church of Rome and of its ministers. Either for political, moral, personal or doctrinal reasons, all of our characters harboured some degree of opposition to the Catholic establishment and/or its members. Thus, whether the deponents were members of a higher 'clerical' rank, or simply sympathisers, they were aware of holding a position of alterity, of being 'outsiders'. In professing an alternative creed they presented themselves as legitimate holders of truth, while at the same time reversing the semantics of persecution (as in the case of the Cathars). This attitude and belief is demonstrated very well in a famous passage of the *Gleisa de Dio*:

Note how all these words of Christ contradict the wicked Roman Church. For it is not persecuted for the goodness or justice which is in it, but on the contrary it persecutes and kills all who refuse to condone its sins and its actions. It flees not from city to city, but rules over cities and towns and provinces and is seated in grandeur in the pomp of this world; it is feared by kings and emperors and other men. Nor is it like sheep among wolves, but rather like wolves among sheep or goats, for it endeavours to rule over pagans and Jews and Gentiles. And above all does it persecute and kill the Holy Church of Christ, which bears all in patience like the sheep making no defence against the wolf.[11]

Only by looking at an interrogation in the light of this aspect of opposition to the established hierarchy are we able to re-read it as an event.

Although this general attitude can be ascribed to all deponents, there is in fact a distinction to be drawn. Not all of them tried simply to

---

[11] 'Nota en cal maniera totas aquestas parolas de Christ son contrarias a-la gleisa maligna romana. Car ela non es persegua per ben ni per justicia que ela haya en si; mas per contrari ela persegh e aoci tot hom que no vol consentir a li sio peccat e a-las soas faituras. Ela non fugis de cita en cita, mas segnoriza las citas e los borcs e las provincias e se sey en grandeça en la ponpa d'aqest mont; e es temuda dels reys e dels emperadors et dels aotres barons. Ni ela non es aisicom las fedas entre los lops mas aisicom son li lop entre las fedas e entre los bocs, car ela se esforça de segnorizar pagans e Judios e gentils e sobre tot el persegh e aoci la sancta gleisa de Christ, la cal sosten tot en-paciencia aisicom fay la feda que non se defent al lop.' *Gleisa de Dio*, Venckeleer (ed.), p. 828; Wakefield and Evans, p. 603.

get themselves out of trouble. For some, as we shall see, a hearing represented the chance to reaffirm their own position in relation to the Church of Rome: an opening, a moment in which they could voice their own choice of alterity. This attitude is visible in the depositions given by higher members of the Cathar hierarchy; by nobles adhering to Catharism, or simply strongly opposed to Roman interference in French affairs; or by relapsed heretics who did not deny – even under interrogation – their firm belief in the Good Men. If on the one hand we sometimes find evidence of this kind of attachment to personal beliefs and independence, on the other hand many of the believers seem to have made the choice (which is ultimately a 'political' one) to be governed by other priorities. These priorities were themselves, their families, their patrimony and their homes, in line with the traditional sociological tripartition of the 'boundaries of security' (domain, body, house).[12] The depositions reveal both fear and challenge/resistance.

THE PROBLEM OF PERCEPTION: A READING MODEL

In 1985 Mary Douglas produced a remarkable study which unveiled the mechanisms which lead individuals, as actors in a social and cultural system, to take risks and responsibilities relating to themselves and the group to which they belong.[13] According to her study, risk-taking choices first of all mirror and are direct consequences of the choice of system to which a person belongs (in the case of our heretics, the choice of belonging either to the dominant or to the alternative system). Whichever this choice is, however, the individual's ultimate boundaries of choice are dictated – especially in the case of lower-class individuals, or people who are not part of a ruling elite – by narrow margins of fear, which very often are related merely to the physical dimension, that is, to the likelihood of personal survival. The reason for such narrow margins is the overall limitation of individuals' liberty, which is strictly controlled by the ruling system. Through codes and law the powerful define very precisely how far the individual can go, and how much anyone is allowed to challenge the common frame of reference.

According to this reading of social dynamics, therefore, the relationship between risk-taking strategies and power is *directly* proportional, in that the higher the degree of power, the wider the margins of one's risky choices; and the lower one's social status, the more restricted are

---

[12] Tuan, *Landscapes,* p. 206.
[13] M. Douglas, *Risk Acceptability According to the Social Sciences* (London, 1985).

the boundaries one is prepared to cross. The powerful can afford to be worried about, and measure their actions against, loftier ideals and collective aims, while the powerless mostly care about mere survival or the safety of their patrimony. Yet, at the same time, the relationship between power and actual risk is *inversely* proportional. The less one's power, the weightier the responsibilities of an individual *per se* in every 'social action'[14] in which he or she engages – for instance, the higher the risk of being unprotected against retaliation and corruption of the legal system in place.

If applied to our trial depositions, this schema looks useful. Setting aside the first part of the equation for later discussion, the second part is immediately relevant to us. The degree of actual risk the deponents had to face when confronting the inquisitorial mechanism depended on how weak they were in relation to it. First of all, during the trial, as individuals they faced at least two opponents: the inquisitor and his partner, or the inquisitor and the notary/scribe. Secondly, the great majority of deponents, even when nobles, were of lower status than the inquisitors. Finally, the primary choice they made, choosing to adopt a dissident system of belief (even if to varying extents), placed them automatically in a weak position in the eyes of the Roman Church's ministers. It is this implicit weakness in the deponent's status that makes every instance of 'reaction' to the inquisitors even more remarkable. Even though unaware of this, whenever the deponents draw comparisons with the already established mechanisms of the religious system they criticise, they display a degree of autonomous choice.

Moreover, when talking about 'power', we should not forget that – at least in the case of Catharism – power was located also within the counter-hierarchy, and not only in relation to political dynamics or church positions. The power exerted by a Cathar bishop or 'priest' within their own community dictated their own reactions to risk. Thus the responses of Good Men or Good Women have to be weighed differently from those of common believers or sympathisers. A higher degree of commitment to their beliefs should be ascribed to them, and consequently a stronger resistance to recanting. Of the forty-five people quoted in this chapter as 'evidence', around two-thirds belonged to 'powerful' backgrounds – nineteen nobles, churchmen, squires and the like, and twelve others belonged to the religious elite of Catharism ('priests', deacons). This leaves only one-third of them about whom we do not know enough. It seems that, to a considerable extent, the people under investigation who

---

[14] Douglas means by 'social action' every decision taken in a social framework, even those related to questions of mere existence and/or subsistence.

provide evidence of risk-related sentiments, belonged to a rather homogeneous group where the elite were prevalent.

This confirms Douglas's theory of inverse proportionality of risks and social background: the higher the social background, the stronger the inclination to risk-taking strategies, while the lower the actual risk. Nobles, squires, bailiffs and priests would have less interest in concealing their attitudes, feelings or thoughts against the Church and churchmen because of their own position, in virtue of which they were less at risk. Good Men and Women, whose main purpose was the dissemination of the Word of Truth, were similarly less prone to lying, but for different reasons. Their commitment to truth did not favour lying as a way of escaping justice. Good Men and Women did hold positions of counter-power, but when in front of the inquisitors this meant a low status. Within their own system of reference of course, the Cathar church, their power was effective and could exert pressure upon common believers.

Another element which contributes to a more nuanced picture, is the typical multi-tasking of dissenters, which we have discussed in the previous chapters. One person could be at the same time a hostel owner and a bishop, or a weaver and a messenger, or a messenger and a spy. Attitudes to risk might vary because of this overlapping of roles; and people handling such a challenging existence might have been more prone to risk, and more used to risky situations. Nevertheless, reconstruction of their multifaceted, role-related attitude to risk and fear is too difficult for the historian. Our knowledge of each individual case is too limited to allow for multi-tasking in individual cases, and only in a small minority of them are we aware of this element. What is available to us is only a tiny fragment of the whole picture, and we would have to know much more about our actors to achieve such a precise view of their decisions and emotions. We must keep this caveat in mind, but we should also try to draw general lines of assessment, which look at broader dynamics and responses. More will be discussed below, in Section 4.4. ('Fears, risks and reactions').

What is the deponent's own perception of risk? And, should we treat the deponent as an individual, or as a member of a group? What Douglas was referring to was essentially the individual's response and attitude towards situations of risk in a given environment. This is not the only issue we are dealing with. Although we assume the existence of a collective environment which they all shared – that is, the system of values and norms within which deponents operated – their assessment of danger and their risk-taking attitude would vary. Of course, the majority of our deponents were ultimately acting on their own when attending rites, being 'consoled', travelling and getting in touch with heretics. Yet, within this individuality there are different degrees of commitment to the creed. Danielle Laurendeau has divided them into three categories: commitment of conscience (belief in the literal sense of the word), family commitment (belief inherited from family ties) and collective commitment (as part of a shared cultural patrimony).[15] In cases like the theft of the registers in Carcassonne, risk and the relative response to it are faced by an individual who functions as part of a group of 'conspirators'.

Let us focus on this example, bearing in mind that this (as well as all subsequent ones) must be taken as an indicator of a specific situation, and not as a general reflection of attitudes found throughout the depositions.

The theft of the registers of Carcassonne[16] is illuminated by Douglas's theory, and gives us a clear idea of the mechanisms leading to decisions about risk-taking, of the contrast between individual and group perceptions, and of the different positions held by the powerful and the powerless. Let us briefly recapitulate the events. In 1282, on the suggestion of and in agreement with some Cathar 'priests', a group of Cathar sympathisers belonging to the ruling elite of Carcassonne decided to organise the theft and the destruction of the inquisitorial registers of interrogation, which were under safe-keeping in the inquisitor's private lodging. Their immediate intention was to destroy any proof of inquisitorial judicial activities in the city and surrounding area. To ensure the success of the enterprise they had already obtained the help of a 'mole', one of the inquisitor's servants, who was able to provide access to the room and the chest where the volumes were kept, but who could not read, and so could not distinguish the important records from other volumes. When an attempt to involve one of the inquisitor's notaries failed, a literate man was approached, who was to go with the servant to choose the appropriate documents.

What we have here is a plan, a subversive action organised by a group (the 'conspirators'). They were acting for and in the interests of a wider community (allegedly, the population and government of Carcassonne), and they were trying to halt activities which were felt to be abuses of power according to a shared system of values. Acting in a group would have diminished the degree of individual risk, not so much because the

---

[15] Laurendeau, 'Des "voix" villageois', p. 284.

[16] For this episode, see J.-M. Vidal, *Un inquisiteur jugé par ses vicimes: Jean Galand et les Carcassonais (1285–6)* (Paris, 1903); M. Lebois, 'Le complot des Carcassonais contre l'Inquisition (1283–5)', in *Actes des XLIe et XXIVe Congrès d'études régionales … 1968*, (Carcassonne, 1970), pp. 159–63 [I have not been able to consult this contribution]; Duvernoy, *Histoire*, pp. 315–17; and J.-L. Biget ('I catari di fronte agli inquisitori', pp. 241–2); Lambert, *The Cathars*, p. 226; also, see above, Chapter 1, pp. 84–6.

possible punishment could be shared (inquisitorial procedure in fact prosecuted those responsible for collective actions as individual offenders), but because the group was composed of individuals who held senior positions within that political and social system. From another point of view, the risks of this particular action could be seen as graver: the collective action was consciously planned as a subversion of an existing and accepted power – the religious one – which was felt to be acting abusively. Evidently, the group of conspirators was here drawing on a totally different series of parameters for evaluation, in order to validate its actions. For some it could have been the survival of their souls, for others, the survival of their autonomy threatened by the deeds of the papal officials. Although all of them shared feelings of contempt and dissatisfaction, they will not have been unanimous in aims or motives.

After ensuring the help of a 'mole', the group approached a literate man, the 'bookwriter' (*scriptor librorum*) Bernard Agasse, who was invited to collaborate in the plan which supposedly had a moral basis. With his help, it could 'do a great service to the whole region' (*faciens magnum bonum toti terre*).[17] Agasse was also offered a 'great reward' (*magnam mercedem*) – material compensation. He willingly accepted, at first, but required reassurance on two points: that the 'mole' knew what he was doing, and that he was trustworthy (*si illa persona erat bene certa, et si bene poterat confidere de ipsa*).[18] On the other hand, Bernard of Laguarrigue, the 'mole', required greater reassurance: first and foremost a warranty of his payment, then an assurance of secrecy and finally a collective oath (*Domine, ego volo esse securus de hoc quod mihi promissum est dare, et volo quod istum bene secretum, et quod omnes iuremus*; and again, below *Domine, ego volo securus esse primo de peccunia mihi promissa antequam faciam aliquid*).[19] With these two men, a different perspective from that of the other conspirators becomes evident: the literate man and the servant were reacting as individuals, and as men of a lower social class, to the risks of the plan. The conspirators had high moral and political aims: to free Carcassonne from the 'extreme confusion' (*confusio maxima*) it was in; to put a stop to persecution; and to 'bravely defend themselves' (*viriliter se defendere*) against the abuses of the religious ministers. In contrast, the moral concerns faded in Agasse's view, and vanished in that of Laguarrigue. The latter, responding to an offer of remuneration, 'did not want to do it for such a small price', and asked for his reward to be doubled A debate arose over this payment, possibly indicating a conflict of priorities, and after much talk one of the

---

[17] D26, f. 212v.
[18] Ibid.
[19] D26, f. 213v.

'conspirators', Sanx the archdeacon, shouted, 'My Lords, let us not force him, let us give the aforesaid Bernard two hundred pounds *turonenses!*'[20] The discussion ended.

The different ratings of risk by the men of the Carcassonne establishment, the literate collaborator and the 'mole' are very clear. They demonstrate that an individual's reward for such a risk has to be measured against different priorities. His own responsibility as a key character in the theft – different in the 'mole' (material subversion and treason), and in the literate (putting his competence at the service of the conspirators); his possibly different perception of the moral level of the enterprise; and ultimately, his personal safety. Laguarrigue priced his own fears at 200 pounds. Here, Laguarrigue put his own material reward ahead of his religious community's gain: he in fact confessed to have been (or to be, we shall never know) a 'consoled heretic and elder son among those heretics who call themselves the Church of Albi',[21] claiming for himself the rank of a member of the highest clergy. Laguarrigue was presumably appointed as a servant of the inquisitors on the basis of his alleged conversion from and renunciation of Catharism. His risk as an individual was thereby increased since, if caught, he would be considered as 'relapsed' (*relapsus*), and therefore liable to execution, while Agasse, who had no previous convictions on his record, would merely have to pay a fine or perform a penance. Membership of the most committed and hard-line group of Cathar acolytes did not prevail over personal preoccupations.

Was this an isolated case? Regrettably, it is the only example where the data permit such a detailed analysis of the individual and collective assessment of such an enterprise and the risks it entailed.

In other instances the evidence is more plain and does not offer such a nuanced portrait of the events and thoughts leading to the incriminating action. Other episodes, which have enjoyed greater popularity over the years, mainly due to their political relevance and their bloody outcomes, offer less scope for reconstructing personal and collective motivations. I am thinking here, first and foremost, of the Montségur and Avignonet cases.

The killing of inquisitors William Arnold and Stephen of St Thibéry in 1242 and the following siege of Montségur of 1243–4 sparked vigorous inquiries into the perpetrators of these rebellious acts. In the first case, the renowned inquisitor William Arnold of Montpellier, a Dominican active in Toulouse and Carcassonne in the 1230s, and responsible for

---

[20] 'Domini, non faciamus vim, demus predicto Bernardo ducentas libras turonenses', D26, f. 269v.
[21] 'Fuerat hereticus consolatus et filius maior inter illos hereticos qui se dicunt Ecclesiam Albiensem', D24, f. 246r.

some episodes of harsh persecution against Catharism – as in Moissac in 1234 – together with his Franciscan co-inquisitor and nine officials and servants, were murdered in Avignonet. The action was the result of a targeted plot carried on by a party of conspirators led by Peter Roger of Mirepoix, son-in-law of Raymond of Pereille, the lord of Montségur. The Dominican inquisitor, for his zeal and ability as a jurist, embodied the institution who illegitimately invaded spaces of power and autonomy in the Montségur area. His killing was meant to infer a lethal blow to the tribunal, and to those supporting it.[22] As a follow-up, the stronghold of Montségur, built around 1204 by Raymond of Pereille and ever since one of the focal points of assembly of the Cathar community, was put under siege by Louis IX, locally organised under the leadership of the sene-schal of Carcassonne, and the support of the archbishop of Narbonne and the bishop of Albi. Of the 415 people found in the castle at its fall, in March 1244, over a half were constituted by Good Men and Good Women, some of them high up in the Cathar hierarchy, such as Bertrand Martin, Cathar bishop of Toulouse, and Raymond Agulher, bishop of the area of Razès. This military action *did* infer a lethal blow to Cathar ecclesial organisation and resulted in a mass-execution at the end of the siege.[23] Recrudescence of inquisitorial persecution was the inquisitors' response to Avignonet, exactly as it happened after the killing of Peter of Castelnau in 1209. This went hand-in-hand with a harsh military response from the supporters of the papacy in Languedoc. The similar-ity with the aftermath of the Crusade of 1209–29 goes further: after the fall and stakes of Montségur, the heroic resistance of Cathar clergy and supporters, coupled with widespread reluctance towards matters of faith being handled by military campaigns, guaranteed that Catharism could enjoy a significant revival among the population.

It is clear from the political and religious significance of these two episodes how the inquisitors were preoccupied with setting up wide-spread inquiries and the interrogations of the conspirators. In both cases the subversion was led by, or planned under the patronage of, a noble or group of nobles and influential knights. The individual acted not as a representative of the group – 'one for all' – but as one *among* a group of actors. In the Avignonet slaughter it was not Raymond of Pereille on his own who killed the inquisitors. Raymond, himself a son and son-in law of Good Women, was the catalyst of criticism against the inquisitors and their methods. It was him who gave the church officials support and

---

[22] See Barber, *The Cathars*, pp. 148–9, 154–5; Lambert, *The Cathars*, pp. 166–9.
[23] The most extensive treatment of this episode is still Z. Oldenbourg, *Massacre at Montségur* (New York, 1961); see also Barber, *The Cathars*, pp. 156–7; Lambert, *The Cathars*, pp. 72–5, 106–7, 167–9.

money and provided shelter, thus partially diverting (at least in the mind of the conspirators) the focus of responsibility onto himself. The actual perpetrators of the killing were acting as a group, backed by a noble, they therefore appeared less prone to doubts, and got their material reward by looting and sacking the inquisitors' possessions. Even so, another obstacle hinders our understanding of the dynamics in this case. No record appears in the Doat depositions of any statement of motives behind the action, the making of covert preparations before the killing, through letters and secret meetings. [24] Though the inquisitors were interested in individual responsibilities and utterances ('who did what', 'who said what'), they were even more concerned to establish every individual's degree of involvement by way of determining their legal status and for the reconstruction of the mechanism of the plan.

The siege of Montségur, on the other hand, saw the destruction of the town and the killing of all the main responsible actors. The inquisitors had no chance to interrogate suspects, and the only ones left to put on trial were a few survivors, or those lucky enough to escape – marginal actors, apostates (here we should assume 'for real', given the extreme nature of the situation) or simply onlookers living in the village without any specific role. [25] The Carcassonne case remains, therefore, as the unique testimony of this dynamic of risk-handling between single actors and groups.

THE PROBLEM OF WORDS

Putting one's fear into words is a difficult matter; but the close link between emotions and words has been demonstrated by social scientists, who talk about emotions as elements of language. [26] Furthermore, all that is left of our deponents' fears in trial records are little phrases scattered here and there throughout the hundreds of folios of the Doat registers. They are conditioned by psychological pressure, either to speak or to conceal the words in one's mind; by inquisitors' interest in or indifference to what deponents want to say; by the relevance of a confession of fear within a certain enquiry; and, finally, by the inquisitors' perception of

---

[24] As stated in several occasions, this study deliberately refers to Doat only, and brings in other deposition material only when necessary to highlight particular points. Ms Toulouse 609 includes information on the Avignonet episode (e.g. 85v), however, such information does not alter my point in this context.

[25] On numbers, and assessment of the interrogations post-Montségur, see L. Albaret, 'L'anticléricalisme dans les registres d'inquisition de Toulouse et Carcassonne au début du XIVe siècle', *Cahiers de Fanjeaux* 38 (2003), pp. 447–70, p. 451.

[26] Scruton, *Sociophobics*, p. 18, where emotions are outlined as fundamental elements of language.

what the deponents' words really meant. After all, in this context, words could do more to hide than to articulate a witness's feelings.

And yet, the deponents also knew the power of words. At times words could be extremely frightening to them, at other times they could be used and manipulated to their advantage. We have noted the laconic proverb where two friends recognised that 'men catch oxen by their horns and peasants by their tongue'.[27] But there is an alternative perspective, a different appreciation of the importance of words and the handling of words, in D25. Here, Raymond Bastier of Caraman recalled the advice of a friend, Raymond Guillaume, about the tactics to use with words and the inquisitors. It was not necessary to confess everything to them at once, and 'he himself ... would have only insinuated it to brother Bernard of Villèle of the Order of Preachers, and that would have the same value'.[28] In Bastier's deposition, words have a value. A deponent has to 'pay' some words to the inquisitor, like a tax, no matter what the words effectively say. It is better to 'pay' this tax by gaining the best result with the smallest amount of compromise. To 'insinuate' or 'suggest' does not mean to 'say'. The inquisitor would have known, and he, the deponent, would not have committed the recordable action of 'saying' or 'declaring' something.

Once again, why is language important in this context, in the analysis of feeling fear? According to Bastier's interpretation, words appear as a way to play on risk, a way to work the system to one's advantage, and not just as a source of inequality and fear, as the old proverb about oxen and peasants seemed to suggest. The same attitude is displayed by Bernard of Villeneuve, a squire, who was instructed by Pons *de Manso* of Fayac not to accuse him, but rather to mention some names of people from Fayac who had already been condemned to the stake. Pons 'asked ... that he [Bernard] should hide him [Pons] from the aforesaid events, suggesting to him that he should say it [i.e. "to make the same accusation"] about others from Fayac, who had been burned. And were he [Bernard] to have spent anything in going to the inquisitors, he [Pons] would repay him the expenses'.[29]

But there is more to it. When dealing with words and feelings, the omnipresent gap between the inquisitor's and the deponent's words, and the simultaneous desire to hide oneself and one's aims behind these words are once again evident. A classic example is provided by the careful notes

---

[27] Above, Chapter 1.

[28] 'Quia ipse Raymundus Guillelmi insinuaret fratri B[ernardo] de Villela Ordinis Predicatorum, et valeret tantundem', D25, f. 230r.

[29] 'Rogavit ... quod celaret ipsum de premissis, suggerens ei quod poterat illud dicere de aliis de Faiaco qui erant combusti, et si expenderet aliquid eundo ad inquisitores, quod ipse redderet sibi expensas,' D26, f. 75v.

of Gui's *Manual,* where he warns inquisitors of the cunning strategies of the heretics, and advises on how to counteract them.[30] Quite apart from the sophisticated strategies highlighted by Gui, and before them, there are the instinctive human reactions of both parties. To put it bluntly, in the records we can read what the deponents *declare* they fear, which may be different from what they *actually* fear; we can imagine the fear which the inquisitor subtly encourages with his words, but also his effort to prevent this fear from jeopardising the enquiry and the successful gathering of information. Church officials struggled for decades to locate the thin line between these two forces, a difficulty which is attested by Gui's words. This is a game of hide-and-seek, not only for the parties to the game, but even more for historians trying to figure out the degree of 'pollution' these words impose on their understanding of feelings.

We have established the deponents' awareness of the risks and advantages hidden in words. Of course, the inquisitors knew this only too well. However, the oath formula recorded in some of the depositions allows us to go a step further: it shows the inquisitor's understanding of how the intrinsic value of a deposition could be hindered by obstacles, pressures felt *by the deponents* which could compromise the validity of a confession or the utility of a declaration. For this reason, the inquisitor asks 'whether [the witness] has confessed the above items [under the pressure of someone] imploring [them] or bribery, or out of fear, hatred or love of any person, or under influence or harshness of torture'.[31] What the inquisitor assumes his deponents might fear are external pressures ('imploring or bribery'), feelings for somebody ('fear, hatred or love'), and the psychological/physical pressures of the trial ('influence or harshness of torture'). It is a concise yet exhaustive list of possible obstacles, the fears which he assumes can affect the deponents' free speech.

We find a parallel to the inquisitor's formal concerns in the words recited during the 'heretication' rite by Cathar believers on their deathbeds. At this key moment of life both as a human being and as a Cathar adept, the believer had to promise to avoid a series of actions – eating certain foods, sexual intercourse and swearing oaths, and so on – and also to promise that they 'would never leave the sect for fear of fire, water or any other kind of death'.[32] We cannot be sure how far the formulaic character of this phrase derived from inquisitors' imposition of

---

[30] Gui, *Le manuel,* part V, Mollat (ed.), transl. WE, pp. 375–445.

[31] For instance, see D26, f. 215v: 'si prece vel precio timore, odio et amore alicuius persone seu suggestione seu tormentorum asperitate confessus est predicta'.

[32] Many occurrences, nearly all cases of reported 'hereticatio' quote 'quod numquam dimitteret sectam eorum per ignem, vel aquam, vel timorem alterius generis mortis' (for example D23, f. 82r).

uniformity on phrases that in reality varied more, or whether this was in reality a ritual phrase that hardly varied. Whatever the case, behind it lay the worst nightmare of the Cathar establishment. While the inquisitor worried about compromising the legal value of the deposition and the reliability of the declarations, the Cathars were concerned about desertion and betrayal of the 'oath of purity' through fear of death. In both cases formulaic expressions hide a fear of fears.

How far these lists of worries corresponded with the deponents' mental list, and dictated their use of words, or guided their risk-taking strategies is difficult to ascertain. As we have said, the fears which one admits to might not be the fears one actually does fear. Moreover, fears are rather a personal matter, and each individual has his or her own priorities. Once again the case of the Carcassonne registers can shed some light on this question. When facing the risk of becoming involved in the plot, Bernard Agasse and Bernard Laguarrigue declared their aim of getting assurances about the secrecy, compensation and trustworthiness of the participants. They were looking for a guarantee that they would not feel fear in the future: not feeling afraid about their own visibility, about not getting money and about spies in the group.

On the one hand, there is the inquisitorial reading of this problem. What concerned the inquisitor, according to the *formula*, is that what appeared to be the witness's true words might have been extorted through some kind of pressure. His aim, let us not forget, was the recovery of 'what happened' and 'who was there', in order to establish the extent of the deponent's involvement, and therefore the degree of his or her moral transgression. Gui said of mistakes: 'his [the inquisitor's] conscience torments him if an individual is punished who has neither confessed nor been proved guilty; ... it causes even more anguish to the mind of the inquisitor ... if by their wily astuteness they escape punishment, to the detriment of the faith, since thereby they are strengthened, multiplied, and rendered more crafty.'[33] The inquisitor therefore had to be both practical and ethical, his frame of reference the wider interests of the local community and the Christian faith. Equally, for the Cathar clergy, moral issues, in this instance the unity of the Church and the believer's observance of his or her moral code, were the overriding preoccupation; thus the believer's frame of reference is similarly collective and doctrinal. Moreover, in both cases we must assume a projected 'ideal model' behind the texts: the 'ideal deposition/enquiry', the 'ideal heretication/heretic'. Two abstractions which have to be set against real events and behaviours.

---

[33] Gui, *Le manuel*, 'Preface'; WE, p. 377.

On the other hand, the deponents' worries and fears are that *particular* individual's concerns. They do not go beyond the boundaries of personal advantage and safety, and although secrecy could be said to be an issue involving the broader community (for instance, inasmuch as one is either excluded or included and accepted into the community itself as a full member), it is always in respect to the individual that this issue is taken into consideration.

The two perspectives do not match *in words*: although fear is assumed by both parties, it is done so on different grounds and with different priorities in mind. What the inquisitor assumed to be an obstacle to the true recording and reconstruction of the facts, in parallel with the Cathars' obsession with the purity of the nearly-deceased, was not what worried the common believer. Regrettably, the weakness and scarcity of our evidence prevents us from understanding whether the imbalance changes if the deponent happens to be a 'priest' or somebody involved at a more serious level with the Cathar hierarchy or civil community, or whether Bernard Laguarrigue – the 'mole' of the Carcassonne plot who rated his own fears at two hundred pounds – has to be taken as a unique example of cowardice and selfishness.

We have another subtly disguised problem to consider when it comes to words. Words of law, such as manuals, legal consultations (*consilia*) and papal bulls, aim at setting out one or more lines of thought, and the pastoral behaviour appropriate for church officials. These present an ideal form of the penal scenario a deponent would have to take into account when planning a strategy of risk-taking. But reality was another matter – the degree to which this scenario was actually realised in practice. The social background, milieu and mentality of the deponents would have an effect on the real playing out of this scenario. While it is not usually possible to discern or measure these in our evidence, we need always to be alert to them and to be wary of superficial reading of the sources.

Words are therefore tools either to hide or preserve knowledge; they codify assumptions and ideals, and are the vehicle of a strategy. It is hard to detach these factors and assess how they related to actual feelings: the perception of words lies ultimately in the 'ears of the listener'. Yet there are other words which certainly affected both parties' view of fear and risk at a different level and on different occasions: the words heard during preaching or confession by each individual believer, and those written in the treatises and *summae* which were read by the inquisitors and the priests.[34] This is not the place to embark on a study of the significance

---

[34] The literature on preaching and the anti-heretical activity is vast. See, for instance, 'La prédication en Pays d'Oc', *Cahiers de Fanjeaux* 32 (1997); for a recent survey, B.M. Kienzle, *Cistercians, Heresy*

and influence of ideas and texts of the highly literate. Currently in vogue in the study of medieval emotions is the analysis of lives of saints, commentaries, manuals and tracts. Such sources are crucial for reconstructing what the elite and the philosophers thought about fear, and what they wanted to advertise to the lower strata of society; but in exploring heresy trials we are moving on a different level.

Let us see why. What we have in our depositions are answers to specific questions about events and people or, at most, digressions away from the answer's theme, and free interpretation of a question. It is very unlikely that inquisitors showed any interest in the theoretical issue of 'what the deponents feared', unless such a feeling could in some way interfere with the questioning and its purpose, the inquiry as a whole. Moreover, we must not forget that fears, as excuses ('I did/did not do this through fear'), and even if irrelevant to the main issues, could be perceived as ways of avoiding having to tell the truth. Nevertheless, fears as obstacles to accurate reporting of the facts ('the deponent declared/did not declare this because influenced by fear'), and as a way to disguise and minimise one's actions ('the deponent declared they had done something through the pressure of fear, saying this in order to diminish their own responsibility') *did* interest the inquisitors, and this appears in the recording of the hearings. These concerns dictate what parts of the original dialogue were thought worth including in the written account.

Although we can suppose that each believer, whether inquisitor or deponent, was well acquainted with that 'Catechism of Fear' which, from the mid-twelfth century permeated and shaped all aspects of religious life, cultural expressions and visual imagery,[35] the fears portrayed in our sources are qualitatively different. They are practical, everyday, down-to-earth concerns, 'real' cares about money, feelings about another, worries for one's personal immunity or safety, which we too might have if caught in a similar situation. 'High-style' literate words seem to be a world apart from our depositions. Even though 'real fears' were there, in our characters' minds, when they did not seem to relate to the inquiry, or to the inquisitor's interests, and did not seem to affect deponents' decisions to act or to speak, they do not appear in the records.

---

and the Crusade in Occitania 1145–1229 (York, 2001); J. Byrd, 'The construction of Orthodoxy and the (de)construction of heretical attacks on the Eucharist in "Pastoralia" from Peter the Chanter's circle in Paris', in *Texts and the Repression of Medieval Heresy*, pp. 45–61; L. Paolini, 'Domenico e gli eretici', in *Domenico di Caleruega e la nascita dell'ordine dei frati predicatori: Atti del XLI Convegno storico internazionale (Tòdi, 10–12 October 2004)*, Spoleto, 2005, pp. 297–326.

[35] This is a very neat expression coined by S. Menache, 'The catechism of fear and the cult of death', in *The Vox Dei: Communication in the Middle Ages* (New York and Oxford, 1990), pp. 78–97.

FEARS, RISKS AND REACTIONS

What, then, are our deponents afraid of? What are they used to, and what goes beyond the usual? How do they declare or overcome these obstacles? And, indeed, to what extent were they perceived as obstacles, rather than facts of life? People's imagination in this sense was rich and painted in contrasting, strong colours. Peasants especially, but also townspeople, were accustomed to natural events, to an almost total precariousness of living conditions, and also to everyday images of war and violence.[36] Moreover, the public spectacle of penance, common in towns and villages both for lay and ecclesiastical offences, certainly exerted an influence on the perception of punishment.[37] In this context, the inquisitor's open speech performed in the town's main square, or a public declaration of guilt followed by the display of the offender, did not have quite the same impact as we could expect it to have on a modern Western audience.[38]

---

[36] Fumagalli, *Landscapes*, ch. 1, 6 and 7.

[37] Recently, Trevor Dean has criticised the tendency displayed by historians of crime and punishment to stress this visual and violent aspect of medieval history. Dean reckons that 'historians who have sought out sensational material and described it using impressionistic methods have created and maintained an image of the Middle Ages as *the* age of violence, when latent aggression could suddenly flare up, and when the population lived in constant fear of bandits and highway robbers' (T. Dean, *Crime and Justice in Late Medieval Italy* (Cambridge, 2007), p. 8). In fact, the danger of such a methodology is a real one. However, although our knowledge of the *perception* of violence by individuals is very limited, two important elements cannot be denied. The first, the public aspect of penance and judgements (for example the inquisitors' *sermones generales* and the public declaration of penances). The second, their impact on the population. For general reference, see R.W. Kaupfer, *War, Justice and Public Order: England and France in the Later Middle Ages* (Oxford, 1988); R. Bartlett, *Trial by Fire and Water: The Medieval Judicial Ordeal* (New York, 1986); A. Zorzi, 'Rituali di violenza, cerimoniali penali, rappresentazioni della giustizia nelle città italiane centro-settentrionali (secoli XIII–XV)', in P. Cammarosano (ed.), *Le forme della propaganda politica nel Due e Trecento*, ('Collection de l'École Française de Rome' 201), (Rome, 1994), pp. 395–425; 'Rituali e cerimoniali penali nelle città italiane (secc. XIII–XVI)', in J. Chiffoleau, L. Martines and A. Paravicini Bagliani (eds.), *Riti e rituali nelle società medievali* ('Collectanea' 5), (Spoleto, 1994), pp. 141–57; G.G. Merlo, 'La coercizione all'ortodossia: comunicazione e imposizione di un messaggio religioso egemonico (sec. XIII–XIV)', *Società e Storia* 10 (1980), 803–23 [also in French, 'Coercition et Orthodoxie: modalités de communication et d'imposition d'un message réligieux hégémonique', in *Faire croire. Modalités de la diffusion et de la réception des messages réligieux du XIIe au XVe siècle*, ('Collection de l'École Française de Rome' 51) (Rome, 1981), pp. 101–18]; Given, *Inquisition*, pp. 72–85.

[38] One further basic distinction is necessary here between televised audiences and first-hand observers. Within contemporary society, one thing are those communities where hanging, stoning to death, beheading and other forms of capital punishment are equally shared – and sadly, frequent – images. These, as the medieval audiences, have physical experience of a spectacularisation of penance, death and punishment. Another thing is the mediatic visualisation of the same episodes, which pays the price of the filtering and censorship of images reaching us after the cuts of television news broadcasters, and – most of all – through the physical filter of technology such as computers and televisions.

Moreover, feelings, by their nature, cannot be assumed to be consistent throughout one's life, or in response to different situations. In general, the undoubted pressure exerted by an interrogation in front of church officials is most likely to have had a very varying impact on different people's feelings, and on their consequent decisions to hide or disclose evidence. To obtain a fuller picture of the presence of fears and risks in people's lives, historians should add the continuous fluctuation of the political situation in Languedoc, with its unstable alliances and balance of power.[39] Although it is not the purpose of this study to embark into a contextualisation of heresy within the social environment of Languedoc, like others have done successfully,[40] a brief overview on the 'actors in the play' is important in order to set the few snippets of deposition in their appropriate context of power balance and socio-economic interaction. John Mundy has demonstrated that heretics and their sympathisers were related to the Languedocian nobility or to local clergy and members of religious orders, to different extents, either directly through family ties or simply as people standing on the same side of the barricade. In particular, the intermarriages between the main local noble houses (most of all the counts of Toulouse, but also the viscounts of Carcassonne and Béziers, and the counts of Foix) had created a net of family-based alliances within which Catharism had enjoyed a huge success. Mundy's studies on Toulouse have highlighted the popularity Catharism exerted particularly within the knightly town families (Castelnau, Gameville and Villeneuve are among the most frequently quoted in the *Doat Collection*) but also among 'burgher families of the patriciate', who enjoyed wealth and land possession outside Toulouse, and whose members often served as consuls in the town government. In general 'a disproportionate adhesion on the part of the wealthier classes'.[41] Although this picture is a product of the sources available to historians, it is important to note that such a deep rooting of Catharism into higher social strata and political

---

[39] For a concise and effective overview of this issue, see J.-L. Biget, 'Hérésie, politique et société en Languedoc (vers 1120–vers 1320)', in Berlioz, J. (ed.), *Le Pays Cathare: Les religions médiévales et leurs expressions méridionales* (Paris, 2000), pp. 17–79.

[40] See J.H. Mundy, *Society and Government in Toulouse at the Age of the Cathars* (Toronto, 1997); J.B. Given, *State and Society in Medieval Europe: Gwynedd and Languedoc under Outside Rule* (Ithaca and London, 1990); Id., 'Factional politics in a medieval society: a case study from fourteenth-century Foix', *Journal of Medieval History* 14 (1988), pp. 233–50; Laurendeau, 'Des "voix" villageois'; Lansing, *Purity and Power*; C. Taylor, *Heresy in Medieval France: Dualism in Aquitaine and the Agenais, 1000–1249* (Woodbridge, 2005).

[41] J.H. Mundy, *The Repression of Catharism at Toulouse: The Royal Diploma of 1279* (Toronto, 1985), pp. 54–61, quote at p. 60. Mundy also sketches the history of twenty-two of the most prominent families of the town, all connected with Catharism, and mingled together by marriages, at pp. 131–303.

alliances superimposed religious loyalty to a pre-existing net of other loyalties: the seigneurial bond between higher and lower families within the county, the family ties between clans who were linked by intermarriages, the duties involving political positions within the town elite (the example of the consuls is a clear one) and the economic interests connected to the land and its property.

Moreover, these loyalties fluctuated in time. The counts of Toulouse Raymond VI (1194–1222) and Raymond VII (1222–49) provide a good example of this fluctuating relationship with Catharism and its protection or persecution. Raymond VI was seen as one of the key characters behind the killing of Peter of Castelnau, papal legate, in 1209. However, he was later reconciled with the pope at the very beginning of the Crusade. His son, who swore alliance to the pope in 1222, was later on responsible for two episodes of 'betrayal' in 1229 and 1235.[42] Another good example is provided by the events linked to the Trencavel family. Once viscounts of Béziers and Carcassonne, the Trencavels lost their lordship of that area with the treaty of Paris of 1229. The vice-county was thus reorganised into the seneschalsy of Carcassonne. The family and their allies embarked in a resistance against the decision, aiming at re-establishing their power on the Carcassonne area. However, when their attempt was definitively crushed in the early 1240s, some allies such as the Niorts and the de Termes changed side, and chose to back the king.[43]

This brief excursus shows that political events could place one or the other party on the winning side, with alliances varying within the groups. Dissenters enjoyed a climate of widespread toleration, sometimes open support, before the Crusade. Members of the noble families were accepted as Good Men and Good Women, for example Esclarmonda of Foix, sister of count Raymond Roger, the count's own wife Philippa and his aunt Fays of Durfort were all ordained and chose to reside in Cathar houses.[44] Such a deeply entrenched link with non-conformists, fostered and tolerated by the local nobility, suddenly provided the mark of outlaws during and after the Crusade.[45]

Despite the intricate and multi-layered net of loyalties, placing each character within one or more than one group at a time, there is one occasion in which individuality is most important. All of the deponents were either captured, summoned to respond *individually* to accusations or spontaneously gave their testimony to the court. Even though

---

[42] Barber, *The Cathars*, pp. 43–57; Lambert, *The Cathars*, pp. 60–9.
[43] Lambert, *The Cathars*, pp. 168–9.
[44] On noblewomen and their link to Catharism, see A. Brenon, *Les femmes Cathares* (Paris, 1992).
[45] See Barber, *The Cathars*, pp. 34–70, 141–50; Lambert, *The Cathars*, pp. 60–9, 73–80, 102–7; Duvernoy, *L'histoire*, pp. 237–56, 258–66.

their responsibility for a specific action could be shared with others, inquisitorial law operated on a one-to-one basis: effectively each suspect stood in isolation in front of the pope's agents.[46] Because of this, and for the reasons outlined above, it is no surprise that the fears appearing in our records are mainly about self-preservation. In other words, treated as individual offenders, their fears are those of being attacked as individuals; their reactions and individual responses to those fears.

This basic concern is clear in the following example. Peter Ferreol of Trébons was one of the many who amended his initial deposition after a period of 'reflection'. We have already met him in the first chapter, where he declared that his first confession had not been recorded by the notary.[47] In going back to the court for the third time, he was well aware of how one should deal with the inquisitors; he knew that, if he voluntarily confessed everything he knew, he could plea-bargain with them. According to this sort of 'calculus of decisions', he carefully weighed his actions and measured the risk he was taking: he wanted reassurance that, before his deposition, the inquisitors would guarantee his immunity and would not touch his patrimony. The following phrase, a visible 'textual result' of his calculations, appears in the record of his hearing. 'He is guaranteed that he will not have any penance imposed by which he might lose his own body or possessions, if he gives full deposition on the crime of heresy by next Tuesday.'[48] Peter's decision to assess risk and to work out a risk-taking strategy was not taken in a panic attack: he had weighed up the pros and cons of confessing something, and deposed according to this very basic calculation.

Several examples in the depositions give clear evidence of the deponents' fears for their lives, whether openly declared or hidden behind a fear of being betrayed, 'sold' or being associated with suspicious persons. The believers of Puylaurens were scared. According to Gaucelin of Miraud, 'one time, because of the burning of a man of Puylaurens, who was called *Estelo*, who was burnt with two women heretics who had been found in his, *Estelo's* house, all the believers were terrified of heretics, so that they did not dare to host them'.[49] After the massacre of Avignonet, the knight

---

[46] Despite the obvious additional pressures imposed by this one-to-one mechanism, J. Paul has argued that such a confrontation eventually produced realistic end-results ('L'hérésie au village dans la diocèse de Carcassonne au milieu du XIIIe siècle', *Cahiers de Fanjeaux* 40 (2006), pp. 255–82, at pp. 256–8). Although Paul's position can be endorsed to some extent, there's a degree of generalization which does not take into appropriate account the singularities of each personal attitude towards any specific situation and towards the authority.

[47] See above, Chapter 1.

[48] 'Assecuratus quod non habebit penitentiam propter quam amittere debeat corpus aut bona sua, si infra diem martis proximo futuram plene confessus fuerit de crimine heresis', D26, f. 66r.

[49] 'Quodam vice, propter combustione cuiusdam de Podio Laurentio qui vocabatur Estelo qui fuerat combustus cum duabus hereticabus que invente fuerant in domo eiusdem Estelo, territi fuerunt

Arnold Roger of Mirepoix was questioned about the killing and other links with heresy. He told the inquisitors that the people of Avignonet, who in the past had been supportive of the 'heretics' to whom they used to bring food and other goods, had ceased to provide them, as 'for the last six years or so they [the citizens of Avignonet] had not dared to go there for fear of the *gallici*'.[50]

As evident from these instances, the advent of the Crusades (1209–29) and of the king's supporters, followed by the institution of the papal inquisition (1233), definitely represented *the* turning-point in the life of Cathar communities. A brief parenthesis is necessary here to remind us of the key dynamics of these two decades. After the killing of the papal legate Peter of Castelnau (1209), a Cistercian sent to the area with the express purpose of carrying on anti-Cathar preaching, Innocent III's efforts were directed to convincing the king, Philip II, of the necessity of a more radical and effective campaign – crusade-like – against Catharism and its supporters. Failing this, he turned to nobles of the region of Francia, among which soon emerged Simon of Montfort, originally from the Île-de-France, near Paris. Until his death in 1218, de Montfort became the spiritual and military leader of a party of other northern nobles, mainly drawn from his same area, who led a military campaign addressed mostly to the Languedocian nobility (counts of Toulouse and Foix, and viscounts of Béziers and Carcassonne, the Trencavels). The campaign enjoyed approval, blessing and privileges granted by the papacy to the Crusades against the muslims. Although after the first few years the campaign arose suspicion within the papacy as to the effective religious drive behind the numerous sieges and killings – for instance Innocent III in May 1213 revoked crusading privileges to those participating in de Montfort's campaign, and effectively reprimanded him for his indiscriminate violence – mass-executions could still be carried on publicly in 1210 at Minerve and in 1211 at Lavaur and Les Cassès. After de Montfort's death, in 1218, his son Amaury and the dauphin Louis, son of king Philip II, took the lead of the campaign. Although the southern forces did gain territory in the early 1220s, Louis was able to pursue his agenda much more freely at his father's death (1223), and his impact on Languedocian dynamics of power eventually meant the surrender and even change of side of some former supporters of the Trencavels and of the counts of Toulouse, who sided with the crown.[51]

---

omnes credentes hereticis ita quod non audebant tenere hereticos', D23, f. 112r.

[50] 'A sex annis citra usquequo non fuerint ibi ausi venire timore gallicorum', D22, f. 146v.

[51] Barber, *The Cathars*, pp. 120–40; Lambert, *The Cathars*, pp. 102–11; Oldenbourg, *Massacre*, pp. 1–27, 132–76.

The crusade meant effectively the start of a different political environment, where the papacy could interfere in matters of heresy without passing through the authority of the local church. This element, together with the atmosphere of increased mutual fear, undoubtedly transformed the pattern of proselytism and the ecclesial habits of Catharism. A comparison of the evidence in earlier registers such as D21–3 with the later ones shows many differences. Disputations and preaching moved away from squares and streets to the homes of sympathisers, woods and huts. What had previously represented an extremely successful and organised alternative to Catholicism, managing to exist side-by-side with it, now became quintessentially dangerous and 'other'.

Also, with the active intervention of the *crucesignati* as Crusaders of the pope, political issues and dynamics came to the fore to such an extent that political alliances and/or rivalries overlapped with religious and doctrinal ones. Douglas's model must now take into account that pressures on one side and fears on the other were now following political patterns as much as religious ones.

In addition, from the Crusade onwards, people were forced to take up clearer positions in their religious and political choices. All that 'grey area' of floating believers, uncertain listeners, lukewarm sympathisers was pushed into a more defined framework: either in or out, pro or against, for one or for the other. There was less space for indecision, no time for dwelling on doctrinal disputes, and even less tolerance of uncertainty. No one could claim any longer, 'I did not know'.

The situation is clearly outlined by Pons of Magrefort. He declared that 'before the coming of the crusaders' the heretics 'lived publicly, and without worries, because they were wary of nobody',[52] as – according to Berbegueira of Puylaurens – 'no-one denied contact or admittance to the heretics'.[53] One could cite many examples of a change in attitude, of the spreading climate of mutual mistrust and suspicion, with its inevitable consequences for people's behaviour and feelings, especially the growth of fear. Peter of Cabanil, once in the presence of heretics, 'did not adore the aforesaid heretics, nor did the others, as he saw, because people were afraid of each other, because they were not friends'.[54] Philippa of Francarville testified that 'when Francarville was captured by the French and destroyed, she and her husband and her nanny, Guillelme, went to

---

[52] 'Stantes publice … indifferenter ita quod a nemine sibi cavebant ante primo adventum crucesignatorum', D23, f. 86r/v.
[53] 'Nullus vitabat accessum vel introitum ad hereticos', D24, f. 136r.
[54] 'Interrogatus dixit quod ipse testis non adoravit dictos hereticos nec alii ipso teste vidente, quia timebat sibi adinvicem, quia non erant amici', D24, f. 28r.

the aforementioned *clusellum* for fear of the French'.[55] Bertrand Martin, Cathar deacon and renowned preacher – and thus liable to harsher treatment once in court – 'did not dare to stay on in the land of the King'.[56] Esquiva of Auriac and her son Ademar 'came to the heretics and said to them that they [the heretics] had been sold, and that, for the love of God, if they were to be captured they should not reveal her'.[57] Raymond Raseire of Auriac was invited to see heretics in a friend's house, but asked for a woman to be sent away as he did not dare see heretics in her presence 'because he feared her' ('timebat de ipsa').[58] And again, the list includes Bertrand of Alamans, who with two other men visited a couple of heretic women living in a 'hut' ('cabana') next to the village and urged 'that they go away from there, because they could not well stay, and they were next to the road and because of them a great danger was hanging over the village of Calvairac. And the heretics replied that they would go'.[59]

The Crusade represented therefore the turning-point after which freedom of belief and profession was never the same again, thus making the years 1209–33 exceptionally significant in this sense. However, all Cathar history was punctuated by moments of high tension which coincided with a rapid heightening of suspicion and mutual fear. One clear case is represented, once again, by Montségur. Arpaix of Ravat reveals how 'there was suspicion among men and women in Montségur, that Bertrand of La Baccalarie, who made machines, had come to the aforesaid village on behalf of the Count of Toulouse or for his men'.[60] Some used this climate of reciprocal mistrust to serve their own purposes, as appears in James Given's detailed study of the plot against William Tron. In this famous case, two arch-enemies, both notaries at Tarascon, William Tron and Peter of Gaillac, accused each other of heresy. Peter of Gaillac came from a family of Cathar believers, had known Peter Autier, the famous Good Man, and was probably sentenced to imprisonment in

---

[55] 'Cum Francartvila caperetur a francigenis et dirueretur, ipsa testis et maritus ipsius testis et Guillerma predicta nutrix ipsius testis venerunt ad dictum clusellum propter timorem francigenorum', D23, f. 258v. The heretics had been given some land to work, and built this *crusellum*, where the context suggests a little hut or shelter.

[56] 'Non erat ausus remanere in terra domini Regis', D24, f. 89r.

[57] 'Esquiva de Auriaco et Ademars, filius eius, venerant ad ipsas hereticas et dixerant eisdem hereticabus quod vendite erant, et quod amore Dei si caperentur non discooperirent ipsam', D23, f. 183r.

[58] D23, f. 183v.

[59] 'Quod recedent inde quia minus bene stabant ibi, et erant iuxta viam et possent propter ipsos magnum periculum imminere toti castro de Calvairac, et heretice responderunt quod in procinctu erant recedendi,' D23, f. 68v.

[60] 'Suspicio erat hominum qui erant in castro Montis Securi et mulierum quod Bertrandus de la Bacalairia qui faciebat machinas venisset in dicto castro ex parte Comitis Tholosani vel suorum', D22, f. 263r.

Carcassonne by the inquisitor Geoffroy of Ablis. Later on he became some kind of 'informer for the inquisitor', and started his campaign against his colleague William Tron, who, on more than one occasion, had denigrated him publicly for his non-conformist past. Eventually, the inquisitor, this time Jacques Fournier, discovered how this private rivalry had turned into a personal campaign, and how Peter of Gaillac had gathered a little party of followers who set a well-organised plot against Tron.[61] Such a climate of mistrust, and the possibility of legitimising mistrust and hatred through reciprocal accusations of heresy, undermined the bonds within communities and families, in an era when – as demonstrated since *Montaillou* – 'l'engagement réligieux est affaire de lineage et non de choix personnel'.[62]

In parallel with political instability and floating political patterns, safety for believers and Good Men and Women followed zigzagging patterns of highs and lows in the following decades. Lambert talks of a period of increased security in the late 1220s, then of the 'revival' of Catharism leading to Montségur in 1244, but with peaks of persecution between the 1230s and 1240s. In addition, we must take into account that, even in times of persecution, good or bad conditions for Cathars, both believers and sympathisers, followed uneven patterns throughout France. Lambert writes of a general 'meridional tolerance and unwillingness to draw sharp lines between heresy and orthodoxy' which 'resurfaced in various places'.[63] Consequently, rising tensions were a repeated phenomenon, together with the uneven geographical spread of 'levels of tension' throughout the area under enquiry. We should probably think in terms of people becoming accustomed, after the period 1209–29, to an atmosphere of constant alternation between relief and tension, and to the existence of clusters of relative safety for dissenters. Among these, first and foremost, was Italy where the alliance between the ghibelline cities provided a net of safe havens for refugees, and where the anti-papal front under the leadership of Oberto Pallavicino and Ezzelino of Romano lasted up until 1266–7.[64] Also, places like Montségur for some time, certainly from 1229 to its fall in 1244, and the areas dominated by the family of the Niorts, south of Carcassonne, up to their defection to king

---

[61] J. Given, 'Factional politics in a medieval society: a case study from fourteenth-century Foix', *Journal of Medieval History* 14, I (1988), 233–50; see my analysis of the case in Chapter 1.
[62] E. Le Roy Ladurie, *Montaillou: Cathars and Catholics in a French Village 1294–1324* (Harmondsworth, 1978), esp. pp. 24–52; the quote is taken from Biget, 'Hérésie et politique', p. 26.
[63] Lambert, *The Cathars*, p. 134.
[64] See Roach, *The Devil's World*, pp. 149–58; Lambert, *The Cathars*, pp. 171–214; Lansing, *Power and Purity*, pp. 13, 139–41; Barber, *The Cathars*, pp. 164–8; Duvernoy, *L'histoire*, pp. 165–83, esp. pp. 175–83.

Louis II in the early 1240s,[65] of Caraman, Lanta, Lavaur and Castelsarrasin over several decades. In the southern part of the lands of the count of Toulouse, the Cathars had deacons in Lanta, Villemur, Labecède, St Félix, Caraman, Auriac, Montmaur, Puylaurens and Vielmur. In general, up to the breakdown of the southern alliance against the Crown (mid-1240s), Catharism was able to find shelter in all the lands where supporters of the count of Toulouse and his southern allies could enjoy a reasonable degree of autonomy from the crown's influence.[66]

There are a few explicit mentions of fear of the *inquisitors* driving our deponents into flight. This may be due to the reasons listed above. Among those attesting to this specific kind of fear is Rixende of Mireval of Graulhet, who had been captured and brought to trial. She openly confessed to having fled her home 'for fear of the inquisitors'.[67] So did Arnold Raymond, who fled to Catalonia driven by this fear *(timor inquisitorum)*,[68] Arnold Richer of Narbonne *(metu inquisitionis)*[69] and Arnolde of Lamothe and her sister – both ex-Good Women – who, 'because of too much fear of persecution' *(pre nimio timore persecutionis)*, left the Cathars, started to eat meat again and asked for reconciliation from the local bishop.[70]

I have not found statements of fear of the trial itself, or of the emotions it generated. However, one curious deposition shows a bizarre association between friars and natural calamities. Peter Perrin of Puylaurens was frightened by storms which – he heard – were connected to the arrival of the Friars Minors and Preachers, who caused social and environmental damage. Somehow he cleverly managed to divert the paternity of this belief to another source, a reliable, literate *auctoritas,* thus lightening the burden on his own shoulders. On a very stormy day, he says, 'He heard Bernard of Lavaur, notary of Soual, saying once that lightning and hailing used not to fall so frequently at the time when the heretics lived in this land as they do now – but since we live with the Minors and the Preachers, they fall more frequently than they used to. And he said this then because it was darkening, and he, and others who were there, were afraid of the hail.'[71]

---

[65] Lambert, *The Cathars*, p. 169; Roach, *The Devil's World*, p. 115.

[66] Lambert, *The Cathars*, p. 169.

[67] 'Timore inquisitoris', D25, f. 176v.

[68] D26, f. 147r.

[69] D23, f. 140r.

[70] D23, f. 6v. In fact, it was a 'calculated conversion', as stated by Lambert, a 'private transaction' with the bishop of Cahors which subsequently led to a quiet return to Catharism and its rituals (Lambert, *The Cathars*, p. 132).

[71] 'Audivit Bernardum de Vauro, notarium Assoal[is], dicentem quadam vice quod fulgura et tempestates non solebant cadere ita frequenter sicut modo faciunt tempore quo heretici manebant

These immediate concerns regarding personal survival and possessions, however, were not exclusively related to the risk of falling into
the inquisitors' net or into the hands of the 'Gallici' (northern French).
Deponents reveal fears resulting from the pressures exerted by their
belonging to an alternative/rival unit. Fear of transgression, of possible retaliation, is felt with regard to the Cathar community as well.
Just as with the Catholic Church, through breaking the rules and bonds
of loyalty of their new community individual Cathars risked becoming estranged from it. Anthropology has explained this phenomenon and
pointed out that the mechanism by which individuals within a given cultural structure or system fear betrayal of the group, the transgression of a
collective system of rules and values, is directly proportional to the depth
of their sense of belonging to that group.[72] There must have been lukewarm believers on both sides, for whom such estrangement did not cause
much trouble; but there were also committed adherents who genuinely
cared, first and foremost the Good Men and Women. This concern with
transgressing applies to Cathar communities where – in the same way
as a sense of being the target of unjust persecution acted as 'ideological
glue', and the fear of persecution bonded the group together[73] – contra-
vention of internal codes and moral rules was a cause of major concern
among the clergy. Peer pressure to perform according to the new, shared
belief must have been instilled in consciences through constant preaching, in a life where one's own identity depended so much on belonging.
The idea of contamination of the true belief was not one which was only
found among Catholics.

For example, the possibility of the Cathar *consolamentum* being administered repeatedly in cases where believers recovered from a spell on their
deathbed, shows how the structure tried to overcome the imperfection
of human nature, taking transgression of the rules for granted. It could
be considered as mirroring the Catholic pattern of confession–admission
of wrongdoing–penance, a mechanism which could be repeated many
times.[74] Despite the possibility of repeating the *consolamentum*, in practice
this scenario was better avoided, given the difficulties and risks of moving 'priests' around, and the many chances of things going wrong. The
knight Saix of Montesquieu, among others, told the inquisitors about
two Cathar priests' concern about relapses, when they did not think it

---

in terra ista – sed postquam sumus cum Minoribus et Predicatoribus, cadunt frequentius quam
solebant. Et hoc dixit tunc quia obscurabatur, et timebant ipse, et alii qui erant ibi, de tempestate',
D25, f. 216v.
[72] Tuan, *Landscapes*, p. 213 and ff.
[73] See the discussion on this point in Tuan, *Landscapes*, p. 210.
[74] See discussion on *consolamentum*, above, Chapter 1.

appropriate to administer the *consolamentum* to a dying woman because 'the said heretics feared that, in case she lived, the … ill woman would not be able to observe [the precepts] of their sect'.[75] The same happened to Bernard Fort[76] and Peter Escafre: each of them was not consoled 'because he did not think he would die' (*quia non putabat mori*).[77] Another interesting case, this time individually tailored, concerns the famous heretic Esclarmonde, mother of Bernard Otho, who was allowed to eat meat and behave as she felt appropriate, in order to avoid arrest.[78] To this category belong all the examples of ex-Good Men and Women who used 'calculated conversions' in order to escape a period of particular harshness, and who returned to Catharism when the worst was over: for example, the already cited Arnolde and Peirona of Lamothe.[79]

Application of the rules, again, was a matter of personal judgement; its evaluation relied upon differing levels of toleration and flexibility on the part of the officials. Esclarmonde's permission to break the rules, in its exceptionality, shows 'in negative' how the system to which she belonged took decisions according to a scale of worries which took into account each individual case, and established a hierarchy of priorities. For instance, in the case of dying believers who were denied the *consolamentum*, the main preoccupation was that, by breaking the moral code of the group, they might lose their integrity. In Esclarmonde's case, however, the Good Men were more afraid of losing her through her being captured by the inquisitors acting suspiciously and then being killed. This also shows anxiety about breaking the unity of the group; not so much a moral concern as a matter of church organisation where the loss of a core member – as Esclarmonde must have been – could affect and compromise the existence of entire Cathar communities. It is as though the 'Good Men' were saying, 'We cannot afford this risk: the price to pay for her breaking our code of belief (only ostensibly, not in her heart) is lower than the risk of losing her.'

Such anxiety to keep the group together is attested not only where the hierarchy took measures to prevent or limit transgression and apostasy, but also in other cases, where fear of breaking up the internal unity of the groups results in different outcomes and attitudes towards the Inquisition and the Cathars. This generalisation needs a caveat. In the snippets of depositions that bear upon this, there might also be a certain apologetic

---

[75] 'Timebant dicti heretici quod dicta infirma, si viveret, non posset observare sectam eorum', D24, f. 132v.

[76] D24, f. 30r.

[77] D24, ff. 33v–34r.

[78] See D21, f. 34v.

[79] See Lambert, *The Cathars*, p. 132.

tone, in attempts to minimise one's actions through pleading fear. It is necessary to point these out: there is no reason to exclude the possibility that to some extent fear (as well as other considerations) could have driven these confessions.

Adalaix of Massabrac, giving testimony in 1244 just after the siege of Montségur, was in the village herself when it was taken by the pope's allies. She told the inquisitors that she had previously converted back to the Catholic faith and abandoned her old congregation (*deseruit sectam hereticam*) in order to get married. She should therefore have been considered safe. However, she claimed, 'because of the coming of lord Imbert of Beaujeu and of the bishop of Clermont to those parts, she [...], fearing for herself, took flight and went into the castle of Montségur', where she was captured.[80]

As a new church, Catharism enrolled enthusiastic clergy, who showed not only strong belief, but also a high degree of commitment towards their brethren and the ideals they shared with them. It is true that Adalaix was summoned to court after being caught in a rather compromising situation, and that her concern to 'call herself out' by claiming to be no longer a heretic must have dictated her statements to some degree. Nevertheless, it is not unlikely that the potential danger she was facing was what impelled Adalaix – and with her, many others – to act as she did, driven by stress and panic, and that the prospect of estrangement from the Cathar community mattered more to her than the fear of being caught by the inquisitors. After all, she had believed that her soul would be saved through the Cathars. Still, salvation was more important than being married, when facing an exceptional situation such as the long Montségur siege. Even if we cannot be sure about her, certainly individuals *like* her will have felt strong pressures from both sides to comply with established rules. It is known that, during the final phase of the siege, about twenty people voluntarily asked for the *consolamentum* in the fortress. Brotherhood and internal cohesion had worked to such an extent upon people's minds, convincing them that it was better to die consoled, than to flee marked forever by the shame and sin of flight. Both the rival institutions wished to retain the highest number of believers they could, and as proselytising was common on both fronts, people will also have been hammered by psychological pressures from both sides.

We have evidence of threats and pressures as when, for example, the knight Guiraud Colom declared that some heretics, knowing of his intention to capture them, told him, 'Beware that you said those things

---

[80] 'Propter adventum domini Imberti de Belloioco et episcopi Claromontensis ad partes istas, ipsa testis timens sibi arripuit fugam et intravit castrum Montis Securi', D24, f. 203 and ff.

[i.e. "the accusations he made"] with evil intention, and for this you shall now lose your life.'[81] This reappears when Raymond Boer excused the incompleteness of his previous declarations to the inquisitors by saying that 'he hid all he knew about heresy from the said inquisitors out of fear, since William de L'Île, knight of Laurac, had threatened him, the witness, that he would experience a misfortune if he revealed anything [about heresy] to the said inquisitors'.[82] Threats were therefore many sided. People were exposed to them from the Church (warning about moral transgression and spiritual and physical punishment), from their own brotherhood (pressures about diminishing or breaking internal cohesion, or betraying their fellows), local powers-that-be (either for or against the dissenters) and also from family ties (pressures to preserve and protect one's family, or to establish priorities where family came before religious belonging). To this list we must add pressures coming from superior social groups. A threat made by a local knight must have sounded graver than threats made by one's peers. Mundy's dissection of the social and political patterns of Toulouse has detailed this complicated framework of hierarchical groupings, thus highlighting the possibilities of various pressures exerted top-down on to the low levels. Toulouse can be taken as a representative example of all possible combinations existing – to say it with Mundy – 'in the age of the Cathars'. For instance, on the basis of their place of residence, the hierarchy *milites–burgenses–rustici*; on the basis of religious confession, the polarity Christians–Jews; and again, the seigniorial chain (viscounts, *comitores, vasvassores, milites, rustici*); in business, the disparity between businessmen and their *mancipii* (partners not owning any of the merchandise); in families, differences between members of a house and their *familiares* (domestics) who 'ranged between persons of authority and even privilege to slaves', but also between family members, old and young, men and women, close or far relatives; and lastly, the clergy–laity dichotomy. Although not explicitly recorded in public and private charters, these differences existed in fact and were evident in the treatment reserved to individuals belonging to different groups when facing the law, or in the mechanisms of adoption of family names among relatives, which is witness of 'the strength of family solidarity'.[83]

When Atho of Baretges, a bailiff of the count of Toulouse, was warning the people of Moissac not to accept the sentences of William Arnold and Stephen of St Tibéry, unless they wanted their own persons and

---

[81] 'Sciatis quod male dixisti ista, et ad huc propter hoc amittetis vitam', D23, f. 152v.
[82] 'Celavit dictis inquisitoribus omnia que sciebat de heresi propter timorem, quia Guillelmus de Insula miles de Lauraco comminatus fuit ipsi testi quod infortunium veniret ipsi testi si revelaret aliquid dictis inquisitoribus', D23, f. 148v.
[83] Mundy, *Society and Government*, pp. 45–7, 49–54, 60–6, 76–9, 154–7, 174–6.

possessions to be seized,[84] the threat must have sounded quite concrete to the audience.

Guiraud Gallart was warned that his eyes would be in danger if he revealed anything about three local men,[85] and Gaillard Ruby of Montgaillard explained his actions by reference to the 'prayers and incantations of his said brothers',[86] while Pons Faure acted 'more out of fear than love' (*plus timore quam amore*).[87] Peter Fogasset of Caraman would have been willing to collaborate with the inquisitors, but did not do so 'for fear that they [the heretics] would kill him, since although he wanted to capture them, he did not dare'.[88] Perhaps we should also read in this light the various declarations by deponents who had 'hosted heretics as they [the deponent] had been compelled to do so'.[89] This does not sound unlikely, and it gives strength to the inquisitor's claims that 'fear of someone' (*timor alicuius*) could hinder a true and honest deposition.

Whatever the origin and focus of fears, there is clear and consistent evidence of a 'reaction' with regard to the system and its ministers. Clear examples of the reluctance to comply with the inquisitors' guidelines and sentences can be seen particularly in Toulouse, where the support of count Raymond VII and the city consuls to Frederick II from 1235 guaranteed a sympathetic environment to all anti-papal undercurrents, and ultimately, a safer environment to non-conformity. This hostile tendency culminated in the open opposition to the work of the inquisitors, with several episodes of trials being jeopardised by the lack of collaboration between the tribunal and the local authorities. In particular, the aversion to the Dominican William Arnold and the Franciscan Stephen of St Thibéry, escalated from the blatant disregard of their sentences, to the expulsion of the Dominicans from Toulouse, to the killing of the two in 1242.[90]

Aside from general politico–religious unease, some more specific features of the 'business of peace and faith' seem to have stirred particular opposition. Among them, the practice of exhumation of people recognised as heretics only posthumously, which is recorded in Languedoc ever since the 1230s, was perceived as an open provocation, an illegitimate

---

[84] The episode is analysed more thoroughly below.
[85] 'Dixit tamen quod Aimericus de Bressols et Arnaldus et Vitalis adiuraverunt ipsum qui loquitur per fidem suam et in periculo oculorum quod nichil diceret de eis inquisitoribus', D22, f. 18r.
[86] 'Propter preces et incantationes dictorum fratrum suorum', D26, f. 56r.
[87] D24, f. 118v.
[88] 'Pro timore ne interficerent, quia quamvis vellet ipse testis caperet eos, non esset ausus', D23, f. 335r.
[89] For instance, D24, f. 16r.
[90] Lambert, *The Cathars*, pp. 125–7.

abuse perpetrated by the tribunal. The repeated attacks on the inquisitor Arnold Catalan in Albi in 1234 are recorded evidence of this hostility.[91] In general, it seems that the establishment of the Inquisition in 1233 as an 'exceptional tribunal' provoked openly rebellious attitudes. For instance, episodes such as the rebellions of 1233 in Narbonne, 1234 in Albi and 1235 in Toulouse.[92] These attitudes, fuelled by growing resentment against church officials, dotted the whole of the post-Crusade period, reflecting the highs and lows of political relationships between church members and political power. One example is the changing attitude of Raymond VII of Toulouse towards Cathar supporters. He backed and even concretely helped the hunt for suspects in the immediate aftermath of the treaty of Paris (1229) then, since 1235, radically changed side, following his support to Frederick II and, by mid-1242 to a political coalition against the Capetian monarchy. Raymond VII's behaviour in the fight against religious non-conformity paid the price of his political moves, caught between the loyalty to his local lords (supporting Catharism) and the wider political patterns of alliance between monarchies, lower lordships and the papacy.[93] In most cases, when organised, rebelliousness enjoyed the backing if not the leadership of local urban oligarchies. Overall, no matter what pressures they were under, the deponents, either as individuals or in groups, do not stand before us as weak and astonished figures. They work their way through the trial, and outside the courthouse they study strategies, try to get the best result with the least harm, now using the system to their own purposes, now collapsing in the face of overwhelming physical or psychological pain. The responses to fear, which result from each individual's risk-taking strategy, can be as diversified as are the cases with which we are dealing. Yet still they react: angrily, cunningly, violently or wisely. On their own or in groups, according to personal or to collective criteria, they take actions that may surprise us: not all of them keep their heads down.

The overriding impression is that exceptional conditions, in combination with the extraordinary nature of an event such as a judicial interrogation, provoked the reactions of extreme behaviour: fear, rebellion, submission and hatred, all of which were felt with intensity.

As demonstrated in Chapter 1, a particular liveliness or expressiveness featuring in the otherwise formulaic depositions is the clear sign of authenticity in the wording. To this category belong all the outbreaks

---

[91] Barber, *The Cathars*, pp. 150–64, recalls the whole process of the escalation of 'resistance' leading to the siege and fall of Montségur.
[92] Biget, 'Hérésie politique', p. 38.
[93] Lambert, *The Cathars*, pp. 126–7; Barber, *The Cathars*, p. 155.

of anger and heartfelt resentment. They are particularly revealing, as one must picture them recurring in front of and in spite of the inquisitors. Indicatively, however, in most cases they are reported second hand. Peter Autier was reported as declaring that he would never recant his beliefs, 'not even if all of his friends were flayed alive in front of him'.[94] Attributed to Fabrissa of Limoux was the statement that she 'knew such things that she would not give away, even if all the flesh of her body were stuck with pins'.[95] Likewise the words of one of the Avignonet conspirators, – according to John Vidal – expressed anger and resentment against the inquisitors themselves. 'He would give naught for all the masses celebrated in Cahors, and if the judge inquisitors sent him to go ahead, he would go behind, and that their excommunication is not worth an egg, because the Church made many false judgements.'[96] Another sympathiser, William Faure, was described as reacting violently to the news coming from Avignonet. 'Now come here, masked, rabid Catholics, we were blind for long, but now we have our sight back, and it [sight] will certainly last more for us than for you.'[97] Here is a defiant attitude towards the authorities which the inquisitor has every interest in keeping as it is, as it could constitute evidence for incrimination.

In all these cases invectives come from people whose involvement in the facts of heresy was quite substantial: one of the last surviving Cathar priests; the daughter of a Good Woman, if not a Good Woman herself; a conspirator in the killing of inquisitors; and an enthusiast for that killing. It makes sense that words of scorn, of commitment to a belief and attachment to its establishment come from these people.

Under this heading of angry and violent responses, two striking examples must be mentioned. These are more than just displays of resentment, as they carry within them lethal personal consequences. Both of them feature a lively recollection of events and a picaresque organisation of the discourse, which serve as highlighters for us. In the first case, an

---

[94] 'Etiamsi omnes amici sui excoriarentur vivi coram ipso', referred in Gui, *Liber sententiarum*, p. 220.

[95] 'Sciebat talia, que non revelaret, etiam si tota caro sua carnis/acubus pungeretur', D25, ff. 43r–v.

[96] 'Quod nichil daret pro omnibus missis que dicuntur apud Caturcum, et si iudices inquisitores mandarent ipsum ire ante, et quod excommunicationem ipsorum non apreciabatur ovum, quia multa falsa iudicia faceret ecclesia', D22, f. 11v.

[97] 'Veniatis huc vos alii mascarat Catholici ravios, nos fuimus diu ceci sed modo recuperavimus visum et duravit (possibly for "durabit"?) de cetero magis nobis quam vobis', D22, f. 11v. The meaning of 'mascarat' presents some difficulties. Although literally 'covered by a mask', its contextualisation and the following punctuation here is a personal interpretation. Possibly William attacks both the hypocrisy and physical aspect of the clergy (where the 'mask' can be seen as a derogatory description for the paraments). This interpretation would also fit with the follow-up: although hypocritical and pompously dressed up in church robes, the Catholics have been uncovered in their true nature, behind their mask and their rich garments, by their opponents.

attempt to 'terrorise' (*bene terrere*) an over-zealous priest ends up with him being killed. Around 1240–1 the men of Caraman, tired of this *capellanus* (chaplain or parish priest) who persecuted heretics, decided to frighten him 'to the point that he would not dare persecute them' anymore. It was the priest's companion, a fellow who used to go around with him to collect tax, who suggested a good place for giving him the fight of his life. The attack was like a military operation, led by several armed men, and it made the priest seek safety in flight. But, in the end, he was killed. The group decided to hide the corpse by throwing it into a well. The witness himself was one of the group, and does not hide his part in it, declaring that he did it 'for love of the heretics' (*amore hereticorum*).[98]

The protagonist in the other example was Atho of Baretges, previously a bailiff of the count of Toulouse. He declared his defiance to the inquisitorial measures of William Arnold and Stephen of St-Thibéry, the Minor (Franciscan). When the two officials publicly pronounced sentences in the village of Moissac, he said 'in public, in the church, that no one should dare to accept these penances from the inquisitors; because he [Atho] would seize their bodies [i.e. of those complying with the sentences] and take possession of their goods'. Also, he declared to the inquisitors themselves that 'the count did not consider them judges, and that they could not show the letters of his [the count's] jurisdiction'.[99]

In both of these violent reactions people do not appear to have been frightened of the power of churchmen. In the second case, the public declaration of hostility was no empty threat. Coming during a period of tension between Raymond VII, the count of Toulouse and the inquisitors, the public attack on the inquisitors' sentences was a reflection of pre-existing enmity between the count and William Arnold, which culminated in William's expulsion from Toulouse in 1235. Hostility and pride intermingle with sheer anger in the records, where the deponents do not even attempt to justify their own actions or cloak them in feeble excuses. Atho's declaration in particular appears in his own deposition, and is not a second-hand quotation reported by others.

In these cases again, Douglas's model proves to be very illuminating. We have an attack organised at the prompting and under the protection of the town's bailiff by the men of Caraman; and a public declaration of control by a bailiff of the count of Toulouse. As in the case of the theft of the Carcassonne registers, a plan organised by powerful men to subvert

[98] D23, ff. 313r–4r.
[99] 'Prohibuit omnibus publice in ecclesia quod nullus est ausus accipere penitentias ab inquisitoribus, quia ipse caperet/eorum corpora et occuparet eorum bona', 'Dicebat etiam inquisitoribus quod comes non habebat eos pro iudicibus, nec ipsi poterant ostendere litteras iurisdictionis sue', D22, ff. 45v–46r.

inquisitorial power can count on the backing and support of the local
military and religious elite. Although all these deponents could count
on having a degree of authority and power over local populations, and
although they too did not hide details of their actions, the attitude displayed in these two examples is far from the grovelling confessions of
Agasse and Laguarrigue, both of whom were broken men. The motivation behind these two examples does not appear to be purely political,
a matter of the local power having sufficient strength and resources to
oppose the churchmen, or hopes of personal gain. A *capellanus*, whose
assiduity in 'grassing on' people outweighed his zeal as a shepherd of
souls, is wiped out – to the advantage of the population. There is a degree
of hatred and sheer cockiness in these witnesses's words that shows open
rebellion. They were reacting to a situation which had gone far beyond
the bounds of acceptability.

In most cases, however, the deponents' responses have a different
tone, at once apologetic, fearful and deferential. This applies to all those
instances when people, in the follow-up to their first deposition, now
confess matters previously denied, and admit to having concealed them
out of 'fear' or 'terror' (*timore, terrore*), or that they had acted from 'stupidity' (*insanitas*), 'folly' (*insipientia*) or 'forgetfulness' (*quod non recolebat*). Here,
their reaction could have been dictated either by real terror, mixed with
submissiveness, or by the desire to secure the interrogator's good graces
or by both. In other words, by a calculation which would have assured
for the deponent at least partial remission of sins.

An example, which is free from the bias of the heresy/orthodoxy
counterpoint, and which helps us understand different responses in risk-
taking, is the case of Arnold of Les Rouzégas, a cleric. Arnold himself had
nothing to do with heresy or heretics, but he suddenly discovered that
some of his past connections could bring his name to the attention of
the inquisitors, and he panicked. What had happened? Some years before
his deposition, he had played a trick on some of his fellow citizens, telling them that during repair work in his house, he had found an 'earthen
vase or pot' (*olla lutea*) in a hole in the wall. As the house had once been
the property of the Templars, he was curious about the contents, which
turned out to be parchment wills left by heretics. On the basis of these
documents, Arnold extorted money from the families of the deceased,
and fled with his wife and the money to Catalonia. In reality, of course,
the wills had all been written by him, and he confessed to the inquisitor
that – in order to make the whole story more credible – he had placed the
parchment documents in a 'little window' 'in the place where he did his
cooking' (*in quadam fenestrula, in loco ubi ille coquinabat*) so that 'blackened
by the smoke they would look older' (*fumo denigrata sunt and antiquiores*

apparerent). So far his fraudulent scheme had not been discovered, but Arnold learnt that some of his victims had been accused of heresy, so he rushed back to France to give a spontaneous[100] deposition about the fake wills, in order – one may suppose – not to be accused of something else. Why this daring action, patently disregarding the law? 'Why did you do it?', asked the inquisitor. Arnold replied and gave his explanation, with its combination of meekness and calculation. 'Because he, the witness, and his wife were poor and were overwhelmed by a penury with which they could not deal, so he thought of a way by which he could ease his poverty.'[101] Again, there were concerns about survival and welfare.

One can detect a slightly more bitter tone in Arnold Cimordan's wordy explanation of why he, a previously convicted rebel against episcopal power, escaped from prison. 'Why did you do it?', asks the inquisitor. The record reports:

Because he did not have his necessities there. For he was not provided for from the goods of the king, because his forfeited possessions had not come to the king, but to the bishop; nor was he provided for from the goods of the bishop, because he did not have a messenger whom he could send frequently enough to the bishop's hall for bread. And when some bread was sent to him from the bishop's house to the prison, he was sent hard bread, and he could not eat it. He also lacked clothes and other necessities.[102]

A third group of reactions can be seen in cases where individuals found a way of 'tricking' the system, escaping accusations or manipulating the existing rules to carry on behaving as they wished. Corruption was probably the quickest way to obtain the silence of witnesses or the non-interference of the authorities. Examples of bribery appear in the records.

Peter Fogasset had approached the bailiff and vice-bailiff of Caraman, offering them a hundred *solidi* of Toulouse each 'so that they would let things be, and would not concern themselves with those who carried off the said heretics, that is the heretics Raymond Fort and his companion, and he [the witness] would do them a service'. Apparently, all the

---

[100] People confessing voluntarily (*sua sponte*) were granted absolution from excommunication and given canonical penances, normally quite lenient ones. If the deponent was a Good Man, he was encouraged to apply for religious status, preferably within the Dominican order, and then to be trained for work as inquisitor. See B. Hamilton, *The Medieval Inquisition* (London, 1981), p. 43.

[101] 'Cum idem testis, ut dixit, et uxor eius essent pauperes et habundarent penurie quibus satisfacere non valebant, cogitavit per quam viam posset sue consulere paupertati', D26, f. 146v.

[102] 'Dixit quod quia non habebat ibi necessaria non enim providebatur/sibi de bonis regis, quia incursus ipsius non pervenerat ad regem, sed ad episcopum, nec providebatur ei de bonis episcopi, quia non habebat nuntium quem posset ita frequenter mittere ad aulam episcopi pro pane. Et quando mittebatur ipsi testi panis de domo episcopi ad murum, mittebatur durus, et non poterat comedere. Carebat etiam vestibus et aliis necessariis,' D25, ff. 220v–221r.

population made contributions towards a collection and they managed to raise the required sum.[103] Two years later Bertrand of Alamans recalled that a couple of captured heretics were handed over to their gaolers by the local bailiffs. Following orders from the local knights and population, he had the delicate task of bargaining for the heretics' escape with the bailiffs, offering them money – a hundred *solidi* of Toulouse apiece – to release the prisoners. The knights and people of Caraman, in fact, feared that this arrest could lead to a wider inquiry, so he acted 'lest the town of Caraman be destroyed if they were to conduct an inquisition against anyone from the said town'.[104] Bertrand succeeded. A sum of 150 *solidi* was gathered through a new collection, and the heretics were released. Caraman could be considered a true bastion of Catharism, where even during the years of the Crusade 'few people died without *consolamentum*', and even at the beginning of the fourteenth century, 'old attachments [to Catharism] were brought into new life' by the mission of the last Cathar missionary, Pierre Autier.[105] However, it was not the only place where corruption occurred. Collections for bribing are recorded in several instances. For example, in 1233 there was a very effective 'whip-round', which led to the quick release of Bertrand Martin, the deacon and renowned preacher.[106] This is telling stuff, attesting the established practice of reactions to the system through acts of suborning and corruption *within* the system itself. It reveals great cohesion among dissenters and a parallel fragmentation among members of the other side.

Whenever reaction is not organised, and when it arises spontaneously among the local population, especially where nobles or officials are not involved, it provides more striking evidence of grassroots initiative and inventiveness. A curious Decameronesque episode is recounted by William Rafard. The messenger of the abbot of Sorèze had captured two renowned heretics, Raymunde Autier and her companion, and was about to take them to prison in Sorèze. While he was preparing for the transfer,

the women of Roquefort got together, and rushing on the said messenger with sticks and rocks, they snatched the aforesaid heretics from his hands and let them go away free. When this had been done, the said messenger returned immediately to the said abbot at Sorèze ... [They] called together there the women of

---

[103] 'Quod dimitterent stare, quod non intromitterent se de illis qui abstulerunt dictos hereticos, scilicet Raymundum Forts et socium eius hereticos, et quod ipse faceret eis servire', D22, f. 334r-v (discussed in Lambert, *The Cathars*, p. 145).
[104] 'Ne destrueretur castrum ipsum de Caramanh nec facerent inquisitionem contra aliquem de ipso castro', D23, ff. 69r–70r.
[105] Lambert, *The Cathars*, pp. 106, 261.
[106] Lambert, *The Cathars*, p. 157.

the said castle – because the men were outside at their work – and asked the said women if it was true that they had taken the said heretics from the aforesaid messenger. And they replied that that messenger had not found or captured any heretics there, but had captured two good women [a play of words here, between good women and Good Women], married, from the castle, whom, like a fool, he accused of being heretics: and that they had taken those women away from him, and no others. And they showed them two married women from the castle, saying that he had captured them; which the two women themselves likewise claimed. The said messenger, on the other hand, said that it was not those women that he had captured and that they had been taken away from him, but without doubt he had captured two heretics whom they had taken away from him. And he did not see them there – because he would know them well. And because the said messenger could not prove his case further, everything ended up in a swindle.[107]

This episode, whose tone is slightly ironic even in the records, sees a group of local women acting in concert – and possibly without much premeditation – against the most authoritative figures of the area: the local lord and the nearby abbot. They attacked a public official, and then maintained their version of events in a public meeting by substituting the characters on the scene. It is a remarkable episode, and not only for the technique of keeping narrative effects within the record; the extent of decision-making and confrontational initiative of these women comes out clearly in this case. Their position as members of a group made corruption unnecessary. Through the tactic of nullification of the messenger's words they were able to achieve the same outcome.

Whether the numerous conversions and abjurations, the feelings of regret or humility which appear in the depositions were genuine or not will never be known for sure. From the number of retractions and second, third or even fourth appearances before the inquisitors, we can see that people involved at various times in heretical business very rarely confessed 'all they knew about facts of heresy and Waldensianism' on the first occasion. Jacques Paul has concluded that most of the 'serial offenders',

---

[107] 'Congregaverunt se mulieres de Ruppeforte, et irruentes in dictum nuntium cum baculis et lapidibus, eripuerunt de manibus eius supradictas hereticas, et fecerunt eas abire liberas. Quo facto dictus nuntius rediit protinus ad dictum abbatem apud Soricinum … Convocaverunt ibi mulieres dicti castri – quia viri erant extra in operibus suis – et quesiverunt a dictis mulieribus an verum esset quod abstulissent dictas hereticas nuntio supradicto. Et responderunt quod nuntius ille non invenerat nec ceperat ibi hereticas, sed ceperat duas bonas mulieres de castro maritatas, quibus, sicut stultus, imponebat quod erant heretice, et quod illas abstulerunt ei, et non alias: et ostenderunt eis duas mulieres de castro maritatas, dicentes quod illas ceperat; quod ipse due mulieres similiter asserebant. Dictus vero nuntius ex adverso dicebat quod non erant ille mulieres quas ipse ceperat, et abstulerant ei, sed proculdubio ceperat/duas hereticas quas abstulerant ei; et non videbat eas ibi – quia bene cognosceret eas. Et quia dictus nuntius non potuit aliter factum suum probare, fuit reductus in trufam', D26, ff. 39v–40v.

after several partial depositions, passed on to abjuration, thus triggering a mechanism of admission and pardon which was much encouraged by the ecclesiastical authorities and jurists, and therefore could not be counter-mended or skipped during the trials.[108] Aside from this, however, there is virtually no insight as to what happened outside the tribunal, apart from the accounts of repeated actions – attendance at rites, meetings, contact with heretics – which are visible retrospectively through the follow-up of the first hearing, and which, as in the first instance, constituted proof of guilt. However, one interesting deposition helps us shed some light on what happened after and as a result of the hearing. It is, once again, a 'reaction', a way to work out an escape strategy, so as to act without incurring any penalty or breaking the law.

Peter of Clauzelles was approached by a man, Ysarn Bonhom, whose mother was seriously ill, feared death and said she wanted to be 'consoled' by the heretics. Ysarn needed help, as he was bound by a promise made to the inquisitor to have no further contact with heretics or heretical affairs. So he asked Peter 'that he, the witness, should take them [the heretics] to the said ill woman, since he, Ysarn Bonhom, would not meddle with her, nor take [the heretics] there; because he had been confessed to brother William Arnold, and had promised him that henceforth he would have no faith in them'.[109]

Some risks were unavoidable. The deponents carried on living and interacting in an environment where Catharism and Catholicism were closely intertwined, and were – alternately – on the 'winning side', depending on the political dynamics. Other risks were not so unavoid-able, as in the curious case of a visit to Rome. A deposition recorded in 1243, and – as usual – relating to facts occurred many years before, tells us of 'Regina Helishonors', the wife of the count of Toulouse, and another noblewoman, Finas, who, accompanied by their personal squire, went to Rome on unspecified business – perhaps pilgrimage, penance or a meeting. On their way they met several heretics and were put up in hos-pices where heretics frequently visited, probably heretical houses. Once in Rome they managed to go daily to the chapel where the pope heard mass, but did not go to see the pontiff. There they met – again, daily – a 'deacon of the heretics dressed like a pilgrim', who had been taken to the chapel by their squire, and they venerated him.[110] These women are

---

[108] Paul, 'L'hérésie au village', p. 256.
[109] 'Quod ipse testis adduceret eos ad eandem infirmam, quia idem Ysarnus Bonushomo non intro-mitteret se de illa, nec traderet inde, quia confessus fuerat fratri Guillelmo Arnaldi, et promiserat ei quod ulterius non haberet fidem in eis', D24 f. 231v.
[110] 'Diaconum hereticorum in habitu peregrini', D23, f. 92r.

probably identifiable as Eleanor, sister of Peter II king of Aragon (thus, 'regina'), and fifth wife of count RaymondVI of Toulouse ([1182]–1226), and the noble Finas.[III] Their action, a deliberate act of risk-taking, was put into place by a most powerful woman, who chose danger in the lion's den. Douglas's equation works here too. The higher the status, the more prone people are to taking risks.

Reactions to the system can therefore be seen in cases where deponents acted in open opposition to the system itself, challenging it consciously and blatantly, or where they took risks connected to their own status as dissenters. Whether they are visible to us through phrases (verbal reactions) or simply as actions confessed during a hearing, the different shades of response from anger to excuse, to open challenge, as little tricks or carefully organised conspiracies, all appear in the records. Bernard Laguarrigue who lived with the inquisitors as a servant was a practising Cathar; he had once been a *filius maior* and betrayed his new employers by attempting to steal the deposition books. Bertrand of Olmière openly made known to his fellow citizens his views on the corruption of clergy and his own free interpretation of the Scriptures without being particularly concerned about secrecy. The killers of Avignonet slaughtered and mocked the inquisitors and their symbols of power by dressing in their gowns and concocting humorous verses about their deaths. Viewed from this angle the traditional two-dimensional picture of the powerless believers is no longer convincing.

At this point we must return to our initial questions. What did people see as the limits of acceptable risk? Did they have limits in their challenge to the institution? What were they? What were their priorities? Ultimately, why did they do it?

We need now to turn away from individuals and particular circumstances. A certain degree of abstraction is necessary, when trying to extrapolate some general conclusions and to assess the usefulness of Douglas's model. In the past as in the present, the outcomes of risk-taking strategies (that is, the actions) have to be taken as the result of a balancing of risk, gain (reward) and the chances of success. In our case there is a common thread which dictated the balancing of these three factors. For both individuals and groups, common people and ruling elite, it was the idea of posing a challenge to the Inquisition, or to the Church, which they felt was abusive and illegitimate.

[III] Finas, wife of the pro-Cathar lord of Tauriac, Isarn, is interrogated in 1244 with her husband in D22 (Isarn's deposition at f. 62r, followed by Finas's at f. 64v); see also A. Brenon, *Les femmes cathares* (Paris, 1992), pp. 169–71; Lambert *The Cathars*, p. 150.

In general, as occurs in times of war, people who felt this struggle to be an extraordinary and exceptional occurrence were more prone to take risks than they would have done in a situation of normality. So, while the levels of risk increased overall, people were generally more prepared to face the challenge, and the acceptable limits were pushed forward. Catholicism and Catharism were effectively at war. Crusade aside, resentment of an illegitimate, alien, occupying power imposing its own will, laws, judgements and men upon their communities exacerbated relationships and undermined the existing connections between laity and clergy. Moreover, the new papal officials, because of the nature of their own court ('extraordinary tribunal') took virtually no account of the existing local dynamics of power. After all, this was precisely the reason why Gregory IX had detached inquisitors from local hierarchies: so that the struggle against heresy would not be obstructed by local authorities. As Barber puts it, 'the first step was to drive a wedge into the façade of community solidarity'.[112]

However, as Douglas suggested, even in wartime or warlike conditions, the levels of risk in subverting authority and its upholders are also variable. The various combinations of elements A, B and C (evaluation of risk, evaluation of gain, evaluation of the chances of success) are affected by standards of living (whether one is rich or poor), and by standards of morality and decency (how much one cares about the moral issues behind this subversion). Moreover, as economists have pointed out, individuals can be further grouped into those who are 'risk-averse', 'risk-neutral', or 'risk-lovers'.[113] The case of Languedoc adds further elements to this basic pattern. At the core is the fact that there were dual systems in operation. By establishing a counter-system (at least in terms of frame of mind) Catharism subverted the polarity of powerful–powerless among the communities supporting it. High or low status *within* the Church of Good Men and Women dictated individuals' priorities and choices so that, for example, a Good Man was more prone to take risks than a common believer. In the first instance, he exposed himself through being ready to undertake all the tasks that went with his status, such as administering sacraments, travelling and preaching, all actions which put him in a more dangerous position in the eyes of the Catholic judicial system. Secondly, by implicitly assuming that – if he were to be caught – his senior status would incur a harsher penance, leading to the stake if he were unwilling to recant and collaborate with his enemies. Thirdly, the commitment to truth of the Good Men and Women put them in a more

---

[112] Barber, *The Cathars*, p. 148.
[113] See D. Begg, S. Fischer and R. Dornbusch, *Economics*, 7th edn. (London, 2003), pp. 184–5.

delicate position, since when under interrogation they were less ready to disclose evidence, lie or disguise their own status. Certainly, some among them would have been 'risk-averse' individuals who did not have the moral fibre, commitment or simply the courage to keep faith. While each of these exceptions needs to be recognised as such and individually assessed by the historian, the broad generalisation still applies.

The polarity powerful–powerless was further complicated by the presence of a third category of holders of power: lay notables of various sorts (urban elites, rural knights, king's men, such as bailiffs, or higher southern nobility, such as the Trencavels or counts of Toulouse). These – and most importantly the combination and overlapping of these within the same geographic territories – did not follow even patterns of alliances throughout the history of Catharism. Systems of lordship and overlordship, common in the Languedoc area, became crucial in this respect during the years of the Albigensian Crusade, when the army led by Simon of Montfort required support and backing from the local nobility. For example, the case of the lord of Montréal and Laurac, Aimery, sheds good light onto this aspect. Although he had made a formal promise of loyalty to Simon of Montfort, Aimery turned his back on him twice – according to Peter of Les Vaux-de-Cernay – in 1209 and 1210, and decided to support the Cathars. Reading more in-depth into Aimery's behaviour, it is easy to see how behind this fluctuating attitude lay a mix of issues involving loyalty and political calculation: the determination not to succumb to the Crusaders, who effectively were leading a military campaign against the southern nobility; the mixed feelings for the roots that Catharism had gradually grown within noble families; the loyalty to the viscount of Béziers, his direct overlord; and the will to retain a certain degree of independence from the viscount himself.[114] However, this example shows how, in analysing the interference and the weight of *a* lay power upon the individuals' decisions, we must keep in mind a series of variables. First of all, that it would be a gross generalisation to attribute to this power the features of a monolithic structure (something like the relationship between kings and lower nobility). Secondly, and consequently, that the assumption of consistency in the lay power's attitude to heresy is superficial and incorrect.

Thus, a reconstruction of the impact and pressures of power (lay and ecclesiastical) upon religious non-conformity is a matter of single case-studies. In other words, unless each individual case is studied *per se*, it is impossible to find consistency and establish *generally* where the pressures were exerted, and by which 'power'. What has been important here is an

---

[114] Barber, *The Cathars*, pp. 34–7.

awareness of how the various powerful could exert pressures on single deponents, and that these pressures could have been both against or in support of dissenters.

Overall, our deponents seem to act according to a range of types of behaviour, depending on the interaction and weighing of the above factors: Douglas's model is further complicated by the different Languedocian case-related specific features. Consider, for instance, the high social position of Pierre Roger of Mirepoix, a noble and a Cathar sympathiser. He ran a high risk of compromising his own position in society and his prestige by following and sheltering Cathars, but he delegated to his men the dirty job of murdering William Arnold and Stephen of St-Thibéry the Minor, risking less in terms of his actions. There is also the role of Bernard Laguarrigue: he faced greater risks as a former convict and as a servant of the inquisitors who was now returning to help his old companions, but he believed he could make up for some of this with the 200 *solidi* he obtained as a reward.

The picture becomes even more complicated when the individual deponent – and in legal terms the individual defendant – is acting within a group. Here one should add to the variables the so-called risk-sharing strategy, which, by splitting the overall risk of the action into a series of smaller segments, makes the burden of the enterprise seem lighter to each of the participants. In fact, this easing off was only at a psychological level since, as we have already pointed out, inquisitorial law operated on a one-to-one basis. Stories such as the murder of the zealously collaborating priest, or the liberation of the two heretics by the women of Roquefort show that, in terms of reaction to the system, individuals felt safer when acting as part of a group. In other words, element C (the evaluation of possible success) seems more favourable to an individual if external factors are involved, such as the political backing of a powerful instigator, as in Avignonet, or the existence of accomplices, as in the previous cases.

What I have called the 'limit of acceptability' of risk follows the combination and development of this pattern. For each of our deponents the limit must be set at a different point, because each person's starting point and balance of initial factors differ. At the same time, in order to estimate each person's priorities historians should follow the same scale of evaluation. If considered side by side, however, despite the prevailing 'powerful' background of our deponents (senior Cathar clergy, squires, knights and so on), we find to our surprise that the priorities against which they weigh their own actions, in other words their personal 'limits of what is tolerable', are measured against the basic three 'boundaries of security' (domain, body and house). However, it is a matter of applying these labels ('domain', 'body' and 'house') to different things. For Raymond of Pereille, the 'catalyst' and perhaps mastermind of the Avignonet slaughter, it was a matter of re-establishing an order altered illegitimately by the inquisitors, who ultimately affected directly his own family (thus preserving his 'house'). For some of his fellow conspirators, perhaps led by a lesser degree of personal involvement, risk was measured against the hope of restoring their political independence (and in so doing, protecting the 'domain'). The extraordinary allowances granted to the Good Women Esclarmonde, Arnalda and Peirona of Lamothe are a consequence of the Cathar hierarchy's measuring risks against the preservation of these women's 'body', but also of the 'body' of their living church. The physical death of each of these women would have meant also the spiritual death of their church. Even the case of the countess of Toulouse, who risked being caught in Rome, in the pope's private chapel, in the presence of a Cathar deacon, shows how this woman, a powerful one, anteposed her spiritual salvation to the loss of her own physical freedom. This is, too, an example of primary concerns of survival taking the lead of one's actions. 'Body' equals in this case 'salvation'.

Within this broad reading of what I called 'primary concerns', a reading which moves them beyond the sphere of 'material considerations', a further specification should be made. Such a simplification of priorities could also be explained by the very nature of the inquisitorial judicial system. In a society where religion was a matter of membership, of ties with lineage and house, and existence as a whole had a meaning in the context of belonging, the Inquisition and its procedure operated a 'judicial dissection', by prosecuting and judging people on a one-to-one basis. The individual was treated as solely responsible for his or her own sins. Left standing alone in front of the pope's law and his men's sentence, people reverted to an individual's fears: body, possessions and house.

What reactions we have found, therefore, be they invectives, actions or plans, are even more revealing of a non-submissive attitude, of a degree of free will present in each individual. In my analysis I have tried to insert new elements into the picture, and to outline a 'grille' of elements to be taken into consideration when evaluating every single occurrence. The clash of systems in medieval Languedocian society, which is reflected in people's fears and their attitude to risk, must be examined not only on a logical and textual foundation, as suggested so effectively by Patschovsky,[115] but also by taking into account the political and social status of our characters.

---

[115] A. Patschovsky, 'Gli eretici di fronte al tribunale. A proposito dei processi-verbali inquisitoriali in Germania e in Boemia nel XIV secolo', in *La parola all'accusato*, pp. 252–67.

'Why did you do it?' asked the inquisitors at the end of a confession. Similarly, we are puzzled by the 'whys', and while identifying with the inquisitors in this quest for answers, we also try to identify with those deponents who 'did it', that is – variously – challenged the establishment, lied, professed a different creed, hosted suspects and 'clergy', escaped and so on. Did they fear? What did they fear?

In this chapter I have tried to make distinctions between people, their attitudes and their values. I have tried to understand which variables influenced the sequence word (recorded and spoken) – fears – evaluation of risk – strategies – actions. In order to do this, a basic contextualisation was necessary, but only insofar as it helped us gain a better understanding of our distinctions.

What is left after this analysis is a series of 'methodological boxes' in which to file our evidence. There is one called 'words hiding evidence', where distinctions must be made between (a) those words which hide willingly actions and responsibilities (like Raymond Guillaume's advice to 'hint' at things while deposing, or Pons of Fayac's alleged suggestion to accuse people already dead); (b) those which hide involuntarily (failure to declare things under pressures by different sources); and (c) those which hide 'mechanically' (due to the irrelevance of the confession to the purpose of a specific enquiry, or to the constraints of legal jargon).

A second box is called 'fears', and within it we must make distinctions between fears driven by individual concerns and fears led by group concerns. On the one hand, Bernard Agasse and Bernard Laguarrigue, the writer and the 'mole' of Carcassonne, feared for themselves, and so did the many other deponents who were afraid of the king's soldiers during and after the Crusade, or feared Atho of Baretges, bailiff of the Count of Toulouse, or even the moral judgement of the Cathar hierarchy when recanting. On the other hand we have Bernard Gui, in his manual of good inquisitorial practice, and the Good Men and Women who were about to decide whether to administer *consolamentum* to dying believers. These feared for the integrity and preservation of their respective churches. So did the conspirators of Avignonet and Montségur, who feared the escalating power of inquisitors and the papacy.

A third box is labelled 'risk-evaluation strategies'. Here historians must take into account personality ('risk aversion', 'risk neutrality' and 'love of risk'), but also whether individuals weighed pros and cons against themselves (thus mainly following Tuan's 'boundaries of security' (domain, body and house), and like Arnold Cimordan who escaped from prison driven by hunger), or against a collective purpose. Examples of the latter include the release of the women of Roquefort, the destruction of the registers in Carcassonne, the killing of Guillaume Arnaud and his companions, and the allowance made by Cathar clergy to the Good Woman Esclarmonde to eat meat and behave like a common believer. Lastly, they must take into account the status of the deponent within each elected group of reference (Good Men and Women as opposed to believers; lords/ citizens; parishioners/clergy). This can be seen in the example of Eleanor of Aragon and Finas's visit to Rome, where they honoured a Good Man dressed as a pilgrim in the pope's chapel.

The same categories apply to the 'actions' box. Actions were taken according to risk-taking strategies, and were their concrete application.

Finally, there is the 'declared words' box. This includes all evidence of declarations of resistance to the Inquisition, ranging from defiance, to self-excuse, to declarations of challenging actions and so on. Such evidence represents an interesting parallel with the 'surpluses' I have identified in Chapter 1. Distinctions must be drawn between (a) open declarations of resistance, driven by the will of the deponents (invectives, confessions of defiant actions); and (b) involuntary declarations, either driven by the technique of the interrogation (confirmation/refutation of pre-existing charges or torture) or torture or by psychological pressure.

Because of the many obstacles in the path of this historical enquiry there are significant limitations in drawing conclusions. The first crux in our analysis is the degree of disguise operated by words, through the many layers of overlapping filters which jeopardise our understanding, and through the game of 'verbal hide-and-seek' between deponent and interrogator. A second crux is that feelings must not be considered as constant, consistent throughout one's life, and although an individual's basic categorisation as 'risk-averse', 'risk-lover' or 'risk-neutral' can be assumed, single occurrences and events could vary their attitudes to risk on specific occasions. The analytical task is unlike that posed by literate sources: in order to understand our characters' fears it is not enough just to contextualise them and deconstruct their language. James Given and Danielle Laurendeau have carefully reconstructed the political dynamics and group strategies behind two specific cases, achieving remarkable results.[116] This huge effort is possible only when a context for each single case is attainable, and it was not the purpose of this chapter. My objective has been to lay out the cards, to display all the possible elements one should consider when looking closer at each single case, and to provide a wide-ranging model of reference deriving from Douglas which can be satisfactorily used in future research.

Some general results, however, appear if one steps back, after operating methodological distinctions, and taking *cruces* into account: the great

---

[116] See above, n. 10.

importance, *but not omnipresence* of inquisitorial 'filters'; the possibility to isolate and read against appropriate context a range of evidence on fears and fear-driven actions; the relevance of Douglas's model in interpreting the individual and group responses to repression of non-conformity; and the revised image of non-conformists themselves, who appear far from non-reactive and passive elements of this religious and political conflict, instead displaying ability to play the system, to react openly to it, and even to let their own emotions lead words and actions.

But behind all these words and feelings, these supposed calculations, textual, verbal and political games, historians and readers of Doat *must* remember that these were people and they had feelings. Like Bernard of Rival who, after giving a full account of his deeds and evasions to the inquisitors, and after abjuring his beliefs, went back to his cell. Having reached the limit of what he was able to suffer – whether consumed by remorse for his act of betrayal or by a sense of guilt for having sinned – he hit his head against the wall, wanting to end it all.

In the same year as above (1273), on the Sunday in Lent, in the evening, the aforesaid Bernard of Rival – detained for a long time and still held in prison in leg-irons, because he was found to have confessed less than fully – was found wounded in the head. And he acknowledged before me, Aton, the aforesaid notary ... that he had hit and wounded himself in the head, wishing to die, and wanting to kill himself.[117]

---

[117] 'Anno quo supra, Domenica in Quadragesima, sero, Bernardus de Rivali predictus, diu detentus, et ad huc existens in carcere compeditus, pro eo quod reperiebatur minus plene confessus, repertus est in capite vulneratus, et recognovit coram me, Athone, notario, supradicto ... quod ipsemet se percusserat et vulneraverat in capite mori desiderans, et se volens interficere', D25, f. 14v.

CONCLUSIONS (AND STARTING POINTS)

A study paying particular attention to methodology risks posing numerous caveats, setting subtle distinctions, dissecting the evidence and being left with the scattered pieces of a broken machine, without the tools to make sense of them. Records, however, should not be seen as crumbs of reality. In our inquisitorial volumes, the pieces are kept together by an inherent consistency. This lies, first of all, in two crucial features underpinning the formation of these texts, but also in their reading.

The first feature is that inquisitors were jurists and legal officials acting on behalf of the papacy. Despite their personal take on the whole business of 'faith and peace' (*negotium pacis et fidei*), their task was to instruct, conduct and record a legal procedure aiming at the establishment of responsibilities in the deviation from religious conformity. Awareness of this aspect makes the process of reading and interpreting inquisitorial records remarkably germane to reading and interpreting records of 'lay' enquiries. Religious and lay crime were intertwined during the Middle Ages, and officials pursuing the finding and punishment of transgressors operated following similar dynamics, and relying on the support of similar – sometimes the same – legal structures and personnel. *For the purpose of our records*, inquisitors were judges and detectives, first and foremost. Then, they were men of the Church committed to the preservation of a common faith, sometimes able psychologists, at other times more interested in legal nuances, or even harsh interpreters of a mission against evil. What we have are judicial records, not pieces of polemical literature.

The second feature is that because of the nature of our texts, officials were interested more in what made the *transgressor* rather than in what constituted a *transgression*. A theoretical formulation of the boundaries between licit and illicit was a job for canon lawyers, jurists and philosophers. Inquisitors were appointed to apply the norm to concrete cases, and to distinguish and discriminate among them. It is thus not surprising that the records do not display interest in theoretical statements, nor in the reasons why people chose non-conformity. The Doat volumes exist to testify to a hunt for people, names, incriminating actions and words. With this purpose in mind, the most useful witnesses to track down were 'messengers', such as Peter of Beauville, Amblard Vassal, Peter Maurel and

Raymond Hughes of Roquevidal.[1] They knew of people involved, family and political links, locations of rites, places of hiding of Good Men and Women, hospices and so on. Confessions of 'messengers' take over folio after folio of the Doat copies. To get hold of them meant a victory for the tribunal, while the capture of a Good Man or Woman, someone who in most cases had a high degree of commitment to their beliefs and the Church, often represented a defeat: a defeat for the inquiry, as they were less likely to confess and involve other members of their church; and a defeat for the Church of Rome, as many preferred to die rather than recant.

So far, for 'what appears in the records'. Readers should not forget, however, that absence can be equally telling. For instance, the depositions do not give information about the process of recuperation, but provide glimpses of evidence on collaborators and spies (such as Marquise of Prouille, ex-Good Woman now 'explorer' for the inquisitor), and names of previous heretics are recorded among the witnesses of interrogations. After recanting, in fact, *all* deponents could prove extremely useful to the inquiry. Converted 'messengers' were extremely useful as informers and could be employed as spies, while ex-Good Men could become the harshest accusers of their previous companions (as in the famous examples of polemicists Anselm of Alessandria and Ranier Sacconi), or act as a deterrent, such as in the cases of those employed by inquisitors during the trials (e.g. Sicard Lunel, former Cathar deacon, employed in several occasions in D25–6).[2] For a deponent, to see a former Good Man sitting as a witness on the opposite side would have meant realising that all possibilities of diverting questions, diminishing responsibilities or lying about practices and rituals were wiped out.

Thus, technical sources assembled by jurists and judicial officials do tell us about what was relevant to the inquiry, but can also tell of how the inquiry was led through minor fragments only accidentally included in the records.

My main goal has been to rebalance the opposition between inquisitors and deponents, to review their interaction and reciprocal attacks, by focusing on three main issues: (a) the characteristic, featuring obsessively in the records, of movements and itinerancy; (b) its side-issue of the structure of non-conformist groupings; and (c) the strategies, motives and dynamics of risk-assessment and fear. Although all these have been tackled by embracing the similitude of a 'hunt' where Church officials were trying to bring under control what they considered to be the viruses for

---

[1] On these messengers, see above, Chapters 2 and 3.
[2] D25, ff. 7v, 14r–v, 28v, 36r, 43r, 66r, 67r, 139r, 148v, 153r.

a possible mass-contamination of Christianity, the roles of 'hunter' and 'prey' appeared not so clear-cut as previously assumed.

Although we have inquisitors and dissidents standing on two clearly separate grounds, there are some attitudes which cannot be ascribed with certainty to one or the other party. This contributes to an initial fragmentation of the whole picture. Among such attitudes we can number the attitude to power – here meant in a Foucauldian way – its deviation, its abuse; and the attitude to freedom of conscience, faith and religious belonging. As for the first, we should not assume that 'power' meant only that imposed by religious authorities onto all believers. It meant also political power with all its priorities and conflicts. The political pattern of alliances in Languedoc, with the constant struggle between local nobility (e.g. the Counts of Toulouse, Béziers, the Trencavels) and the crown, affected the success or defeat of papal initiatives. Again, the shifting of some noble families from one side to the other (e.g. Niorts, de Termes)[3] meant that a constant climate of protection to non-conformity by local nobles must not be assumed tout court. 'Power' also meant community power, the power to exert pressures and to ostracise the 'other' for religious, social or political reasons. A clear example of this can be seen where Aladaix of Massabrac, captured after the siege of Montségur, told the inquisitors about the pressures to turn back to Catharism after her conversion to Catholicism.[4] It also meant power of family ties, which could be so strongly compelling when deciding over personal issues, as witnessed by the example of Gaillard Ruby of Montgaillard, who was 'enchanted' by the prayers of his brothers.[5]

Religious belonging too has nuances. It must have been felt strongly on both the Cathar and the Catholic sides. It carried within it a set of norms regulating adherence to a creed and obedience to its ministers, but also a complex set of psychological implications for all affiliates, a mix of resentment, nostalgia, sense of guilt, anger, awkwardness and confusion, to name but a few. The example of Bernard Faure, who allegedly sent a messenger to convince his daughter, who had joined the Cathars against the will of her parents, to come home, shows some of these mixed feelings.[6] It follows that the inquisitors themselves should be seen, at the same time, as powerful persecutors but also as not-so-powerful targets of rebellion and scorn by the local communities. The stories of the women

---

[3] On these dynamics and examples, see above, Chapter 4.
[4] Chapter 4.
[5] Chapter 4.
[6] See Chapter 1.

of Roquefort tricking the local priest, and of the attack to the zealous *capellanus* of Caraman are very telling.[7]

Further, there was a wide and variegated grey area represented by those who played a double game, acting like collaborators with the inquisitors, while spying on the inquisitors for their companions. In this grey area are also those who had been allowed – by the Cathar hierarchy – a false status of having re-converted to Catholicism (for example the Good Woman Esclarmonde, who was allowed to eat meat by her fellow 'clergy').[8] Instead they were still crucial members of the heretical hierarchy. Other double-game players were those who wanted to appear trustworthy to the dissidents in order to denounce them to the inquisitors and were, in reality, working whole-heartedly for neither side, aiming only to save their own skin (the 'mole' of Carcassonne, Bernard Laguarrigue, for instance, is a clear case).[9]

The reading of Doat has demonstrated that not only is it difficult for a historian to apply rigid categories and labels to the characters encountered, it is also wrong. For instance, let us consider the structure of the dissident church. A crucial role was that of the 'messengers', who moved from one place to another under request of their fellow believers. Mainly, their role was to put communities or familial groups in touch with the 'priests' for the purpose of administering sacraments and preaching. On the one hand, they were important elements of the Church, as they allowed the system to work, and the Good Men and Women to find safe shelter. Still, within that community they carried little religious weight and authority. On the other hand, they were absolutely crucial pieces of the chessboard for the inquisitors, acting as go-betweens with a lot of responsibility within the organisational framework of Catharism. As a consequence – because of this role – they became prime targets of the pope's officials.

The idea of a non-conformist church in particular is currently under heavy fire from those historians who believe that church-like structures (ecclesiastical hierarchy, territorialisation into bishoprics and 'churches', theological currents, organisation of hospitality and assistance) have been attributed to a mass of non-organised dissenters first by the same authority who persecuted them, and second, by those historians endorsing an a-critical reading of church documents, and adopting the same terminology used in those sources ('heretic', 'Cathar', 'dissent').[10] I have

---

[7] See Chapter 4.
[8] See Chapter 4.
[9] See Chapter 4.
[10] See, for instance, M.G. Pegg, 'Heresy, Good Men and nomenclature' in M. Frassetto (ed.), *Heresy and the Persecuting Society in the Middle Ages: Essays on the Work of R.I. Moore* (Leiden, 2006), pp. 227–39, esp. pp. 238–9.

discussed this issue in Chapter 2. One element which needs reaffirming here is the idea of the development of structures of this church, something which is possible only at a conclusive stage. I have noted on more than one occasion that a climate of persecution (the key period here is of course 1209–29, years of the so-called Albigensian Crusade) strengthened a feeling of belonging, thus reinforcing the bonds between the persecuted, and connecting them to the ideology of martyrdom, as stated in the *Gleisa de Dieu*, the manifesto of Catharism. It is also true that the 'living church' encouraged, in times of persecution, the establishment of very active international networks of assistance and support between communities (increasing what I called 'negative' movements). It is true that, at textual level, this is validated by a significant shift of terminology in the records themselves, where believers who, before the Crusade, used to attend *public* preaching and debates in the streets of Languedoc, refer to the time 'after the Crusade' or 'after the advent of the Gallici' as a time of meetings in huts (*cabane*), private houses and wood shacks. There is also a significant increase in mentions of Italian destinations and trips to Italy after particular events such as the killing of inquisitors in Avignonet (see the whole cluster of occurrences in D25–6).

However, we must not fall into the trap of thinking that only because things did not appear in the records, they did not exist. The absence of mention of a network of hospices between Italy and Languedoc, and of their role in hosting refugees, does not mean the absence of an assistance network *per se*. I have in fact counted around fifty instances of structures where heretics were hosted between D22 and D26. These refer both to the pre-Crusade time and after it. Terminology changes ('domus hereticorum' in earlier cases, 'hospicium hereticorum' in later references), and perhaps also the way in which people led these hospices (conventual-like structures before, then possibly transformed into shelters), but the reality of an organisation – however called – remains.

As in other cases, even when studying Cathar organisation, 'what is not there' might be due to the lack of interest of the inquisitors or lack of relevance to that particular enquiry. Could the variations in terminology *also* be put down to an increased terminological awareness, practice of the inquiries and knowledge of these structures by the inquisitors? My point is that, though the structure undoubtedly would have been strengthened, formalised and encouraged by the climate and the feelings sparked by persecution, the idea of a 'living, travelling church' represents the very essence of Catharism, and must have been there (while not necessarily appearing in the records) since its earlier years. Such a structure, derived from a deep belief of belonging, cannot come only as a response to persecution.

Conclusions (and starting points)

The example of ecclesiastical structures helps to clearly define the reason why the contextualisation of examples has been kept to a minimum. Given the nature of the sources – which has been discussed in detail in the Introduction – any gradual transformation of structures cannot be traced if not summarily in content, patchily in time and with different consistency throughout the geographical area under investigation. Changes in political dynamics are thus less relevant here than in microstudies. There seems to be a natural evolution of structures which adds to the fact that records of a Cathar official normative or, indeed, of any record related to this aspect are non-existent. Even events such as the 1226 council of Pieusse, where the new Cathar diocese of Razès was established by bishop Guilhabert of Castres in response to the need for more organisation in that area, seem to have happened without rigorous planning. This natural evolution must refer to some basic chronological indicators, but must also be analysed outside a too stringent contextualisation, which would not allow for general discussion. It seems that, in the absence of textual *auctoritates* and a corpus of law, non-conformist groups followed an agreed set of, say, best practices. This provided the flexibility necessary to adapt their structure to the needs of any particular moment, and to leave individuals relatively free to adhere to the group's common goals and habits.

This analysis of movement and its consequences led to a rather paradoxical picture of Catharism. On the one hand, we can see how a careful reading of the sources did bring a sort of atomisation of actions, choices and individual responses to matters of belief. On the other, however, it seems that all these individualities displayed awareness of a series of common aims and ways to achieve them – a millipede-like structure, rather than a pantomime horse. This makes sense of the apparent contrast between individuals who acted by themselves while sharing common beliefs and objectives, as is particularly evident in Chapter 4, where Douglas's model has provided a satisfactory scheme for the reading of actions and their evaluation. In the analysis of risk management in relation to fear, or fear-induced reactions, there are many apparent inconsistencies. For example, the contrast between individuals' obsessions with their own safety, means of subsistence and possessions on the one hand, and the defiance of authority displayed in some group – or even individual – initiatives, on the other. My 'forensic' analysis of the theft of the registers of Carcassonne is the prime example of this apparent contrast.

To this could be added that such millipede-like behaviour, in the end, made the chances of escaping an organised persecution significantly higher. I am still unsure about this. First, because it seems that both persecuting machine *and* 'heretical' structures underwent a parallel process of progressive standardisation and formalisation. Second, because historiography is still debating whether non-conformity was crushed by persecution, financial policies and political measures put in place by the tribunals (e.g. confiscation of goods, interdiction from public offices), a series of radical political changes cutting off local support to dissent (e.g. the loss of the 'cause of the South' in France, ever since the 1240s, and the fall of the Ghibelline front in Italy since 1266–7) or ultimately a combination of the three, added to an increased disinterest in theological debate. This remains an open question and provides material for further research.

Pointing out these paradoxes and inconsistencies, but also a possible way of reading them within a wider, less inconsistent picture, does not mean that the roles of the 'catcher' and of the 'caught' can be swapped. It only means that historians must adopt a twofold perspective in order to understand events, and must always consider both parties (if one likes the simile of a hunt) as prey and hunter at the same time. Ultimately, this is a duplicity which reflects, perhaps, the duplicity of a mindset, something evident in my study of religious itinerancy (Chapter 3). The roots of a twofold perspective can be clearly seen when treating medieval religious movements as a whole. Incessant movement ('vagrancy' in the words of the polemicists) was not a habit specific and unique to the religion of the Good Men and Women. As a lifestyle it was shared by nearly all the dissident groups, but also – at least in their beginnings – by most of the eleventh- and twelfth-century itinerant preachers, by the 'new' religious orders and by authorised couples of monks or friars within established orthodox communities. Movement had its ideological motivation in the patrimony of beliefs, Scriptures and rites which dissident groups shared with their opponents. The claim of holding the true inheritance of the apostles and of Christ, a claim made by both parties on the basis of the same scriptural authorities, meant to claim legitimacy. When persecuted, it allowed one to carry the palm of martyrdom. Overall, it meant to be called to a life of endless movement, either on a mission or on the run. Because of this common ground of texts and beliefs, which led, however, to such different outcomes, theoretical help was needed. The Church and its ministers needed clearer understanding of such issues. Thinkers and jurists had to be called in to refine the definition of what was and was not allowed. Theory and authority worked side-by-side to draw limits and to shape identities. They gradually defined where the boundaries between true and fake apostolicity should have been placed. Chapter 3 browsed and followed the gradual formation of these boundaries from as early as the eleventh century, but also pointed out the difficulties which arose from its concrete application onto the reality of inquisitions and prevention of dissent, punishment and forgiveness.

Conclusions (and starting points)

Should historians tie the loose ends of their work and provide a complete picture of subjects? Not always, in my opinion. This is the reason why I limited my study to D21–6: I wanted to check the soundness of new methods of enquiry, to provide tools for further research and sketch a revised picture of non-conformity which, in my opinion, responds better to what is left of the trials. Other historians might find this method unsuitable for their sources, might decide to polish or discard it, but hopefully will take into account my considerations.

I cannot resign myself to the emptiness of Bernard of Morlay's phrase, as used in Eco's famous incipit of *The Name of the Rose*, 'Stat rosa pristina nomine. Nomina nuda tenemus.'[11]

---

[11] Bernard of Morlay, *De contemptu mundi*, ed. T. Wright, ('Rerum Britannicarum Medii Aevi Scriptores'), (London, 1872), II, p. 37, quoted in U. Eco, *The Name of the Rose* (New York, 1983), p. 502.

BIBLIOGRAPHY

PRIMARY SOURCES

Collection Doat, Bibliothèque Nationale de France, Paris, vols. 21–6.

Angelo Clareno, *Historia septem tribulationum ordinis minorum*, in F. Ehrle, 'Die Spiritualen, ihr Verhältniss zum Franziskanerorden und zu den Fraticellen', *Archiv für Literatur und Kirchengeschichte des Mittelalters* 2 (1886), pp. 108–64, 249–327.

Baldricus, Episcopus Dolensis, *Vita Roberti de Arbrissello*, PL 162, cols. 1017–57.

Consultatio Petri de Albalat de Tarragona (= Raymundus de Peñafort, *Directorium*), in K.-V. Selge, *Texte zur Inquisition*, Gütersloh, 1967, pp. 50–9.

Bruschi, C. (ed.), Salvus Burcius, *Liber Suprastella*, ('Fonti per la storia dell'Italia Medievale – Antiquitates' 15), Rome, 2002.

D'Alatri, M., *Doctrina de modo procedendi contra hereticos*, in Martène, E. and Durand, U., *Thesaurus novus anecdotorum*, 5 (Lutetiae Parisiorum, 1717), cols. 1795–814.

L'inquisizione francescana nell'Italia centrale del Duecento: con in appendice il testo del 'Liber inquisitionis' di Orvieto trascritto da Egidio Bonanno, ('Bibliotheca Seraphico-Capuccina' 149), Rome, 1996.

Dondaine, A. (ed.), Anselm of Alexandria, *Tractatus de hereticis*, in 'La hiérarchie Cathare en Italie', II, *Archivum Fratrum Praedicatorum* 20 (1950), pp. 308–24 [now in Dondaine, A., *Les hérésies et l'Inquisition*, IV, pp. 234–324].

Raniero Sacconi, *Summa de Catharis et Leonistis seu Pauperibus de Lugduno*, in *Un Traité néo-manichéen du XIIIe siècle, le Liber de duobus principiis, suivi d'un fragment de Rituel cathare*, Rome, 1939, pp. 64–78 [also edited by Sanjek, F., 'Raynerius Sacconi O.P. Summa de Catharis', *Archivum Fratrum Praedicatorum* 44 (1974), pp. 42–60].

Dondaine, A., *Les hérésies et l'Inquisition XIIe–XIIIe siècles. Documents et études*, Variorum Collected Studies 314, Aldershot, 1990.

Douais, C., *Documents pour servir à l'histoire de l'Inquisition dans Le Languedoc*, Paris, 1900.

Duvernoy, J. (ed.), Guillaume Pelhisson, *Chronicon (1229–1244)*, Paris, 1994.

Le régistre de Jacques Fourner, évêque de Pamiers (1318–1325), 2nd edn., Toulouse, 1978 [see also *Inquisition á Pamiers. Interrogatoires de Jacques Fournier, 1318–1325, choisis, traduits du texte latin et presentés par Jean Duvernoy*, Paris, 1966].

Régistre de Bernard de Caux. Pamiers (1246–1247), Bulletin de la Société Ariégeoise des Sciences, Lettres et Arts 1990, pp. 5–108.

Duvernoy, J., *L'inquisition en Quercy. Le registre de pénitences de Pierre Cellan 1241–1242*, Castelnaud-La-Chapelle, 2001.

Bibliography

Eberwin of Steinfeld, *Epistola CDLXXII*, PL 182, cols. 676–80.

Eckbert of Schönau, *Sermones tredecim contra hereticos*, PL 195, cols. 9–102.

Friedberg, E. (ed.), *Corpus iuris canonici: Decretalium collectiones*, reprint, Leipzig, 1955.

Friedlander, A. (ed.), *Processus Bernardi Deliciosi (3 Sept. – 8 Dec. 1319)*, ('Transactions of the American Philosophical Society held at Philadelphia' 86/1), Philadelphia, 1996.

Gaufridus Grossus, *Vita Bernardi Tironensis*, PL 172, cols. 1363–446.

Geoffrey of Auxerre, *Vita Prima Bernardi*, PL 185, cols. 301–68.

Gleisa de Dio, in Venckeleer, T., 'Un recueil Cathare: le manuscrit A.6.10 de la "Collection Vaudoise" de Dublin', *Revue Belge de Philologie et d'Histoire* 38 (1960), pp. 815–34.

Guiraud, J. (ed.), *Les Régistres d'Urbain IV (1261–4)*, Paris, 1904.

Koudelka, V.J. (ed.), *Monumenta diplomatica S. Dominici*, vol. 25, Rome, 1966.

Maisonneuve. H., *Histoire Albigeoise*, Paris, 1951 [French transl. of R. Guébin and E. Lyon *Hystoria Albigensis* (3 vols.; Paris: Societe de l'histoire de France au Moyen Age, H. Champion, 1926–1939)].

Mansi, G.D. (ed.), *Sacrorum conciliorum nova et amplissima collectio*, Graz, 1960 [orig. edn. Florence and Venice, 1758–98].

May, W.A., 'The confession of Prous Boneta heretic and heresiarch', in Mundy, J., Emery, R. and Nelson, B. (eds.), *Essays in Medieval Life and Thought Presented in Honor of Austin Patterson Evans*, New York, 1965, pp. 3–30.

Meersemann, G.G., *Dossier de l'ordre de la Pénitence au XIII* siècle, ('Spicilegium Friburgense' 7), Fribourg, 1961.

Mollat, G. (ed.), Bernard Gui, *Le manuel de l'Inquisiteur*, Paris, 1927.

Moore, R.I. (ed.), *The Birth of Popular Heresy*, Toronto, Buffalo and London, 1995.

Omont, H., 'La Collection Doat à la Bibliothèque Nationale: Documents sur les recherches de Doat', *Bibliothèque de l'École des Chartes* 77 (1916), pp. 286–336.

Ordo processus Narbonensis, in Selge, *Texte zur Inquisition*, pp. 70–6.

Orr, J. (ed.), *Les oeuvres de Guiot de Provins, poète lyrique et satirique*, Manchester, 1915.

Pales-Gobilliard, A., *L'inquisiteur Geoffroy d'Ablis et les Cathares du comté de Foix (1308–1309)*, Paris, 1984.

Paolini, L. (ed.), *Il 'De officio inquisitionis': La procedura inquisitoriale a Bologna e Ferrara nel Duecento*, Rome, 1976.

Paolini, L. and Orioli, R. (eds.), *Acta S. Officii Bononie ab anno 1291 usque ad annum 1310*, ('Fonti per la storia d'Italia' 106), Rome, 1982 – *Index*, Rome, 1984.

Patschovsky, A., *Der Passauer Anonymus: Ein sammelwerk über Ketzer, Juden, Antichrist aus der Mitte des xiii. Jahrhunderts*, MGH, *Schriften*, 22, Stuttgart, 1968.

Ph. Van Limborch (ed.), Bernard Gui, *Liber sententiarum inquisitionis Tholosanae (1307–1323)*, Amsterdam, 1692.

Preger, W. (ed.), Pseudo-David of Aubsburg, *Tractatus de inquisitione hereticorum*, in 'Der Traktat David von Augsburg über die Waldesier', *Abhandlungen der histor. Cl. der Kgl. Bayerischen Akademie der Wissenschaften* 14/2 (1876), pp. 183–235.

Raymundus de Peñafort, *Directorium*, see *Consultatio Petri de Albalat de Tarragona*.

Reichert, B.M. (ed.), *Litterae Encyclicae Magistrorum Generalium ordinis Praedicatorum ab anno 1233 usque ad annum 1376*, Rome, 1900, pp. 15–63.

Revell, E. (ed.), *The Later Letters of Peter of Blois*, ('Auctores Britannici Medii Aevi' 22), Oxford, 1993.

Sauvage, E.P. (ed.), Etienne de Fougères, *Vitae BB. Vitalis et Gaufridi, primi et secundi abbatum Saviniacensium'*, *Analecta Bollandiana* 1 (1882), pp. 355–410.

Bibliography

Sala-Molins, L. (ed.), Eymerich, N. and Peña, F., *Le manuel de Inquisiteur*, Paris and La Haye, 1973.

Scalia, G. (ed.), Salimbene de Adam, *Chronica*, ('Corpus Christianorum. Continuatio Medievalis' 125), Turnholt, 1998 [Engl. transl. Baird, J.L., Baglivi, G. and Kane, J.R. (eds.), Salimbene de Adam, *Chronicle*, ('Medieval and Renaissance Texts and Studies' 40), Birghamton, 1986].

Tardif, A., 'Documents pour l'histoire du processus per inquisitionem et de "l'inquisitio heretice pravitatis"', *Nouvelle Révue historique du droit Français et étranger* 7 (1883), pp. 669–78.

Thouzellier, C. (ed.), *Livre des deux principes*, Paris, 1973.

Tocco, F., *Quel che non c'è nella Divina Commedia, o Dante e l'eresia*, Bologna, 1899.

von Döllinger, I., *Beiträge zur Sektengeschichte des Mittelalters*, vol. II, *Dokumente*, Darmstadt, 1968.

Wakefield, W.E. and Evans, A. (eds.), *Heresies of the High Middle Ages*, reprint, New York, 1991.

Walter Map, *De nugis curialium*, in Gonnet, G. (ed.), *Enchiridion fontium Valdensium*, Torre Pellice, 1958, pp. 122–4.

Zambon, F. (ed.), *La cena segreta: Trattati e rituali catari*, Milan, 1997.

STUDIES

Abbiati, S., 'Intorno ad una possibile valutazione giuridico-diplomatica del documento inquisitorio', *Studi di storia medievale e di diplomatica* 3 (1978), pp. 167–79.

Albaret, L., 'L'anticléricalisme dans les registres d'inquisition de Toulouse et Carcassonne au début du XIVe siècle', *Cahiers de Fanjeaux* 38 (2003), pp. 447–70.

Albaret, L. (ed.), *Les Inquisiteurs: Portraits de défenseurs de la foi en Languedoc (XIIIe–XIVe siècles)*, Toulouse, 2001.

'L'Inquisition et les hérésies dans le Midi de la France au Moyen Âge: essai de bilan historiographique', in *Hérétiques ou Dissidents? Réflexions sur l'identité de l'hérésie au Moyen Âge, Heresis* 36–7 (2002), pp. 145–59.

Alberzoni, M.P., Ambrosioni, A. and Lucioni, A. (eds.), *Sulle tracce degli Umiliati*, ('Bibliotheca Erudita. Studi e documenti di storia e filologia' 13), Milan, 1997.

'Gli inizi degli Umiliati: una riconsiderazione', in *La conversione alla povertà nell'Italia dei secoli XII–XIV. Atti del XXVII Convegno Storico Internazionale (Todi, 14–17 October 1990*, Spoleto, 1991, pp. 187–237.

'San Bernardo e gli Umiliati', in P. Zerbi (ed.), *San Bernardo e l'Italia. Atti del Convegno di Studi (Milan, 24–26 May 1990)*, Milan, 1993, pp. 101–29.

Albini, G., *Città e ospedali nella Lombardia medievale*, Bologna, 1993.

Arnold, J.H., '"A man takes an ox by the horn and a peasant by the tongue": literacy, orality and inquisition in medieval Languedoc', in Cross, C., Rees Jones, S. and Riddy, F. (eds.), *Learning and Literacy in the Middle Ages*, Turnhout, 2001, pp. 31–48.

Inquisition and Power: Catharism and the Confessing Subject in Medieval Languedoc, Philadelphia, PA, 2001.

Assmann, I., 'Monothéisme et mémoire. Le Moïse de Freud et la tradition biblique', *Annales. Histoire, Sciences Sociales* 54/5 (Sept. – Oct. 1999), pp. 1011–26.

Audisio, G., *The Waldensian Dissent: Persecution and Survival c. 1170 – c. 1570*, Cambridge, 1999.

Bibliography

Bailey, M.D., 'From sorcery to witchcraft: clerical conceptions of magic in the later Middle Ages', *Speculum* 76 (2001), pp. 960–90.

Baker, D., 'Heresy and learning in early Cistercianism', in Baker, D. (ed.), *Schism, Heresy and Religious Protest*, ('Studies in Church History' 15), Cambridge, 1972, pp. 93–107.

Barber, M., *Crusaders and Heretics, Twelfth to Fourteenth Centuries*, Variorum Collected Studies 498, Aldershot, 1995.

Bartlett, R., *Trial by Fire and Water: the Medieval Judicial Ordeal*, New York, 1986.

Bascapé, M.G., '"In armariis officii inquisitoris Ferrariensis". Ricerche su un frammento inedito del processo Pungilupo', *Quaderni di Storia Religiosa* 9 (2002), pp. 31–110.

Becamel, M., 'Le Catharisme dans la diocèse d'Albi', *Cahiers de Fanjeaux* 3 (1968), pp. 237–52.

Benedetti, M., 'Frate Lanfranco da Bergamo, gli inquisitori, l'Ordine e la curia Romana', in *Praedicatores Inquisitores*, pp. 157–204.

'Le finanze dell'Inquisitore', in *L'economia dei conventi dei frati minori e predicatori fino alla metà del Trecento. Atti del XXXI Convegno Internazionale (Assisi, 9–11 October 2003)*, Spoleto, 2004, pp. 363–401.

'Le parole e le opere di frate Lanfranco (1292–1305)', *Quaderni di Storia Religiosa* 9 (2002), pp. 111–82.

Berlioz, J., 'La prédication des Cathares selon l'Inquisiteur Étienne de Bourbon (mort vers 1261)', *Heresis* 31 (1999), pp. 9–35.

Bertuzzi, R., *'Ecclesiarum forma'. Tematiche di ecclesiologia Catara e Valdese*, Rome, 1998.

Biget, J.-L., 'Hérésie, politique et société en Languedoc (vers 1120-vers 1320)', in Berlioz, J. (ed.), *Le Pays Cathare: Les religions médiévales et leurs expressions méridionales*, Paris, 2000, pp. 17–79.

'L'anticléricalisme des hérétiques d'après les sources polémiques', *Cahiers de Fanjeaux* 38 (2003), pp. 405–45.

'"Les Albigeois". Rémarques sur une dénomination', in *Inventer l'hérésie?*, pp. 219–55.

'L'extinction du Catharisme urbain: les points chauds de la répression', *Cahiers de Fanjeaux* 20 (1985), pp. 304–40.

'Saint Dominique, la société du Languedoc, les bons hommes et les vaudois (1206–1217)', in *Domenico di Caleruega e la nascita dell'ordine dei frati Predicatori, Atti del XLI Convegno Internazionale di Studi, (Todi, 10–12 Ottobre 2004)*, Spoleto, 2005, pp. 131–79.

'Un procès d'inquisition à Albi en 1300', *Cahiers de Fanjeaux* 6 (1971), pp. 273–342.

Biller, P. and Dobson, B. (eds.), *The Medieval Church: Universities, Heresy and Religious Life. Essays in honour of Gordon Leff*, ('Studies in Church History', Subsidia, 11), The Ecclesiastical History Society, 1999.

Biller, P. and Hudson, A. (eds.), *Heresy and Literacy, 1000–1530*, ('Cambridge Studies in Medieval Literature' 23), Cambridge, 1994.

Biller, P., 'Heretics and long journeys', in Horden, P. (ed.) *Freedom of Movement in the Middle Ages: Proceedings of the 2003 Harlaxton Conference*, ('Harlaxton Medieval Studies' 15) Donnington, 2007, pp. 86–103.

'Medieval Waldensians' construction of the past', *Proceedings of the Huguenot Society of Great Britain and Ireland* 25 (1989), pp. 39–54.

'Northern Cathars and higher learning', in *The Medieval Church: Universities, Heresy and Religious Life*, pp. 25–51.

The Waldenses, 1170–1530: Between a Religious Order and a Church, Variorum Collected Studies 67, Aldershot, 2001.

'"Through a glass darkly": seeing Medieval heresy', in Linehan, P. and Nelson, J. (eds.), *The Medieval World*, London, 2001, pp. 308–26.

'Umberto Eco et les interrogations de Bernard Gui', in Audisio, G. (ed.), *Inquisition et pouvoir*, Aix-en-Provence, 2003, pp. 257–68.

'Words and the Medieval notion of "religion"', *Journal of Ecclesiastical History* 36 (1985), pp. 351–69.

Biscaro, G., 'Inquisitori ed eretici a Firenze (1319–1334)', *Studi Medievali*, n. ser., 2 (1929), 347–75, and 3 (1930), 266–87.

'Inquisitori ed eretici lombardi (1292–1318)', in *Miscellanea di Storia Italiana*, III ser., 19 (1922), 447–557.

Bloch, M., *Feudal Society*, London, 1961 [orig. edn. *La societé féodale: la formation des liens de dépendance*, Paris, 1949].

Bolton, B., 'Poverty as protest: some inspirational groups at the turn of the twelfth century', in *The Church in a Changing Society: Conflict, Reconciliation or Adjustment?*, Uppsala, 1978, pp. 28–32 [repr. in Bolton, B., *Innocent III: Studies on Papal Authority and Pastoral Care*, Variorum Collected Studies 490, Ashgate, 1995, XIII, pp. 1–11].

Borst, A., *Les Cathares*, Paris, 1974 [orig. edn. *Die Katharer*, Stuttgart, 1953].

Bowden, M., 'The persuaders', *Observer Monthly* 19 (October 2003), 28–40.

Boyd, W.K., *The Ecclesiastical Edicts of the Theodosian Code*, New York, 1905.

Boyle, L.E., 'Montaillou revisited: "mentalité" and methodology', in Raftis, J.A. (ed.), *Pathways to Medieval Peasants*, Toronto, 1981, pp. 119–40.

Brenon, A., *Les femmes Cathares*, Paris, 1992.

Le vrai visage du Catharisme, Portet-sur-Garonne, 1988.

'Sincretisme hérétique dans les réfuges Alpins? Un livre Cathare parmi les récueils Vaudois de la fin du Moyen Âge: le manuscrit 269 de Dublin', *Heresis* 7 (1986), 7–23.

Bruce, S.G., *Silence and Sign Language in Medieval Monasticism: The Cluniac Tradition, c. 900–1200*, Cambridge, 2007.

Brufani, S., *Eresia di un ribelle al tempo di Giovanni XXII: il caso di Muzio di Francesco d'Assisi*, Spoleto, 1991.

Bruschi, C., and Biller, P. (eds.), *Texts and the repression of Medieval Heresy* ('York Studies in Medieval Theology' 4), York, 2002.

Bruschi, C., 'Decostruzione testuale nel *consilium* agli inquisitori di Carcassonne del 1330 (Paris, Bibliothèque Nationale de France, *Collection Doat*, vol. 32)', in De Matteis, M.C. (ed.), *Ovidio Capitani: quaranta anni per la storia medioevale*, 2 vols., Bologna, 2003, vol. II, pp. 137–50.

'Gli inquisitori Raoul de Plassac e Pons de Parnac e l'inchiesta tolosana degli anni 1273–80', in *Praedicatores Inquisitores*, pp. 471–93.

'Il "Liber Suprastella" (1235), fonte antiereticale piacentina. L'ambiente ed il motivo di produzione', *Archivio Storico per le Province Parmensi*, 4th ser., 49 (1997), 405–27.

'Inquisizione francescana in Toscana fino al pontificato di Giovanni XXII', in *Frati minori e inquisizione. Atti del XXXIII Convegno internazionale (Assisi, 6–8 Ottobre 2005)*, Spoleto, 2006, pp. 287–324.

Bibliography

'La memoria dall'eresia alla riammissione. Le cronache quattrocentesche degli Umiliati', *Mélanges de l'École Française de Rome* 115 (2003), pp. 325–40.

'"Magna diligentia est habenda per inquisitorem": precautions before reading Doat 21–26', in *Texts and the Repression of Medieval Heresy*, pp. 81–110.

review of J.H. Arnold, *Inquisition and Power*, in *Journal of Ecclesiastical History* 55 (2004), pp. 576–7.

Byrd, J., 'The construction of Orthodoxy and the (De)construction of heretical attacks on the Eucharist in "Pastoralia" from Peter the Chanter's circle in Paris', in *Texts and the Repression of Medieval Heresy*, pp. 45–61.

Cameron, E., *Waldenses: Rejections of Holy Church in Medieval Europe*, Oxford, 2000.

Camporesi, P., *The Fear of Hell: Images of Damnation and Salvation in Early Medieval Europe*, Cambridge, 1991.

Capitani, O., *Catharisme: l'édifice immaginaire*, ('Collection *Heresis*' 7), Carcassonne, 1998.

'Da Volpe a Morghen: riflessioni eresiologiche a proposito del centenario della nascita di Eugenio Dupré-Theseider', *Studi Medievali*, III ser. (1999), pp. 305–21.

Cazenave, A., 'Aveu et contrition. Manuels de confesseurs et interrogatoires d'inquisition en Languedoc et en Catalogne (XIIIᵉ–XIVᵉ siècle)', in *La piété populaire au Moyen Age: Actes du 99ᵉ congrès national des sociétés savantes (Besançon, 1974)*, Paris, 1977, I, pp. 333–52.

Chaytor, H.J., 'The Medieval reader and textual criticism', *Bulletin of the John Rylands Library* 26 (1941–2), pp. 49–56.

Clanchy, M.T., *From Memory to Written Record: England 1066–1307*, 2nd edn., Oxford and Malden, MA, 1993.

Coleman, J., *Ancient and Medieval Memories: Studies in the Reconstruction of the Past*, Cambridge, 1992.

Colish, M.L., *Medieval Foundations of the Western Intellectual Tradition 1000–1400*, New Haven, CT and London, 1997.

Constable, G., 'Opposition to pilgrimage in the Middle Ages', in *Religious Life and Thought (11th–12th Centuries)*, Variorum Reprints, London, 1979, pp. 125–46.

Constable, O.R., *Housing the Stranger in the Mediterranean World: Lodging, Trade and Travel in Late Antiquity and the Middle Ages*, Cambridge, 2003.

Corsi, D., '"La Chiesa nella casa di lei". Eretiche ed eretici a Firenze nel Duecento', *Genesis. Rivista Italiana delle Storiche* 1/1 (2002), pp. 187–218.

Corti, M., 'Models and antimodels in medieval culture', *New Literary History* 10/2 (1979), pp. 339–66.

Costen, M., *The Cathars and the Albigensian Crusade*, Manchester, 1997.

da Milano, I., 'Vita evangelica e vita apostolica nell'adesione dei riformisti sul papato del secolo XII', in *Problemi di Storia della Chiesa. Il Medioevo dei secoli XII–XV*, Milan, 1976, pp. 21–72.

d'Alatri, M., *L'inquisizione francescana nell'Italia centrale del Duecento: con in appendice il testo del 'Liber inquisitionis' di Orvieto trascritto da Egidio Bonanno* ('Bibliotheca Seraphico-Capuccina' 149), Rome, 1996.

Davis, N.Z., *Fiction in the Archives: Pardon Tales and Their Tellers in Sixteenth-Century France*, Stanford, CA, 1988.

'Les conteurs de Montaillou (note critique)', *Annales. Economie, Société, Civilisation* 34 (1979), pp. 61–73.

The Return of Martin Guerre, Cambridge, MA and London, 1983.

Dean, T., *Crime and Justice in Late Medieval Italy*, Cambridge, 2007.

Del Col, A., *L'Inquisizione nel patriarcato e diocesi di Aquileia 1557–1559*, ('Inquisizione e Società'. Fonti 1), Trieste, 1998.

'Minute a confronto con i verbali definitivi nel processo del Sant'Ufficio di Belluno contro Petri Rayther (1557)', *Quaderni di Storia Religiosa* IX (2002), pp. 201–37.

Delumeau, J., *La peur en Occident: une cité assiegée (XIVe–XVIIIe siècles)*, Paris, 1978.

Le peché et la peur: la culpabilisation en Occident (XVIIIe–XIXe siècles), Paris, 1983 [Engl. edn. *Sin and Fear: The Emergence of a Western Guilt Culture 13th–18th Centuries*, New York, 1990].

Dereine, C. 'Les prédicateurs "apostoliques" dans les diocèses de Thérouanne, Tournai et Cambrai-Arras durant les années 1075–1125', *Analecta Praemonstratensia* 59 (1983), pp. 171–89.

Dickson, G., 'Encounters in medieval revivalism: monks, friars and popular enthusiasts', *Church History* 68/2 (1999), pp. 265–93.

Diehl, P., 'Overcoming reluctance to prosecute heresy in thirteenth-century Italy', in *Christendom and its Discontents*, pp. 47–66.

Dondaine, A., 'La hiérarchie Cathare en Italie', *Archivum Fratrum Praedicatorum* I 19 (1949), pp. 280–312; II–III 20 (1950), pp. 234–324.

'Le manuel de l'Inquisiteur (1230–1330)', *Archivum Fratrum Praedicatorum* 17 (1947), pp. 85–194.

'L'origine de l'hérésie médiévale. A propos d'un livre récent', *Rivista di Storia della Chiesa in Italia* 20 (1950), pp. 47–78.

Dossat, Y., 'La répression de l'hérésie par les evêques', *Cahiers de Fanjeaux* 6 (1971), pp. 217–51.

'Le 'Bûcher de Montségur' et les bûchers de l'Inquisition', *Cahiers de Fanjeaux* 6 (1971), pp. 361–78.

'Les Cathares au jour le jour. Confessions inédites de Cathares Quercynois', *Cahiers de Fanjeaux* 3 (1968), pp. 259–98.

'Les Cathares d'après les documents de l'Inquisition', *Cahiers de Fanjeaux* 3 (1968), pp. 71–104.

Les crises de l'Inquisition toulousaine au XIIIe siècle (1233–1273), Bordeaux, 1959.

'Les Vaudois méridionaux d'après les documents de l'Inquisition', *Cahiers de Fanjeaux* 2 (1967), pp. 207–26.

'Types exceptionnels de pélerins: l'hérétique, le voyageur déguisé, le professionnel', *Cahiers de Fanjeaux* 15 (1980), pp. 207–25.

'Une évêque Cathare originaire de l'Agenais: Vigoreux de la Bacone', in *Eglise et hérésie en France au XIIIe siècle*, Variorum Collected Studies 147 (Aldershot, 1982), XIII, pp. 623–39.

'Une figure d'inquisiteur: Bernard de Caux', *Cahiers de Fanjeaux* 6 (1971), pp. 153–72.

Douais, C., *Documents pour servir à l'histoire de l'Inquisition dans la Languedoc*, Paris, 1900.

Douglas, M., 'Introduction', in Douglas, M. (ed.), *Witchcraft, Confessions and Accusations*, London, New York, Sidney, Toronto, Wellington and Tavistock, 1970, pp. xiii–xxxviii.

Risk Acceptability According to the Social Sciences, London, 1985.

Risk and Blame: Essays in Cultural Theory, London and New York, 1992.

Bibliography

Dunbabin, J., *Captivity and Imprisonment in Medieval Europe 1000–1300*, Basingstoke and New York, 2002.

Dupré-Theseider, E., 'Le Catharisme Languedocien et l'Italie', *Cahiers de Fanjeaux* 3 (1968), pp.299–316 [also in 'Il Catarismo della Linguadoca e l'Italia', in *Mondo cittadino e movimenti ereticali*, pp.233–59, 345–60].

Mondo cittadino e movimenti ereticali nel Medioevo, Bologna, 1978.

Duvernoy, J., *Inquisition à Pamiers: Interrogatoires de Jacques Fournier, 1318–1325, choisis, traduits du texte latin et presentés par Jean Duvernoy*, Paris, 1966.

'La prédication dissidente', *Cahiers de Fanjeaux* 32 (1997), pp.111–24.

La religion des Cathares, Toulouse, 1976.

'Le Catharisme: l'unité des eglises', *Heresis* 21 (1993), pp. 15–27.

L'histoire des Cathares, Toulouse, 1979.

Dyer, C., 'Work ethics in the fourtheenth century', in Bothwell, J., Goldberg, J. and Ormrod, W.M. (eds.), *The Problem of Labour in Fourteenth-Century England*, Woodbridge and York, 2000, pp.21–41.

Eco, U., *The Name of the Rose*, New York, 1983 [orig. edn. *Il nome della Rosa*, Milan, 1980].

Esch, A., 'Évangélisme et hérésie. (Table ronde)', *Cahiers de Fanjeaux* 34 (1999), pp. 223–47.

'Gli interrogatori di testi come fonte storica. Senso del tempo e vita sociale esplorati dall'interno', *Bullettino dell'Istituto Storico Italiano per il Medio Evo* 105 (2003), pp. 249–65.

'Évangélisme et hérésie. (Table ronde)', *Cahiers de Fanjeaux* 34 (1999), pp. 223–47.

Evans, A.P., 'Hunting subversion in the Middle Ages', *Speculum* 33 (1958), pp. 1–22.

Febvre, L., 'Comment reconstituer la vie affective d'autrefois? La sensibilité et l'histoire', *Annales d'histoire sociale* 3 (1941), pp. 5–20.

Fentress, J. and Wickham, C., *Social Memory*, Oxford, 1992.

Feuchter, J., *Konsuln und Büßer: die stadtischen Eliten von Montauban vor dem Inquisitor Petrus Cellani (1236/1241)*, Tübingen, 2007.

Fichtenau E., *Heretics and Scholars in the High Middle Ages, 1000–1200*, University Park, PA, 1998, [orig. edn. *Ketzer und Professoren, Häresie und Vernunftglaube im Hochmittelalter*, Munich, 1992].

Finke, L.A. and Shichtman, M.B. (eds.), *Medieval Text and Contemporary Readers*, Ithaca, NY and London, 1987.

Foote, D., 'How the past becomes a rumor: the notarialization of historical consciousness in Medieval Orvieto', *Speculum* 75/3 (Jul. 2000), pp. 284–314.

Foreville, R., 'Innocent III et la Croisade des Albigeois', *Cahiers de Fanjeaux* 4 (1969), pp.184–217.

Forné, J., 'Approche pluridisciplinaire du concept de "dissidence"', *Heresis* 36–7 (2002), 279–92.

Francica, I., 'Gli Umiliati a Bologna nel '200: forme e significati di una "religio attiva"', *Atti e Memorie della Deputazione di Storia Patria per le Province di Romagna* 45 (1994), pp. 271–93.

Freedman, P. and Spiegel, G.M., 'Medievalism old and new: the rediscovery of alterity in North American studies', *American Historical Review* 103 (1998), pp. 677–704.

Freedman, P., *Images of the Medieval Peasant*, Stanford, CA, 1999.

Friedlander, A., *The Hammer of the Inquisitors: Brother Bernard Délicieux and the Struggle Against the Inquisition in Fourteenth-Century France*, Leiden, 2000.

Bibliography

Fumagalli, V., *Landscapes of Fear: Perceptions of Nature and the City in the Middle Ages*, Cambridge, 1994 [orig. edn. *Quando il cielo s'oscura: Modi di vita nel Medioevo*, Bologna, 1987].

Garnett, G. (ed.), *Law and Jurisdiction in the Middle Ages*, London, 1988.

Geary, P., *Phantoms of Remembrance*, Princeton, NJ, 1994.

Ginzburg, C., *The Cheese and the Worms: The Cosmos of a Sixteenth-Century Miller*, London, 1980, [orig. edn. *Il formaggio e i vermi*, Turin, 1976].

'The Inquisitor as anthropologist', in *Clues, Myths and the historical Method*, Baltimore, OH, 1989 [orig. edn. *Miti, emblemi, spie: morfologia e storia*, Turin, 1986], pp. 156–64.

Given, J.B., 'A Medieval Inquisitor at Work: Bernard Gui, 3 March 1308 to 19 June 1323', in Cohn, S.J. and Epstein, S.A. (eds.), *Portraits of Medieval and Renaissance Living: Essays in Honour of David Herlihy*, Ann Arbor, New York, 1996, pp. 207–32.

'Factional politics in a medieval society: a case study from fourteenth-century Foix', *Journal of Medieval History* 14 (1988), pp. 233–50.

Inquisition and Medieval Society: Power, Discipline and Resistance in Languedoc, Ithaca, NY, and London, 1997.

'Social stress, social strain and the inquisitors of medieval Languedoc', in *Christendom and Its Discontents*, pp. 67–85.

State and Society in Medieval Europe: Gwynedd and Languedoc under Outside Rule, Ithaca, NY, and London, 1990.

'The inquisitors of Languedoc and the medieval technology of power', *American Historical Review* 94 (1989), pp. 336–59.

Gonnet, G., 'Le cheminement de Vaudois vers le schisme et l'hérésie (1174–1218)', *Cahiers de Civilisation Medievale* 19 (1976), pp. 309–45.

Graham-Leigh, E., 'Justifying deaths: the chronicler Pierre des Vaux-de-Cernay and the massacre of Béziers', *Medieval Studies* 63 (2001), pp. 283–303.

Greco, A., *Mitologia Catara. Il favoloso mondo delle origini*, ('Uomini e mondi medievali' 3), Spoleto, 2000.

Grieco. A.J. and Sandri, L. (eds.), *Ospedali e città. L'Italia del centro-nord, XIII–XIV secolo*, Florence, 1997.

Griffe, E., *La Languedoc Cathare et l'Inquisition (1229–1329)*, Paris, 1980.

Grundmann, H., 'Ketzerverhöre des Spätmittelalters als quellenkritisches Problem', *Deutsches Archiv für Erforschung des Mittelalters* 21 (1965), pp. 519–75.

Religious Movements in the Middle Ages, Notre Dame and London, 1995 [orig. edn. *Religiöse Bewegungen im Mittellter*, 2nd edn., Darmstadt, 1961].

Guillemain, B., 'Les Papes d'Avignon. Les indulgences et les pélerinages', *Cahiers de Fanjeaux* 15 (1980), pp. 257–68.

Guiraud, J., *Histoire de l'Inquisition au Moyen Age*, II, Paris, 1938.

Gurevich, A., *Categories of Medieval Culture*, London, 1985.

Medieval Popular Culture: Problems of Belief and Perception, Cambridge, 1988.

Halbwachs, M., *On Collective Memory*, Chicago, IL, 1992.

Hamilton, B. and Hamilton, J. *Christian Dualist Heresies in the Byzantine World c. 650–1405*, Manchester, 1998.

Hamilton, B., *Crusaders, Cathars and the Holy Places*, Aldershot, 1999.

Monastic Reform, Catharism and the Crusades (900–1300), Variorum Collected Studies 97, Aldershot, 1979.

Religion in the Medieval West, London, 1986.

Bibliography

'The Cathar Council of Saint-Félix reconsidered', in *Monastic Reform, Catharism and the Crusades (900–1300)*, IX, pp. 23–53.

'The Cathars and Christian perfection', in *The Medieval Church: Universities, Heresy and Religious Life*, pp. 5–23.

'The Cathars and the seven churches of Asia', in Howard-Johnston, J.D. (ed.), *Byzantium and the West c. 850 – c. 1200*, Amsterdam, 1988, pp. 269–95.

'The legacy of Charles Schmidt to the study of Christian dualism', *Journal of Medieval History* 24 (1998), pp. 191–214.

The Medieval Inquisition, London, 1981.

'Wisdom from the East', in *Heresy and Literacy*, pp. 38–60.

Hassel, J.W., *Middle French Proverbs, Sentences and Proverbial Phrases*, ('Subsidia Medievalia' 12), Toronto, 1982.

Hours, H., 'Émeutes et émotions populaires dans les campagnes du Lyonnais au XIIIe siècle', *Cahiers d'histoire* 9 (1964), 137–53.

Housley, N.J., 'Politics and heresy in Italy: anti-heretical crusades, orders and confraternities 1200–1500', *Journal of Ecclesiastical History* 33 (1982), pp. 193–208.

Hyams, P., *Rancour and Reconciliation in Medieval England*, Ithaca, NY, 2003.

Illich, I., *In the Vineyard of the Text*, Chicago, IL, 1993.

Jimenez, P., 'Relire la charte de Niquinta', *Heresis* 23 (1994), pp. 1–28.

Justice, S., 'Inquisition, speech and writing: a case from Late Medieval Norwich', in Copeland, R. (ed.), *Criticism and Dissent in the Middle Ages*, Cambridge, 1996, pp. 289–322.

Kaelber, L., 'Weavers into heretics? The social organisation of early thirteenth-century Catharism in comparative perspective', *Social Science History* 21 (1997), pp. 111–37.

Kaupfer, R.W., *War, Justice and Public Order: England and France in the Later Middle Ages*, Oxford, 1988.

Kelly, H.A., 'Inquisition and the prosecution of heresy: misconceptions and abuses', *Church History* 58 (1989), pp. 439–51.

Kieckhefer, R., 'The office of Inquisition and Medieval heresy: the transition from personal to institutional jurisdiction', *Journal of Ecclesiastical History* 46 (1995), pp. 36–61.

Kienzle, B.M., *Cistercians, Heresy and the Crusade in Occitania 1145–1229*, York, 2001.

'Holiness and obedience: denouncement of twelfth-century Waldensian lay preaching', in Ferreiro, A. (ed.), *The Devil, Heresy and Witchcraft in the Middle Ages, Essays in Honor of J.B. Russell*, Leiden, 1998, pp. 259–78.

'Preaching as touchstone of orthodoxy and dissent', *Medieval Sermon Studies* 42 (1999), pp. 18–53.

'The prostitute-preacher. Patterns of polemic against medieval Waldensian women preachers', in Kienzle, B.M., and Walker P. (eds.), *Women Preachers and Prophets Through Two Millennia of Christianity*, Berkeley, Los Angeles and London, 1988, pp. 99–113.

Knuuttila, S., *Emotions in Ancient and Medieval Philosophy*, Oxford, 2006.

La prédication en Pays d'Oc, *Cahiers de Fanjeaux* 32 (1997).

Lambert, M., 'Catharisme et bon sens populaire', *Heresis* 6 (1993), pp. 193–214.

Medieval Heresy: Popular Movements from the Gregorian Reform to the Reformation, 3rd edn., Oxford and Malden, MA, 2002.

The Cathars, Oxford, 1998.

Bibliography

Langmuir, G.A., 'The tortures of the body of Christ', in *Christendom and its Discontents*, pp. 287–309.

Lansing, C., *Power and Purity: Cathar Heresy in Medieval Italy*, New York and Oxford, 1998.

Laurendeau, D., 'Des "voix" villageois dans les registres d'Inquisition', *Cahiers de Fanjeaux* 32 (2006), pp. 283–306.

Le Roy Ladurie, E., *Montaillou: Cathars and Catholics in a French Village 1294–1324*, Harmondsworth, 1978 [orig. edn. *Montaillou, village Occitain de 1294 à 1324*, Paris, 1975].

Lerner, R.E., *The Heresy of the Free Spirit in the Later Middle Ages*, Berkeley, Los Angeles and London, 1972.

Lobrichon, G., 'Arras, 1025, ou le vrai procès d'une fausse accusation', in *Inventer l'hérésie?* pp. 67–85.

'L'évangelisme des laïques dans le Midi (XIIIe–XIVe siècle)', *Cahiers de Fanjeaux* 34 (1999), pp. 291–310.

Lomastro Tognato, F., *L'eresia a Vicenza nel Duecento*, Vicenza, 1988.

Lupieri, E., 'Modelli scritturistici di comportamento ereticale. Alcuni esempi dei primi tre secoli', *Atti dell'Accademia Nazionale dei Lincei, Memorie. Classe di Scienze morali, storiche e filosofiche*, 383 (1986), ser. VIII, XXVIII, 7, pp. 403–50.

Maire Vigueur, J.C. and Paravicini Bagliani, A. (eds.), *La parola all'accusato*, Palermo, 1991.

Maisonneuve, H., *Études sur les origines de l'Inquisition*, Paris, 1960.

Manselli, R., 'Dolore e morte nella esperienza religiosa catara', in *Il dolore e la morte nella spiritualità dei secoli XII e XIII, Atti del V Convegno Internazionale di Studi (Todi, 7–10 Ottobre 1962)*, Todi, 1967, pp. 235–59.

'Évangélisme et mythe dans la foi Cathare', *Heresis* 5 (1985), pp. 5–17.

'Gli Umiliati lavoratori della lana', in *Produzione, commercio e consumo dei panni di lana (nei secoli XII–XVIII), Atti della II settimana di studio dell'Istituto di Storia Economica F. Datini*, Florence, 1976, pp. 231–6.

'La religiosità popolare nel Medio Evo: problemi e metodi', in *Studi sulle eresie del secolo XII* ('Studi Storici' 5), Rome: Istituto Storico per il Medio Evo, 1975, pp. 1–18.

L'eresia del Male, Naples, 1963.

'Testimonianze minori sulle eresie: Gioacchino da Fiore di fronte a catari e valdesi', *Studi Medievali*, III ser., 18 (1977), pp. 567–83.

Manteuffel, T., *Naissance d'une hérésie. Les adeptes de la pauvreté volontaire au Moyen Âge*, Paris and La Haye, 1970.

Martineau, F., 'Deux principes antagonistes et un Sauveur: les Cathares Italiens du XIII siècle et le "Liber de duobus principiis"', *Heresis* 29 (1999), pp. 7–29.

Martìnez Millàn, J., 'En torno al nascimiento de la Inquisiciòn Medieval a traves de la censura de libros en los reinos de Castilla y Aragòn (1232–1480)', *Hispania* 40 (1980), pp. 5–35.

Menache, S., 'The catechism of fear and the cult of death', in *The Vox Dei: Communication in the Middle Ages*, New York and Oxford, 1990, pp. 78–97.

Merback, M.B., *The Thief, the Cross and the Wheel: Pain and the Spectacle of Punishment in Medieval and Renaissance Europe*, Chicago, 1999.

Bibliography

Merlo, G.G., 'Controllo ed emarginazione della dissidenza religiosa', in *Francescanesimo e vita religiosa dei laici nel '200, Atti del VII Convegno Internazionale (Assisi, 16–18 October 1980)*, Assisi, 1981, pp. 367–88.

Eretici e inquisitori nella società piemontese del Trecento, Turin, 1977.

'I registri inquisitoriali come fonti per la storia dei grupi eretecali clandestini: il caso del Piemonte bassomedievale', in Tilloy, M., Audisio, G. and Chiffoleau, J. (eds.), *Histoire et clandestinité du Moyen Age à la Première Guerre mondiale, Colloque de Privas (May 1977)*, Albi, 1979, pp. 59–74.

Identità valdesi nella storia e nella storiografia ('Valdesi e Valdismi medievali' II), Turin, 1991.

'Il senso delle opere dei frati Predicatori in quanto "inquisitores hereticae pravitatis"', *Quaderni di Storia Religiosa* 9 (2002), pp. 9–30.

'La coercizione all'ortodossia: comunicazione e imposizione di un messaggio religioso egemonico (Sec. XIII–XIV)', *Società e Storia* 10 (1980), pp. 803–23.

Valdesi e valdismi medievali: Itinerari e proposte di ricerca, Turin, 1984.

Merlo, G.G. (ed.), *Eretici ed eresie medievali nella storiografia contemporanea, Bollettino della Società di Studi Valdesi* 174, Torre Pellice, 1994.

Esperienze religiose e opere assistenziali nei secoli XII e XIII, Turin, 1987.

Miller, W.I., *The Anatomy of Disgust*, Harvard, MA, 1998.

The Mystery of Courage, Harvard, MA, 2000.

Mirow, M.C. and Kelly, K.A., 'Laws on religion from the Theodosian and Justinianic codes', in R. Valantasis (ed.), *Religions of Late Antiquity in Practice*, Princeton, NJ and Oxford, 2000, pp. 263–74.

Molinier, C. *L'Inquisition dans le Midi de la France au 13 et au 14 siècle*, Paris: Sandoz, 1880.

'Rapport à M. le Ministre de l'Instruction publique sur une mission exécutée en Italie de février à avril 1885', *Archives des missions scientifiques e littéraires*, III ser., 14 (1888), 133–336.

Molnàr, A., *Storia dei Valdesi, I, Dalle origini all'adesione alla Riforma*, Turin, 1974.

Monter, W., *Judging the French Reformation: Heresy Trials by Sixteenth Century Parlements*, Cambridge, MA, 1999.

Moore, R.I., 'Heresy, repression and social change in the age of Gregorian reform', in *Christendom and Its Discontents*, pp. 19–46.

The Formation of a Persecuting Society: Power and Deviance in Western Europe, Oxford, 1987.

The Origins of European Dissent, London, 1977.

Morawski, J. (ed.), *Proverbes Français antérieurs au XVe siècle*, Paris, 1925.

Muessig, C.A., 'Les sermons de Jacques de Vitry sur les Cathares', in *Cahiers de Fanjeaux* 32 (1997), pp. 69–83.

Mundy, J.H., *Society and Government in Toulouse at the Age of the Cathars*, Toronto, 1997.

The Repression of Catharism at Toulouse: The Royal Diploma of 1279, Toronto, 1985.

'Village, town and city in the region of Toulouse', in Raftis, J.A. (ed.), *Pathways to Medieval Peasant*, Toronto, 1981, pp. 141–90.

Oldenbourg, Z., *Massacre at Montségur*, New York, 1961 [orig. edn. *Le Bûcher de Montségur*, Paris, 1959].

Omont, H., 'La Collection Doat à la Bibliothèque Nationale: Documents sur les recherches de Doat', *Bibliothèque de l'École des Chartes* 77 (1916), pp. 286–336.

Bibliography

Orioli, R., 'L'eresia dolciniana', in *L'eresia a Bologna fra XIII e XIV secolo*, vol. II. '*Venit perfidus heresiarcha*'. *Il movimento apostolico-dolciniano dal 1260 al 1307*, Rome, 1988.

Pales-Gobillard, A., 'Passages du Languedoc en Italie a l'occasion du jubilé du 1300', *Cahiers de Fanjeaux* 15 (1980), pp. 245–55.

Paolini, L. and Orioli, R., *L'eresia a Bologna fra XIII e XIV secolo*, ('Studi Storici' 93–96), 2 vols., Rome, 1975.

Paolini, L., 'Domenico e gli eretici', in *Domenico di Caleruega e la nascita dell'ordine dei frati predicatori. Atti del XLI Convegno storico internazionale (Tòdi, 10–12 October 2004)*, Spoleto, 2005, pp. 297–326.

'Domus e zona degli eretici. L'esempio di Bologna nel XIII secolo', *Rivista di Storia della Chiesa in Italia* 35 (1981), pp. 371–87.

'Esiti ereticali della conversione alla povertà', in *La conversione alla povertà nell'Italia dei secoli XII–XIV. Atti del XXVII Convegno storico Internazionale (Tòdi, 14–17 October 1990)*, Spoleto, 1991, pp. 127–86.

'Gli eretici e il lavoro: fra ideologia ed esistenzialità', in *Lavorare nel Medioevo: Rappresentazioni ed esempi dall'Italia dei secoli X-XVI, Atti del XXI Convegno storico internazionale (Tòdi, 12–15 October 1980)*, Tòdi, 1983, pp. 111–67.

'Inquisizioni medievali: il modello italiano nella manualistica inquisitoriale (XIII–XIV secolo)', in Maranesi, P. (ed.), *Negotium fidei: Miscellanea di studi offerti a Mariano d'Alatri in occasione del suo 80° compleanno*, ('Bibliotheca Seraphico-Capuccina' 67), Rome, 2002, pp. 177–98.

'Le finanze dell'Inquisizione in Italia (XIII–XIV sec.)', in *Gli spazi economici della Chiesa nell'Occidente mediterraneo (secc. XII–metà XIV), Atti del XVI Convegno internazionale di studi (Pistoia, 16–19 May 1997)*, Pistoia, 1998, pp. 441–81.

'Le Umiliate al lavoro. Appunti fra storiografia e storia', *Bullettino dell'Istituto Storico Italiano per il Medio Evo e Archivio Muratoriano* 97 (1991), pp. 229–65.

'L'eresia Catara alla fine del Duecento', in *L'eresia a Bologna fra XIII e XIV secolo*, vol. I.

'L'eresia e l'inquisizione. Per una complessiva riconsiderazione del problema', in *Lo spazio letterario del Medioevo*, 1/2, pp. 361–405.

'L'eretico, avversario politico', in Cardini, F. and Saltarelli, M. (eds.), '*Per me reges regnant*'. *La regalità sacra nell'Europa Medievale*, Bologna and Siena, 2002, pp. 263–73.

Parmeggiani, R., 'Un secolo di manualistica inquisitoriale (1230–1330): intertestualità e circolazione del diritto', *Rivista Internazionale di Diritto Comune* 13 (2002), pp. 229–70.

Pasztor, E., 'Predicazione itinerante ed evangelizzazione nei secoli XI–XII', in *Evangelizzazione e culture, Atti del Congresso Internazionale scientifico di Missionologia (Rome, 5–12 December 1975)*, Rome, 1976, vol. II, pp. 169–74.

Paul, J., 'La procédure inquisitoriale à Carcassonne au milieu du XIIIe siècle', *Cahiers de Fanjeaux* 29 (1994), pp. 361–96.

'L'hérésie au village dans la diocèse de Carcassonne au milieu du XIIIe siècle', *Cahiers de Fanjeaux* 40 (2006), pp. 255–82.

'Heresy, Good Men and nomenclature', in Frassetto, M. (ed.), *Heresy and the Persecuting Society in the Middle Ages: Essays on the Work of R.I. Moore*, Leiden, 2006, pp. 227–39.

'On Cathars, "Albigenses" and Good Men of Languedoc', *Journal of Medieval History* **27**/2 (2001), pp. 181–95.

Bibliography

Pegg, M.G., *The Corruption of the Angels: The Great Inquisition of 1245-1246*, Princeton, NJ and Oxford, 2001.

Peters, E., *Torture*, Philadelphia, PA, 1985.

Pohl, C.D., *Making Room: Recovering Hospitality as a Christian Tradition*, Grand Rapide, MI and Cambridge, 1999.

Powell, J.M., 'Religious diversity and communal politics in thirteenth century Italy', in *Portraits of Medieval and Renaissance Living*, pp. 363–81.

Praedicatores Inquisitores I, The Dominicans and the Medieval Inquisition. Acts of the 1st International Seminar on the Dominicans and the Inquisition (Rome, 23–25 February 2002), Rome, 2004.

Prosperi, A., *Tribunali della coscienza. Inquisitori, confessori, missionari*, Turin, 1996.

Rachman, S.J., *Fear and Courage*, 2nd edn., New York, 1980.

Reyerson, K., 'Medieval hospitality: innkeepers and the infrastructure of trade in Montpellier during the Middle Ages', *Western Society for French History Proceedings* 24 (1997), pp. 38–51.

The Art of the Deal: Intermediaries of Trade in Medieval Montpellier, Boston, MA, 2002.

Roach, A., 'Penance and the making of the Inquisition in Languedoc', *Journal of Ecclesiastical History* 52 (2001), pp. 409–33.

'The Cathar economy', *Reading Medieval Studies* 12 (1986), pp. 51–71.

The Devil's World: Heresy and Society 1100–1300, Harlow, 2005.

Roquebert, M., *Les Cathares: De la chute de Montségur aux derniers bûchers*, Paris, 1998.

Rosaldo, R., 'From the door of his tent: the fieldworker and the inquisitor', in Clifford, J. and Marcus, G.E. (eds.), *Writing Culture: the Poetics and Politics of Ethnography*, Berkeley, Los Angeles and London, 1986, pp. 77–97.

Rosenwein, B. (ed.), *Anger's Past: The Social Uses of an Emotion in the Middle Ages*, Ithaca, NY, 1998.

Rosenwein, B., *Emotional Communities in the Early Middle Ages*, Ithaca, NY, 2006.

'Emotional Space', in Jaeger, C.S. and Kasten, I. (eds.), *Emotions and Sensibilities in the Middle Ages*, Berlin, 2003, pp. 287–303.

'Emotions in history', *Bulletin du Centre d'Études Médiévales*, Auxerre, 2002, pp. 87–97.

'Eros and Clio: Emotional paradigms in medieval historiography', in H.W. Goetz and J. Jarnut, (eds.) *Mediävistik im 21. Jahrhundert: Stand und Perspektiven der internationalen und interdisziplinären Mittelalterforschung*, Munich, 2003, pp. 427–41.

'I sentimenti', in Romagnoli, D. (ed.), *Il Medioevo Europeo di Jacques Le Goff*, Milan, 2003, pp. 347–53.

'The places and spaces of emotion', in *Uomo e spazio nell'Alto Medioevo. Settimane di Studio del Centro Italiano di Studi sull'Alto Medioevo 50*, Spoleto, 2003, pp. 505–36.

'Worrying about emotions in history', *American Historical Review* 107 (2002), pp. 821–45.

Rouse, M.A. and Rouse, R.H., 'The schools and the Waldensians: a new work by Durand of Huesca', in *Christendom and Its Discontents*, pp. 86–111.

Rowling, J.K., *Harry Potter and the Prisoner of Azkaban*, London, 1999.

Rubellin, M., 'Au temps où Valdès n'était pas hérétique: hypothèses sur le rôle de Valdès à Lyon (1170–1183)', in *Inventer l'hérésie?*, pp. 193–218.

Runciman, S., *The Medieval Manichee*, Cambridge, 1946.

Bibliography

Rusconi, R., '"Forma Apostolorum": l'immagine del predicatore nei movimenti religiosi francesi e italiani dei secoli XII e XIII', *Cristianesimo nella storia* 6.3 (1985), pp. 513–42.

Šanjek, F., 'Le rassemblement hérétique de Saint-Félix de Caraman (1167) et les églises Cathares au XIIe siècle', *Revue d'Histoire Ecclesiastique* 67 (1972), pp. 772–9.

Scharff, T., 'Eterodossia come "variante" dell'evangelizzazione nella prospettiva delle fonti dell'Inquisizione', in *Alle frontiere della Cristianità. I frati Mendicanti e l'evangelizzazione tra '200 e '300. Atti del XXVIII Convegno Internazionale (Assisi, 12–14 October 2000)*, Spoleto, 2001, pp. 41–59.

Scruton, D.L. (ed.), *Sociophobics: The Anthropology of Fear*, Boulder, CO and London, 1986.

Selge, K.-V., 'Discussions sur l'apostolicité entre Vaudois, Catholiques et Cathares', *Cahiers de Fanjeaux* 2 (1967), pp. 143–62.

Sherry, J.E.H., *The Laws for Innkeepers for Hotels, Motels, Restaurants and Clubs*, Ithaca, NY and London, 1993.

Shogimen, T., 'From disobedience to toleration: William of Ockham and the medieval discourse of fraternal correction', *Journal of Ecclesiastical History* 52 (2001), pp. 599–622.

Smail, D.L., 'Hatred as a social institution in late-medieval society', *Speculum* 76 (2001), pp. 90–126.

Sneddon, S., 'The role of the notary in some heresy depositions from 1270s Toulouse' (forthcoming).

Solvi, D., 'La parola all'accusa. L'Inquisizione nei risultati della recente storiografia', *Studi Medievali*, III ser., 39 (Jun. 1998), 367–95.

'Santi degli eretici e santi degli inquisitori intorno all'anno 1300', in Golinelli, P. (ed.), *Il pubblico dei santi. Forme e livelli di ricezione dei messaggi agiografici. Atti del III Convegno di studio dell'Associazione Italiana per lo studio della santità, dei culti e dell'agiografia (AISSCA) (Verona, 22–24 October 1998)*, Rome, 2000, pp. 141–56.

Stock, B., *Augustine the Reader: Meditation, Self-Knowledge, and the Ethics of Interpretation*, 2nd edn., Harvard, MA, 1998.

'History, literature and medieval textuality', *Yale French Studies* 70 (1986), pp. 7–17.

Listening for the Text: On the Uses of Past, Baltimore, OH and London, 1990.

The Implications of Literacy: Written Languages and Models of Interpretation in the 11th and 12th centuries, Princeton, NJ, 1987.

Taylor, C., *Heresy in Medieval France: Dualism in Aquitaine and the Agenais, 1000–1249*, Woodbridge, 2005.

Tedeschi, J., 'Inquisitorial sources and their uses', in *The Prosecution of Heresy: Collected Studies on the Inquisition in Early Modern Italy*, Binghamton, NY, 1991, pp. 47–88.

Théry, J., 'Les Albigeois et la procédure inquisitoire: le procès pontifical contre Bernard de Castanet, évêque d'Albi et inquisiteur (1307–1308)', *Heresis* 33 (2001), pp. 7–48.

'L'hérésie des bons hommes. Comment nommer la dissidence réligieuse non vaudois ni béguine en Languedoc (XIIe–début du XIVe siècle)?', *Heresis* 36–7 (2002), pp. 75–117.

Thouzellier, C., *Hérésie et hérétiques: Vaudois, Cathares, Patarins, Albigeois* ('Storia e Letteratura, Raccolta di Studi e Testi' 116), Rome, 1969.

Tocco, F., *Quel che non c'è nella Divina Commedia, o Dante e l'eesia*, Bologna, 1899.

Bibliography

Trawkowski, S., 'Entre l'orthodoxie et l'hérésie: 'vita apostolica' et le problème de la désobéissance', in *The Concept of Heresy in the Middle Ages (11th–13th c.)*, Proceedings of the International Conference (Louvain, May 1973), Leuven, 1976, pp. 157–66.

Tuan, Y.-F., *Landscapes of Fear*, Oxford, 1979.

Ullmann, W., 'Historical introduction to H. C. Lea, "The Inquisition of the Middle Ages"', in *Law and Jurisdiction in the Middle Ages*, pp. 11–51.

'Reflections on medieval torture', in *Law and Jurisdiction in the Middle Ages*, pp. 123–37.

'The defence of the accused in the medieval Inquisition', in *Law and Jurisdiction in the Middle Ages*, pp. 481–9.

Uomini e donne in comunità, Quaderni di Storia Religiosa 1 (1994).

Vauchez, A., '"Cura animarum". I laici nella Chiesa', in *Apogeo del papato ed espansione della cristianità (1054–1274)*, ('Storia del Cristianesimo' 5), vol. V, Rome, 1997, pp. 707–32.

La sainteté en Occident aux derniers siècles du Moyen Age, ('Bibliothèque des Ecoles Françaises d'Athènes et de Rome', 241), Rome, 1988.

'Les origines de l'hérésie cathare en Languedoc, d'après un sermon de l'archevêque de Pise Federico Visconti († 1277)', in *Società, istituzioni, spiritualità: Studi in onore di Cinzio Violante*, 2 vols., vol. II, Spoleto, 1994, pp. 1023–36.

Vidal, J.-M., 'Le tribunal de l'Inquisition de Pamiers. Notice sur le registre de l'évêque Jacques Fournier', *Annales de St Louis-des-Français* 8 (Oct. 1903), pp. 377–435.

Un inquisiteur jugé par ses victimes. Jean Galand et les Carcassonais (1285–6), Paris, 1903.

Violante, C., 'Eresie nelle città e nel contado in Italia dall'XI al XIII secolo', in Zerbi, P. (ed.), *Studi sulla cristianità medievale: Società, istituzioni, spiritualità*, Milan, 1975, pp. 349–79.

Wakefield, W. L., 'Heretics and inquisitors: the case of Auriac and Cambiac', *Journal of Medieval History* 12 (1986), pp. 225–37.

'Les assistants des inquisiteurs témoins des confessions dans le manuscrit 609', *Heresis* 20 (1993), pp. 57–65.

'Some unorthodox popular ideas of the thirteenth century', *Medievalia et Humanistica* n.s., 4 (1973), pp. 25–35.

Waugh, S. and Diehl, P. (eds.), *Christendom and its Discontents: Exclusion, Persecution and Rebellion, 1000–1500*, Cambridge, 1996.

Weinberger, S., 'Writing, memory and landholding in medieval Provence', in *Portraits of Medieval and Renaissance Living*, pp. 175–87.

Wickham, C., *Courts and Conflict in Twelfth-century Tuscany*, Oxford, 2003 [Orig. edn. *Legge, pratiche e conflitti. Tribunali e risoluzione delle dispute nella Toscana del XII secolo*, Rome, 2000].

'"Fama" and the law in twelfth-century Tuscany', in Fenster, T. and Smail, D. (eds.), *Fama: The Politics of Talk and Reputation in Medieval Europe*, Ithaca, NY and London, 2003, pp. 15–26.

'Gossip and resistance among the Medieval peasantry', *Past and Present* 159 (1998), pp. 3–24.

Wood, N., 'Memory on trial in contemporary France. The case of Maurice Papon', *History of Memory* 11 (1999), pp. 41–76.

Zagorin, P., *Ways of Lying: Dissimulation, Persecution and Conformity in Early Modern Europe*, Cambridge, MA and London, 1990.

Zanella, G., *Hereticalia: Temi e discussioni*, ('Collectanea' 7), Spoleto, 1995.

Itinerari ereticali: Patari e Catari tra Rimini e Verona, ('Studi Storici' 153), Rome, 1986.

'Malessere ereticale in Valle Padana (1260–1308)', *Rivista di Storia e Letteratura Religiosa* 14/3 (1978), pp. 341–90 [also in *Hereticalia*, pp. 15–66].

Zanoni, L., *Gli Umiliati nei loro rapporti con l'eresia, l'industria della lana ed i comuni nei secoli XII e XIII sulla scorta di documenti inediti*, 2nd edn., Rome, 1970.

Zerner, M. (ed.), *Inventer l'hérésie? Discours polémiques et pouvoirs avant l'Inquisition*, ('Collection du Centre d'Études Médiévales de Nice' 2), Nice, 1998.

L'histoire du Catharisme en question: le 'concile' de St Félix, 1167, ('Collection du Centre d'Études Médiévales de Nice' 3), Nice, 2001.

Zerner, M., 'Au temps de l'appel aux armes contre les hérétiques: du "Contra Henricum" du moine Guillaume aux "Contra hereticos"', in *Inventer l'hérésie?*, pp. 119–55.

Zorzi, A., 'Rituali di violenza, cerimoniali penali, rappresentazioni della giustizia nelle città italiane centro-settentrionali (secoli XIII–XV)', in Cammarosano, P. (ed.), *Le forme della propaganda politica nel Due e Trecento*, ('Collection de l'École Française de Rome' 201), Rome, 1994, pp. 395–425.

'Rituali e cerimoniali penali nelle città italiane (secc. XIII–XVI)', in Chiffoleau, J., Martines, L. and Paravicini Bagliani, A. (eds.), *Riti e rituali nelle società medievali*, ('Collectanea' 5), Spoleto, 1994, pp. 141–57.

INDEX

Index

Baretges, wife of Peter Grimoard,20, *see also* Peter Grimoard
Barrau of St Martin, squire, 31
Bastide of the 'Seven Springs', 68
Beatrix, wife of Arnaud Guillem, 78, *see also* Arnaud Guillem
Belestar, 29
Belibaste, 95
Benedetti, Marina, 6, 53
Benedictine rule, 118, 119
Berbegueira,32, 33, *see also* Loubenx
Berbegueira of Puylaurens, 165
Berenger of Montagut, 77, *see also* Peter of Montagut
Bergamo
　Waldensian meeting, 121
Bernard Agasse, 151, 152, 157, 177, 187
Bernard Arquer, 27
Bernard Barre of Sorèze, 16
Bernard Faure, 38, 39, 192
Bernard Fort, 170
Bernard Garrigue, 68
Bernard Gui, inquisitor, 20, 21, 89, 112, 113, 156, 157, 187
　works, 89, 112, 156
Bernard Hugues, 80, 82
Bernard Laguarrigue, 22, 151, 152, 157, 158, 177, 182, 185, 187, 193
Bernard of Camon, 32
Bernard of Caux, inquisitor, 94
Bernard of Ceseratz, 90
Bernard of Clairvaux, 58, 60, 111
Bernard of Laval of the Lantarès, 68
Bernard of Lavaur, 168
Bernard of Morlay, 197
Bernard of Ravat, 30
Bernard of Rival, 142, 189
Bernard of Roquefort, 83
Bernard of Saint Martin, 31
Bernard of Tiron, 100, 117
Bernard of Villèle, inquisitor, 155
Bernard of Villeneuve, 155
Bernard Otho, 79, 91, 170
Bernard/Gerald Bonuspanis, 132
'Bertacius', *see* Matfred of Puylaurens
Bertrand Martin, 98, 135, 153, 166, 179
Bertrand Martin, Cathar bishop, 30
Bertrand of Alamans, 38, 39, 166, 179
Bertrand of La Baccalarie, 166
Bertrand of Olmière, 182
Bertuzzi, Roberta, 8, 65
Béziers
　coucil of, 89
　viscounts of, 161, 162, 164, 184, 192, *see also* Languedoc
Bible

translations, 36–7
Biller, Peter, 4, 5, 121
Bloch, Marc, 142
Bologna, 76, 114
　University, 4
Bona of Puy, 30
Bonella of Florence, 77
Bonet of Cuneo, 77
Bonhom, 27
Bulgaria, 56

Cahors, 68, 86, 175
Calvairac, 166
Camporesi, Piero, 143
Capetian monarchy, 174
Caraman, 155, 168, 173, 176, 179
Castelnau, 161
Castelsarrasin, 168
Castres, 92
Catalonia, 58, 168, 177
Carcassonne, 4, 150, 151, 152, 167
　citizens, 49
　diocese, 16
　hierarchy of, 150–4
　inquisitorial tribunal, 48, 153
　seneschal of, 12, 15, 19, 24, 48, 91, 97, 150, 154, 176, 200, 202, 203, 210
　surrounding area, 48, 162
　theft of registers, 47–8, 49, 150, 154, 157, 158, 187, 193, 195
　and fear, 150–2
　viscounts of, 161, 162, 164, *see also* Languedoc
Cathar sacraments
　and itinerancy, 133–9
　apparellamentum, 121, *see also servitium*
　baptism, 27, 32, 33, 39, 120, 121
　breaking of blessed bread, 121, 138
　consolamentum, 27–9, 39
　melioramentum, 121
　ordination, 28, *see also* consolamentum; hereticatio
　servitium, 121, *see also* apparellamentum
Catharism
　categorisation
　　explorator, 90, 91
　　fautor, 89
　　fugitivus, 93
　　nuncius, 65–74, 79–81
　　receptator, 89, 93
　　relapsus, 152
　clergy, 55
　denial, 8, 65, 193
　doctrine, 7, 33–4, 45
　diffusion, 54–5
　filius maior, 36, 182
　finances, 78–82

Index

Index

Index

Index

Index

Lightning Source UK Ltd.
Milton Keynes UK
UKHW022028101020
371215UK00019B/668